PRIVATE OWNER WAGONS OF BRISTOL & DISTRICT

IAN POPE

Copyright: Ian Pope & Lightmoor Press, 2009

British Library Cataloguing-in-Publication Data. A catalogue
record for this book is available from the British Library
ISBN 978 1899889 36 5
All rights reserved. No part of this publication may be reproduced, stored in a retrieval system
or transmitted in any form or by any means, electronic, mechanical, photocopying,
recording or otherwise, without the written permission of the publisher.

Lightmoor Press
120 Farmers Close, Witney, Oxfordshire, OX28 1NR
Printed by TJ International, Padstow

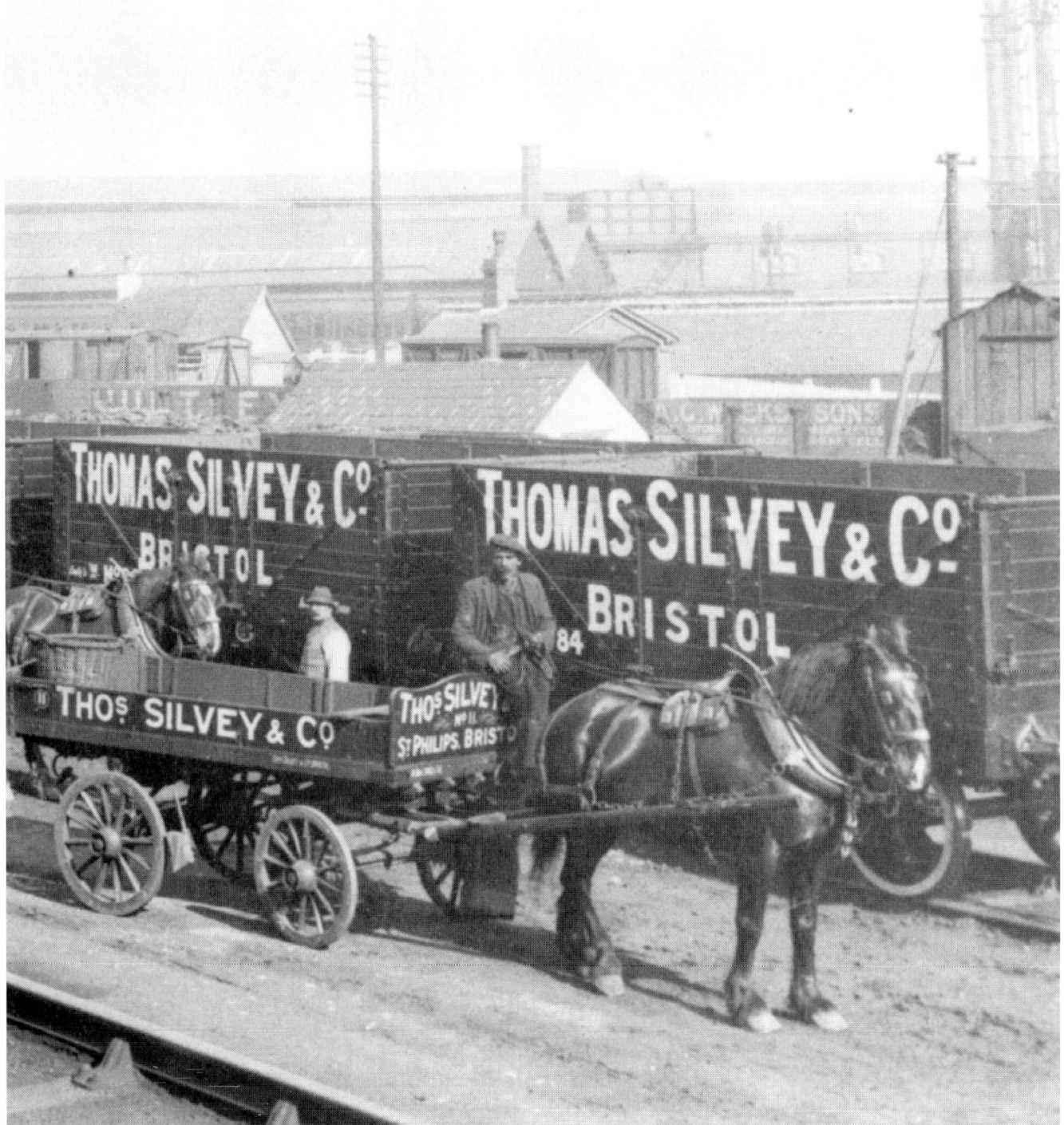

PRIVATE OWNER WAGONS OF BRISTOL & DISTRICT

Lightmoor Press

An Up coal train from South Wales emerging from Patchway Tunnel and passing beneath the A38 overbridge is headed by '28xx class' 2-8-0 No. 2821. Any wagons for the Bristol area would be put off at Stoke Gifford Yard.

G. H. Soole, courtesy Paul Karau

CONTENTS

Introduction 7

The Owners
Ashton Vale Iron & Coal Co. 9
Avon Malleable Iron Foundry Co. 10
John Baker & Sons 10
Lowell Baldwin Ltd 10
Beachim & Balmont 21
Berril & Co. 21
Bird Brothers 21
F. Bird & Co. 22
Bristol & West of England Wagon Co. Ltd .. 22
Bristol Co-operative Society Ltd 23
Bristol Malago Vale Collieries Co. Ltd 23
Bristol Railway Coal Association 25
Bristol Rolling Stock Co. Ltd 25
Bristol Steam Navigation Co. Ltd 25
Bristol Waggon Works Co. Ltd 25
British Coal Co. 26
I. B. Britton 26
Samuel Brookman 27
C. W. Bryant & Co. 30
W. Butler & Co. (Bristol) Ltd 30
Cattybrook Brick Co. Ltd 33
Central Coal Co. 34
Cleeve Coal Co. 35
Clifton Coal Co. 35
Coal Agencies Ltd 36
Coalpit Heath Coal Co. 37
Herbert S. Colborn 39
H. E. Coole & Co. 39
Co-operative Wholesale Society Ltd 40
Dudley & Gibson 41
James Durnford & Son Ltd 44
Edward Edwards 45
Field 45
Fishponds Coal Co. 45
John G. Foster 46
Alfred J. Fudge 46
Herbert J. Fudge 47
S. M. Gael & Co. 47
W. T. Garlick & Co. 47
Gould & Baker 47
Granville, Smith & Co. 47
Gregory & Co. Ltd 47
Oliver J. Gullick 48
H. Hector Hall 50
John Hare & Co. 51
Alfred G. Harris & Co. 51
Hendy & Company 52
C. H. & J. Hewitt 54
Alick Grant Heyward 54
Huntley & Cockram 55
Huntley & Co. Ltd 55
George William Imber & Co. 55
W. F. Jones & Co. 55
B. G. King 55
George Stone Kitson 56
Knee & Co. 56
Robert Lewis 56
Henry Little & Son 56
William Love & Co. 56
Lucas & Co. 56
T. Lucas & Sons 56
John Lysaght Ltd 56
Miles Maudsley 56
Midland Coal Co. [1] 57
Midland Coal Co. [2] 57
Midland Coal Co. [3] 57
William J. Mills 57
A. H. Milton & Co. 59
Edward William Boult Monks 60
Montpelier Coal Co. 60
Thomas Mulford 60
F. G. Mullis & Sons 61
Newport Coal & Coke Co. Ltd 66
T. Nichols & Sons Ltd 66
C. W. Orchard 66
Osborn & Wallis 67
T. Paul & Co. 69
Pepler, Edwards & Co. Ltd 70
Arthur Pepler 71
H. Pepler & Son 71
Poole Brothers 72
James Dillon Pounsbery 73
Pountney & Co. Ltd 74
Princess Royal Colliery Co. Ltd 75
A. Pritchard 75
Redcliff Coal Co. 75
Richard Charles Ring 75
F. Robins & Co. 75
J. Robinson & Co. Ltd 77
F. Sage 77
Sandwell Coal Co. 79
Charles E. Shirley 79
Thomas Silvey & Co. 81
F. H. Silvey & co. 91
Slade & Baker 93
Alfred J. Smith Ltd 95
John Snow & Co. 98
Edwin E. Sohier 100
T. W. Squire 100
Stone & Tinson 100
S. Stone & Co. 100
Eland Sweet 100
Isaac James Tanner 100
Tiley Bros. 101
Lewellin Twining & Co. 101
United Alkali Ltd 104
William Vincent & Co. 106
William Wallis 107
Watkins & Leonard 107
Richard Frank Webb 107
Western Counties Agric. Association Ltd 107
Western Coal Co. 108
Western Petroleum Co. 108
Western Wagon & Property Co. Ltd 108
Wetmore & Bird 109
Robert Wetmore 109
Mark Whitwill & Son 110
Whitwill, Cole & Co. Ltd 110
Williams & Bird 110
Williams & Co. 112

And District: Out to Avonmouth
Bristol Sublimed Lead Co. Ltd 113
Thomas Sharpe 113
E. Baily & Son, Ltd. 113
O. B. 114
National Smelting Co. 115
National Fertilizers Ltd 117

Midland Lines: Mangotsfield to Bitton
Crane & Company 119
Sidney Fussell 119
Golden Valley Paper Mills 120
Kingswood Coal & Iron Co. 120
Mrs E. Lacey 121
Frederick Mayo 121
Arthur Nichols 121
Walter Sheppard 121
Shortwood Brick & Tile Co. 121

Addenda & Errata
Forest of Dean volume
   Osman Barrett 122
   Dean Forest Coal Co. 122
   Dean Forest Consolidated Iron Co. 122
   Forest of Dean Coal Co. 122
   Forest of Dean Stone Firms 122
   Alfred Goold 122
   Thomas Gwilliam 122
   Haywood Colliery Co. 123
   High Meadow Coal Co. 123
   Holmes Bros 123
   Lydbrook Colliery Co. 123
   Lydney Coal Co. 123
   Edward Marmont & Co. 123
   Titanic Iron Co. 123
   Wilderness Portland Cement Co. 123

Gloucestershire volume
Gloucester
   Alexander Crane 123
   T. George & Sons 124
   Gloucester Co-op Ind. Soc. Ltd 124
   Samuel Hipwood 124
   J. Langston & Son 124
   John Knight 124
   Henry Merchant 124
   George Merrylees 124
   Nicholson Bros & Co. 124
   Joseph Scudamore 125
   Lemuel Seyers 125
   W. H. Worth 125
Cheltenham
   John Barrell 125
   Clift & Whiting 125
   Ezra Crook 125
   Hanks & Gwinnell 125
   Henry Jordan & Co. Ltd 125
   J. Lloyd 125
   J. S. Nott 126
   A. G. Stockwell 126
   John Williams & Co. 126
   Henry Workman 126
North of Cheltenham & Tewkesbury
   W. J. Oldacre & Co. 126
   E. W. F. Edgwick 126
   Samuel Healing & Sons 126
   Richard Clifford 126
Cirencester
   Richard Cole 127
   Davies & Attwater 127
Stroud & Nailsworth Branch
   Stroud Gas Light & Coke Co. 127
   Wood & Rowe 127
   Samuel Jefferies & Son 127
   R. Williams 127
Berkeley Road, Yate & Thornbury
   Wickwar Quarries Ltd 127
   Bristol Mineral Co. 127
   Yate Coal & Lime Co. 128
   Tytherington Stone Co. 128
South Wales & Bristol Direct
   Frederick Biss 128
   George E. Dowding 128

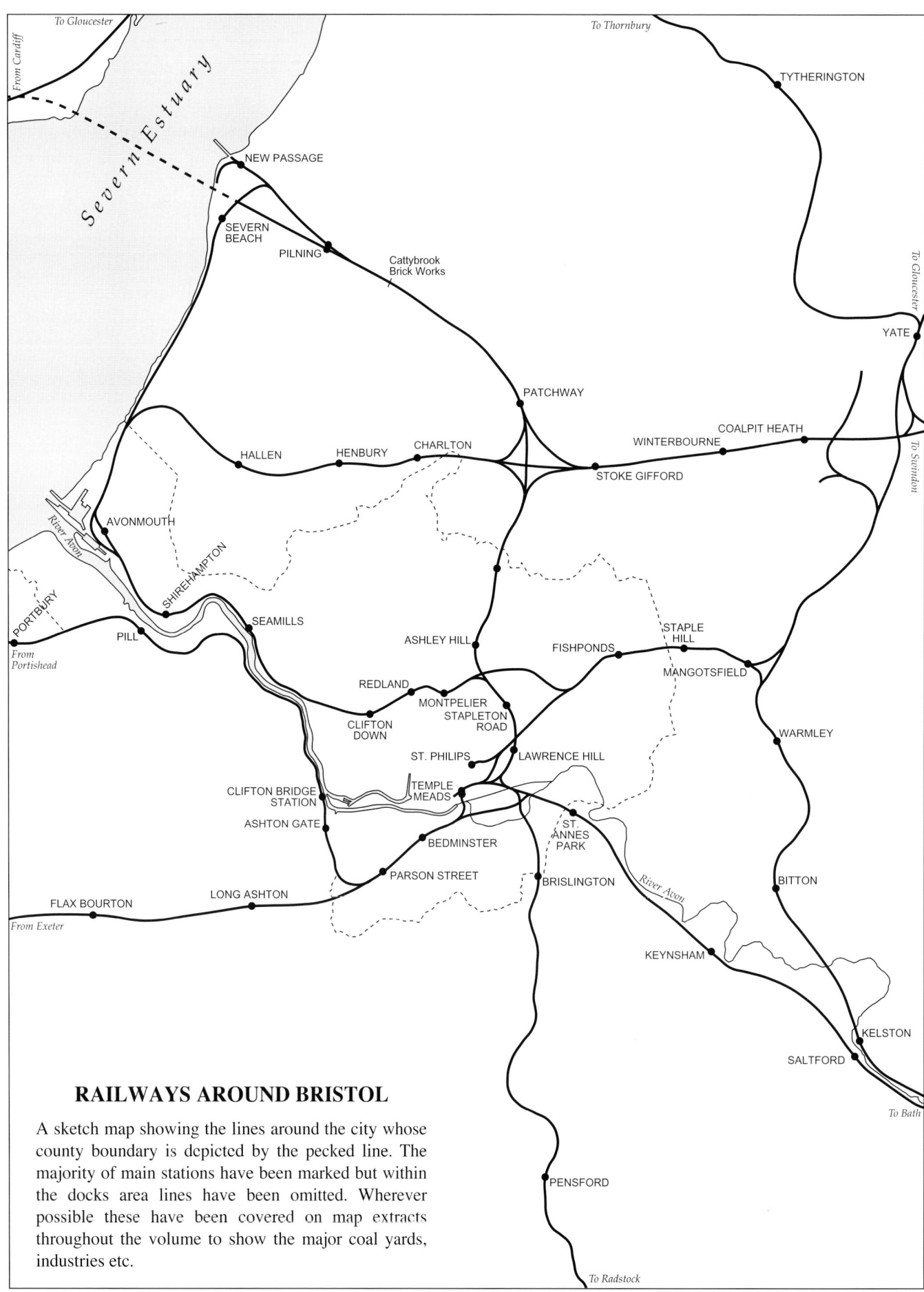

RAILWAYS AROUND BRISTOL

A sketch map showing the lines around the city whose county boundary is depicted by the pecked line. The majority of main stations have been marked but within the docks area lines have been omitted. Wherever possible these have been covered on map extracts throughout the volume to show the major coal yards, industries etc.

INTRODUCTION

THE private owner wagons of Bristol and district completes the trilogy of volumes on wagons connected with Gloucestershire - which is possibly one of the most diverse industrial counties in the country. Bristol in some ways also completes the circle as, like the Forest of Dean, the South Gloucestershire coalfield to the north of the city were served by tramroads linking it to the city itself and to the River Avon. Despite the proximity of the South Gloucestershire coalfield a large amount of coal for the city was also brought up the River Avon from both South Wales and the Forest of Dean and later, once the Midland Railway arrived from Birmingham, the city was opened up for coal from the Midlands coalfields.

The first coal into the city by rail would have come along the Bristol & Gloucestershire tramroad from Coalpit Heath to the north east. Despite being first mooted in 1803 it took until 1828 for the plans to come to fruition with the passing of the Bristol & Gloucestershire Railway Act in June. Even then the northern half of the line was first to open in 1832 allowing coal to be taken from Coalpit Heath to Mangotsfield where the Avon & Gloucestershire Railway made a junction. This line received the Royal Assent on the same day as the Bristol & Gloucestershire and was for a tramroad from Mangotsfield down to the River Avon. This was heavily supported by the Kennet & Avon Canal Co. as it would bring coal down to the river for transshipment. There were to be a number of branches off the main line of the A&G serving collieries in the Willsbridge and Warmley areas and in 1830 sufficient of the line was complete to allow some coal to be brought down to Avon Wharf.

It was not until 1835 that the portion of the Bristol & Gloucestershire between Mangotsfield and the River Avon at Cuckold's Pill, opposite Temple Meads, was opened. It was at Cuckold's Pill (later Avonside Wharf) that a coal wharf was opened for sale of coal into the city. As with the tramroads in the Forest of Dean (see *Private Owner Wagons of the Forest of Dean*) the wagons used on the Bristol & Gloucestershire and the Avon & Gloucestershire had to be clearly identified with their owner's name painted on the sides in white letters at least two inches high.

Bristol will, however, always be associated with the Great Western Railway and Brunel with his broad gauge line to London whose Act was obtained in 1835. The line east as far as Bath opened in August 1840 and through communication to the capital came in June 1841. The Great Western at first determined that the line would carry no coal traffic and, indeed, in the early years there would have been no call for such traffic. It was not until connections were made to South Wales that coal became a regular traffic.

There was also a desire to connect Bristol with Gloucester and thus the Bristol and Gloucester Railway was promoted with Brunel as its engineer. An Act was obtained on the 1st July 1839 for a line from Bristol following the route of the Bristol & Gloucestershire to Westerleigh thence to a junction with the Cheltenham & Great Western Union's line at Standish (see map in *Private Owner Wagons of Gloucestershire*). Whilst having been promoted as a standard gauge line its close connections to the GWR led to it eventually being laid to the broad gauge. The railway opened for traffic in July 1844. This gave a connection to the Birmingham & Gloucester Railway (with the infamous break of gauge at Gloucester) and thus opened the way for Midlands coal to be brought into the City of Bristol. Such traffic apparently commenced in September 1844.

Railway politics then came into play. The Bristol & Gloucester and the Birmingham & Gloucester agreed to amalgamate in 1845 and the GWR made offers to both sets of shareholders but the price could not be agreed upon. A chance meeting led to an offer from the Midland Railway to work the two lines and this came to be in 1846. It was not until 1854 however, that the line was opened as standard gauge and thus gave a direct connection to the Midlands and the north with no break of gauge, albeit the broad gauge rails remained and some GWR goods trains still traversed the route to give access to South Wales via Gloucester and the South Wales Railway, the latter opening in 1854. It was not until the opening of the Severn Tunnel in 1886 that these GWR workings ceased.

The Great Western had lost its stranglehold on Bristol just as the Bristol & Exeter Railway opened in 1844. Initially this had little impact on private owner operation as most coal for the South West still went by sea but an opportunity to get Midland coal directly to Somerset and beyond had been lost to the GWR.

The ability of the GWR to bring coal into the city was increased with the opening of the Bristol & North Somerset line in September 1873 between Bristol and Radstock. This allowed coal from the Somerset coalfield around Pensford and Radstock to be brought to Bristol more easily and this would have had an effect on the markets previously held by the Forest of Dean and Midlands coalfields.

That the Great Western had missed out on a revenue earning traffic to some extent by the Midland taking control of the line north from Bristol is apparent later on when coal merchants and factors such as John Snow, John Williams and later the giants of Silvey and Baldwin, plus the factors who set themselves up further south and west, began using Midlands housecoal and transporting it by rail. Much of this would have come down the Birmingham to Bristol line to the yard at Westerleigh. These traffic flows of coal is an area which has been little investigated, the glamorous express or the humble branch passenger have been heavily studied and documented but the slow, noisy and dirty coal trains have largely been ignored.

The coal trains around Bristol increased with the opening of the Severn Tunnel in September 1886. Most South Wales coal would have passed by en route to London and the South East as much for Bristol consumption still came across the Bristol Channel by sea. This is why many Bristol coal merchants including Osborn & Wallis, Alfred Smith and Thomas Silvey, operated there own fleet of steam and sailing ships.

The one line that seems to have had a large influence on the coal trade in Bristol was the Clifton Extension Railway opened in 1874 which, with goods yards at its stations of Montpelier and Clifton Down, allowed coal merchants easier access to the fashionable suburbs of Clifton, Redland and Montpelier. These had previously been quite a climb for the coal merchants' horses and carts, often necessitating an extra horse and leading to the addition of an extra delivery charge. The number of large houses in the area, all with a fireplace in each room, guaranteed good returns and a large number of merchants set up with depots at one or other, or both, of the stations.

In 1902 it was deemed necessary by the Great Western & Midland Railway Joint Committee who managed the line that an extra coal siding was needed at Clifton Down. To make way for this the goods shed, occupied by a builders merchant, was to be demolished and a new set of rails provided at a cost of £650. The increased accommodation was needed due to the heavy increase in coal traffic which led to complaints from traders about the difficulties of conducting their business with no space when required to bring wagons in. This led to difficulties for the railway companies in having to find storage space elsewhere for the loaded wagons until a berth was available in Clifton Down yard.

To support the case a table was produced showing the coal tonnages handled:

Year	Coal, Coke & Lime	Carted Tons	Not Carted Tons	Mineral Class Tons	Total Tonnage
1895	35,664	103	1,229	5,573	42,569
1896	33,906	64	931	8,082	42,983
1897	37,599	62	1,290	9,781	48,732
1898	40,029	110	1,042	7,850	49,031
1899	43,233	104	1,706	7,635	52,678

Taking the 1899 total of coal, coke and lime alone it would equate to about 4,224 wagon loads at 10-ton per wagon but as most merchants' wagons of this period were of 8-ton capacity it would mean 5,280 loadeds in and 5,280 empties out or somewhere around fifteen loaded wagons arriving per day throughout the year. Again given that coal requirements would be heavier in winter it is obvious that mineral services along the line were busy.

The Clifton Extension Railway also linked through to Avonmouth where a dock was developed in 1877 as the Port of Bristol was hampered by access being up the twisting River Avon. The docks were soon to grow and specialised in grain and banana traffic. The First World War, however, saw a change in the area with a government factory being set up, a picric acid production plant and the start of a zinc smelter. All eventually led to a great increase in rail traffic, mainly tank wagons, and in miles of siding.

The Government wagons used initially at these plants, mainly for the Ministry of Munitions, have not been covered in this volume. Nor have those of the Port of Bristol as they were mainly 'internal users' used only within the docks area.

Should further images of Bristol based wagons emerge from dusty cupboards or family albums, the author would be delighted to see them.

Ian Pope, Witney, 2009

Acknowledgements

This book would not have been possible without the help of many other wagon devotees including Keith Turton, John Horne, Simon Turner, Peter Fidczuk, Richard Kelham and Ed McKenna. It is richer for the business and family recollections given freely by Michael Silvey, Peter Tiley and Neil Tiley and for insights into Bristol from Gerry Nichols. The staff at Gloucestershire Archives and Bristol Records Office patiently dealt with requests for documents and heavy and bulky photograph albums. For photographs I have to thank the Historical Model Railway Society, Trevor Johnson, Neil Parkhouse, John Alsop, Keith Ettle, Steve Grudgings, Roger Carpenter and Paul Karau. To anybody I have missed my sincere apologies. Once more my grateful thanks go to Clare for checking through this volume but all mistakes, errors and omissions are down to the author.

Clifton Down Station with a busy coal yard on the right well screened from the platform. *John Alsop collection*

ASHTON VALE IRON & COAL Co.

For this owner we actually step over the county boundary into Somerset as both the collieries and the iron works operated by the company were right on the edge of the Bristol county boundary. Ashton Vale Colliery was on the west side of the Portishead Branch of the GWR, just south of Ashton Gate Station. Ashton Iron Works was on the opposite side of the line. The line to Portishead was opened in April 1867 and it is likely that sidings for the colliery and iron works were provided from the opening and opened once signalling had been provided.

The iron furnaces were in blast by 1861 and prior to the acquisition of them by the Ashton Vale Iron Co. Ltd, which was incorporated in June 1864, they had been operated successively by Baynton, Knight & Co., Knight, Abbots & Co., and Edwin Knight & Co. There were both Abbot's and Knight's on the board of the new company. The furnaces were finally blown out in 1887 but the iron works continued in use until circa 1893 with the sidings to it being removed by 1904. Ashton Vale Colliery closed in 1906 but a brick works was established on the site.

The company also operated South Liberty Colliery further to the south and served by sidings off the Bristol & Exeter main line and here were also to be established the South Liberty Brick & Tile Works. Coal working at South Liberty appears to have been started in the mid 1750s by the Bedminster Coal Co., coal in the area having been found in 1745.

The date at which South Liberty was acquired by the Ashton Vale Iron & Coal Co. is unknown. A rail connection to South Liberty Sidings was brought into use by February 1873.

South Liberty Colliery closed in 1925 with the brick works continuing until 1963.

In 1875 the Ashton Vale Iron Co. Ltd were advertising in the *Bristol Mercury* for housecoal at the colliery at 15s a ton, delivery to Bristol was an extra 2s 6d to 3s whilst up the hill to Clifton was an extra 3s to 4s. Whether these prices were for taking coal by rail from South Liberty is unknown.

Kelly's *Bristol Directory* for 1902 gives the Ashton Vale Iron Co. Ltd as colliery proprietors with offices at Albion Chambers in Small Street.

On the 8th January 1880 wagons for the Ashton Vale Coal Co. were registered with the GWR. Numbers 100 to 119 had been built in December 1879 by the Bristol Waggon Works Co., whilst numbers 80 to 82 from the same source were registered at the same time. All were of 10-ton capacity with dumb buffers. The company also had twenty wagons on simple hire from the Western Wagon Co. between 1905 and 1914 and possibly as late as 1922.

Unfortunately no images showing wagons for the company, or of the collieries themselves have been seen.

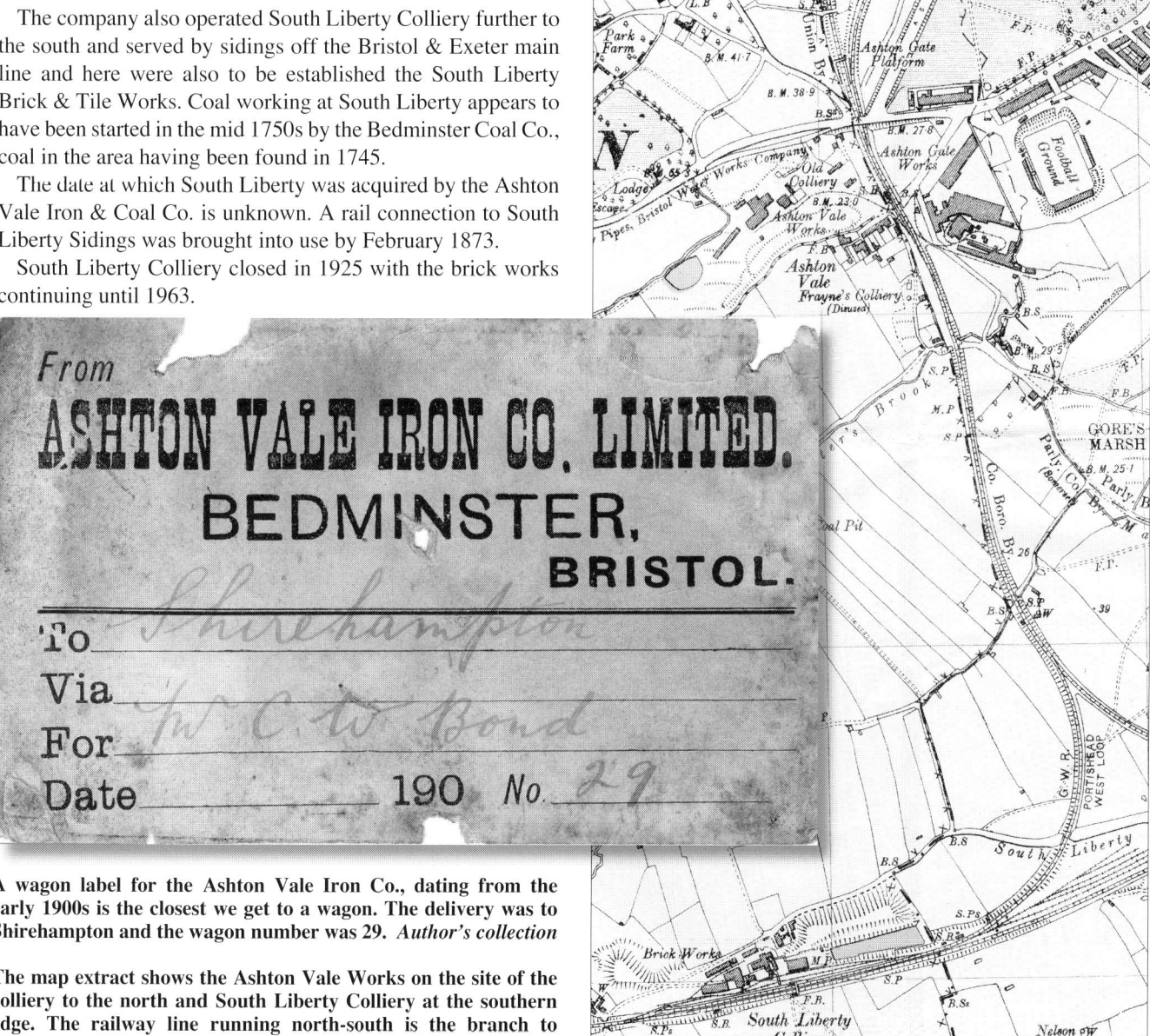

A wagon label for the Ashton Vale Iron Co., dating from the early 1900s is the closest we get to a wagon. The delivery was to Shirehampton and the wagon number was 29. *Author's collection*

The map extract shows the Ashton Vale Works on the site of the colliery to the north and South Liberty Colliery at the southern edge. The railway line running north-south is the branch to Portishead. *Ordnance Survey 6-inch, 1930*

AVON MALLEABLE IRON FOUNDRY Co.

The business can be found in Kelly's *Bristol Directory* for 1914 at Chapel Street, St. Philip's Marsh. Given the title of the business it can be assumed that they were operating a foundry which may have been extant before the limited company was formed in 1899.

The only evidence of wagon operation is that three secondhand 10-ton wagons were taken on temporary hire from the Gloucester RC&WCo. in July 1919. Given that they were on temporary hire it is likely that they were from the wagon company's hire fleet and not relettered for the foundry company. Possibly they were used for one particular purpose, such as the movement of a set of castings, or they might have been for the importation of foundry coke whilst the usual supplier was unable to oblige.

In September 1925 a meeting was held regarding the final winding up of the Avon Malleable Iron Foundry Limited.

JOHN BAKER & SONS

Trade directories from as early as 1902 through to 1914 show John Baker and his sons to have been trading in coal from both Redcliffe Railway Wharf and Pump Lane, Cathay although this latter address had been dropped by 1914. The 1901 census reveals a coal dealer by the name of John Baker, aged 77 although the '& Sons' cannot be identified.

There is, however, no evidence of wagon ownership and it might be that they were just dealing out of the railway yard at Redcliffe taking their coal from one of the larger factors. It is known that coal was acquired both from the Midlands and from Somerset as there are extant wagon labels from Cadley Hill Colliery and Timsbury Colliery. The coal from Timsbury was loaded in a wagon numbered 20 but it is impossible to say if this was a colliery owned wagon or actually one for Baker & Sons.

LOWELL BALDWIN Ltd

The date at which Lowell Baldwin began trading can now be moved to an earlier date than that stated in *Private Owner Wagons of the Forest of Dean*. It is now known that he was in business as early as 1909 or possibly even a year or two earlier.

Lowell Baldwin was born towards the end of 1880 in Bradford, Yorkshire to Richard, a bookeeper, and Martha. In 1901 he could be found working as a 'county court inspector' in Hanley, Staffordshire. He had moved to Bristol by 1908 and he married Louise Beatrice Lucas at the beginning of that year in the city.

It would appear that he may have started trading in coal soon afterwards. At least one wagon was built for him by Hurst, Nelson in 1909 and two wagons were purchased from the Midland RC&WCo. in June 1910. The Western Wagon Co. ledger also has references to payments from 1910 onwards. By 1914 Lowell had a coal factors business based at the Redcliff Railway Wharf with an office address of 6 Redcliff Hill, Bristol.

The unknown plate on the wagon below. In the shape of a letter B with an inset M. – was it an owner's plate?

Hurst, Nelson of Motherwell provided an unknown number of wagons for Lowell Baldwin in 1909 of which number 203 is one. Of seven-plank construction with side and end doors it was registered by the Great Western Railway. The plate to the right of the registration plate, above, is a bit of a mystery.
courtesy HMRS ABP634

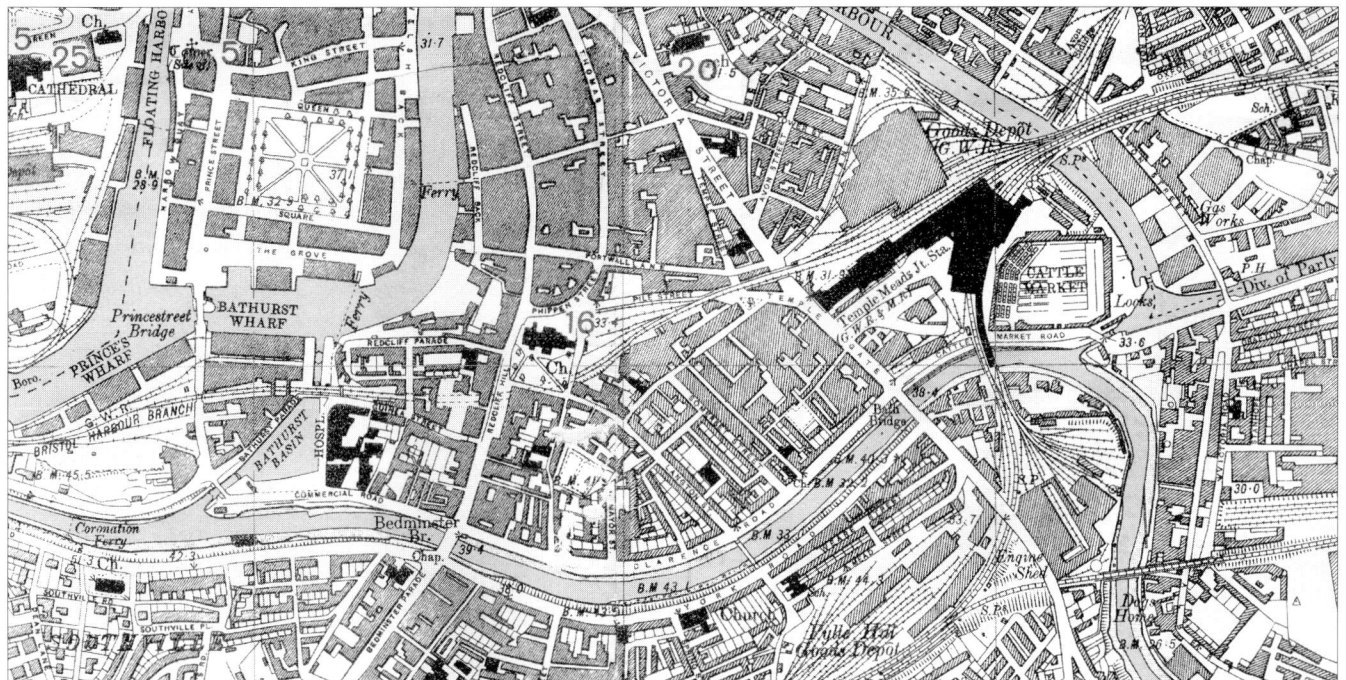

The Redcliff area with Redcliff Railway Wharf, or Redcliff Goods, in the centre. The sidings are off the GWR Harbour Branch which opened in 1872 and which immediately to the west of the sidings enters Redcliff Tunnel which is to the south of the imposing building of St. Mary, Redcliff. Redcliff Hill runs north/south over the top of the tunnel and here were the offices for Lowell Baldwin. At the very top of the map extract, to the north east of Temple Meads Station, can be seen Avon Sidings. Here was the original terminus of the Bristol & Gloucestershire Railway and where from circa 1922 Lowell Baldwin also had a depot having taken over the old Coalpit Heath yard.
Ordnance Survey 6-inch, 1930

The earliest wagon photographed for Lowell Baldwin by the Gloucester Carriage & Wagon Co. was number 1678 in February 1923. It was part of an order for fifty-one new wagons, paid for in cash at £134 each. Of seven-plank construction with side and end doors the latter having angled commode handles fitted. Internal measurements were 16ft 0in. x 7ft 4in. x 4ft 2in. The wagons were painted black with the lettering 'blue white' or pale blue. Notice that it was lettered for Birmingham only. Registration was with the Great Western Railway. *GRC&WCo.*

No. 1712 was photographed in June 1923 and was one of 151 wagons ordered in February and March of that year. Of 12-ton capacity it measured 16ft 0in. x 7ft 4in. x 4ft 2in. and was of seven-plank construction with side and end doors, the latter being fitted with double sloping commode handles. It is impossible to say if any were fitted at the fixed end. Commode handles were used for several reasons, the main one being to allow a shunter or yard man to climb up onto the buffer to check the interior of the wagon for 'foreign' bodies such as sacks left inside. This was important, especially if the wagon owner supplied industrial clients with tipplers as a sack or similar in the conveyor system could wreak havoc. The wagon was painted black with 'blue white' lettering. *GRC&WCo.*

Lowell Baldwin became a limited company in 1921 and this might have been about the time of a great expansion in their business. Interestingly they are only found as a coal merchant in the 1928 *Colliery Year Book*. A 1935 trade directory gives the address as 6 and 8 Redcliff Hill with depots at Redcliff Railway Wharf; Barton Road, St Philips; Gaol Siding and Wapping Wharf. It is also known that he had a depot at Avon Sidings from circa 1922 to the mid 1930s. The 1938 *Colliery Year Book* also lists an office at 14 New Street, Birmingham. Baldwin had, however, been trading in the latter city since at least 1923 as some of the wagons built by Gloucester RC&WCo. were lettered solely for Birmingham. Others were lettered for Bristol & Birmingham and others just for Bristol.

It is possible to built up some idea of the trading patterns of Lowell Baldwin. It is known that he obtained coal from the Forest of Dean, Derbyshire, Leicestershire and Nottinghamshire, plus, of course, South Wales. Extant wagon labels and surviving colliery order books give some idea as to who he was trading with. Coal is known to have been obtained from Ellistown, Snibston, Moira and Desford collieries in Leicestershire; Blackwell and Church Gresley in Derbyshire; Arley (Nuneaton, Warwickshire); Clifton (Nottingham);

Top left: An enlargement out of a full image reproduced in *Private Owner Wagons of the Forest of Dean* which is believed to show Lowell Baldwin, centre, at Eastern United Colliery.
Author's collection

Above & Left: Two wagon labels for consignments of coal from the Forest of Dean to Redcliffe Wharf for Baldwin. Note the two spellings of Redcliff. *Author's collection*

Photographed in January 1926, 2023 was from the batch of fifty 12-ton wagons ordered from Gloucester in December 1925. Again of seven-plank construction with side and end doors but this time no commode handles are fitted. The lettering on the solebar reads: *'For repairs advise Head Office 6, Redcliffe Hill Bristol.'* (note the 'e' on Redcliff) and as the wagons carry no Wagon Repairs Ltd plates we are left to wonder who carried out any repairs necessary. Whilst the body colour remains black lettering is now described as 'pale blue'.

GRC&WCo.

No. 3082 has been rebuilt by Charles Roberts in November 1927 at their works in Wakefield. Originally it had been supplied to the Ministry of Munitions in 1918. Unusually for Baldwin this wagon was finished with a grey body, plain white letters and black ironwork.

courtesy HMRS AAR233

In 1931 five new 20-ton wagons with wooden bodies were bought from the Gloucester RC&WCo. They measured 21ft 1in. x 7ft 1in. x 5ft 6in. and had steel underframes, side, end and bottom doors. Numbers were 4601-4605 and it should be noted that 4601 was lettered differently, bearing the full company name. However, there is always the possibility that the wagons carried the two different names on opposite sides – a feature known from other owners' wagons. These wagons were painted black but now with plain white lettering – they would have looked impressive with pale blue lettering. *GRC&WCo.*

Silverhill (Mansfield, Notts.); Cwmgwrach & Empire, South Wales and Eastern United and Foxes Bridge collieries in the Forest of Dean.

Coke was also dealt with being sourced from some of the collieries dealt with who had coking plants but also from gas works such as Bath.

Clients for the coal and coke were not restricted to Bristol and were spread throughout the West Country. They included Yeovil Gas Works, Southampton Waterworks (coke from Bath), and Gloucester Carriage & Wagon itself. The Torquay Corporation Electricity Works at Newton Abbot and the Swindon Corporation's electricity works were both supplied with coal from Eastern United Colliery in the Forest of Dean.

Lowell Baldwin himself died on the 26th June 1946 when living in Tyndalls Park Road. Louise died 19th June 1950 at 55 Westbury Road.

It is possible that the business was carried on by sons, John and Peter Lowell. The limited company was restructured in

continued on page 20

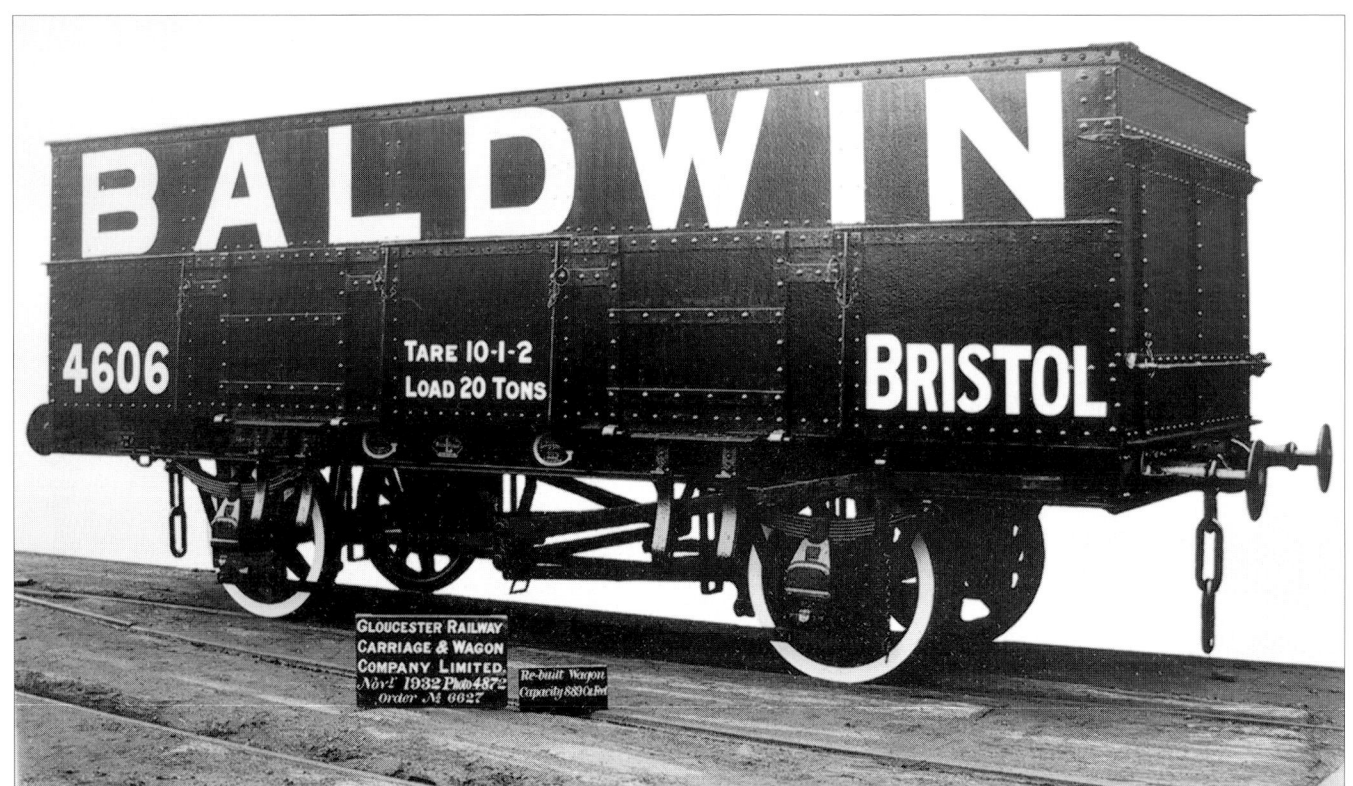

Another batch of 20-ton wagons, this time of all steel construction, was acquired in September 1932 on five years simple hire, this hire being renewed in 1937 seemingly with the addition of an extra wagon. The wagons appear not to have been new in 1932 as the Gloucester board clearly states 'Re-built Wagon Capacity 889 Cu. Feet'. Numbers ran 4606-4610 in a sequence following on the previously seen wooden 20-ton wagons. These wagons also carry Wagon Repairs Ltd plates in the centre of the solebars. Notice also a 2 cwt difference in tare weight between 4606 and 4609.

GRC&WCo.

A pair of coke wagons supplied in 1934 when an order was placed in November for fifty 12-tonners. However, 2030 above was photographed in June and is obviously an older wagon that has come into the works whilst in service for the fitting of the coke rails. One is led to wonder if a new contract had been secured and there was a need to get coke wagons in use before the order for a further fifty was placed. 2030 may be from the 1926 batch of wagons supplied by Gloucester. 3000, below, photographed in December 1934 is lettered to empty to Powell Duffryn's coke ovens at Bargoed. *GRC&WCo.*

Photographed in January 1936 was wagon No. 1538 built to the 1923 RCH specification with side, end and bottom doors. The small italic lettering on the solebar again reads: '*For repairs advise Head Office, 6 Redcliffe Hill, Bristol*'. Registration was by the GWR. Whilst on superficial inspection the lettering on this eight-plank wagon looks identical to that below note how the main lettering on 1584 reaches onto the top plank, the differing position of the fleet number and the Commuted Charge star. *GRC&WCo.*

Photographed in January 1937 and probably part of the order for twenty-five new 12-ton wagons placed in November 1936, is number **1584**. Again the wagon is branded as emptying to the coke ovens at Bargoed suggesting that Baldwin was doing a large amount of business in coke with Powell Duffryn. Lettering on this batch has gone back to being white. *GRC&WCo.*

Two Baldwin wagons are captured on the siding to Clevedon Gas Works off the Weston, Clevedon & Portishead Light Railway. Nearest the camera is a wagon number 23 belonging to the gas works and supplied by Gloucester RC&WCo. in 1932.

courtesy Roger Carpenter collection

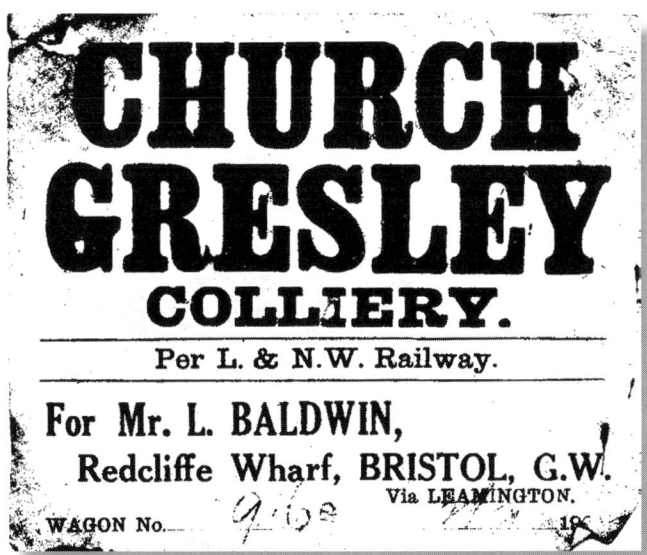

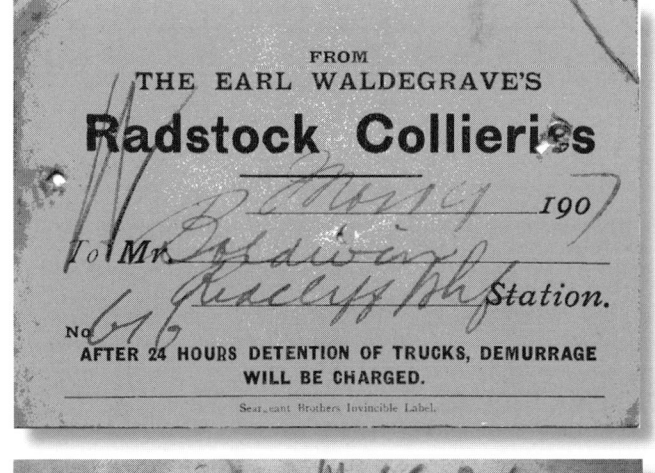

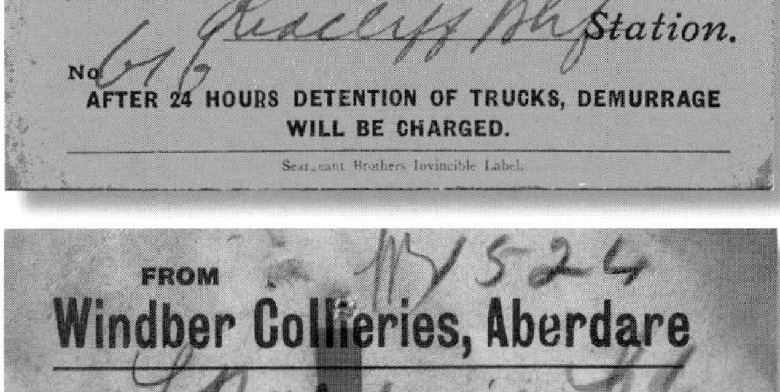

A selection of wagon labels. Church Gresley Colliery was in Derbyshire and dealings must have been frequent for a printed label to be produced. The Radstock Collieries label shows coal was obtained from the Somerset coalfield as well whilst the final label is for Windber Colliery, Aberdare. Baldwin wagons would thus have been seen over a wide area, in coal trains passing through Leamington Spa, along the Bristol & North Somerset line, on the South Wales main line through the Severn Tunnel and coming down the Midland main line from Gloucester. With the strident Baldwin on the wagon sides they certainly stood out in a train as witnessed by the image on the title page. *Keith Ettle & Steve Grudgings*

One thing that can be said about Lowell Baldwin's wagon fleet is that they were consistent in terms of main lettering style and make for very little variation within a train albeit they stand out very well. The livery therefore can be said to work extremely well with the wagons being easily identified from a distance, even when covered in coal dust and grime. *GRC&WCo.*

continued from page 15

March 1952 into Lowell Baldwin (Bristol) Limited and then in April 1968 came the report of the final winding-up of Lowell Baldwin (Transport) Ltd. [Interestingly at the same time and by the same chairman as the Bath Coal Co. and A. H. & S. Bird Ltd, were there connections? Had they been taken over?].

In 1954 Lowell Baldwin was described as an associate company of Amalgamated Anthracite Collieries Ltd and that 'Lowell Baldwin and its many subsidiary companies traded on their behalf throughout the South West of England. By this time of course the company was reliant on British Railways to provide the necessary wagons. They also became part of the BR modernisation and rationalisation plan of the 1960s when many small goods yards and coal sidings were removed. Instead coal distribution centres were built from where coal delivered in bulk by rail was taken by lorry to its destination – even if that meant retracing a wagon's route to a now disused railway goods yard out of which a coal merchant still operated! The coal distribution centre in Bristol was at Wapping Wharf and Lowell Baldwin soon had control over it trading as Western Fuel Co. This traffic ceased in 1987.

In terms of his wagon fleet the earliest known was provided by Hurst, Nelson of Motherwell in 1909. It was a 10-ton wagon with side and end doors, numbered 203 and registered by the GWR. This seven-plank wagon had the name 'BALDWIN' in letters four planks high, and 'BRISTOL' at bottom right.

The next wagon reference found thus far is for two wagons from the Midland Railway Carriage & Wagon Co. in June 1910. The exact details of the order are a little unclear, it suggests that Baldwin had gone to Midland to get finance on two wagons already in his possession. They were purchased by Midland at £40 each and then were relet to Baldwin for seven years at £7 2s each per year.

The next details found are for a number of orders with the Gloucester Railway Carriage & Wagon Co. In November 1918 when thirty-five secondhand 10-ton wagons were taken although the period of the hire was not specified. In February 1923 fifty-one 12-ton wagons were bought for cash at £134 each. The following month saw Gloucester financing one hundred new 12-ton wagons for Baldwin over the seven years purchase period. In November 1925 a further fifty 12-ton wagons were bought new over a ten year period, the total cost coming to £7,000.

Baldwin was not only dealing with Gloucester as in 1924 he took fifty wagons from Charles Roberts & Co., Wakefield with a batch of fifty 12-ton wagons, numbered 1800 to 1849 being delivered in September and October in six batches. All were registered by the LMS and fitted with side and end doors.

22.09.1924	1825-1828	Reg no's 37240-243
05.09.1924	1800-1808	Reg no's 37305-313
12.09.1924	1809-1830	Reg no's 37324-341
10.10.1924	1840-1842	Reg no's 37352-354
30.09.1924	1831-1834	Reg no's 37361-364
	1835-1839	Reg no's 37365-369
10.10.1924	1843-1849	Reg no's 37407-413

During the First World War a large number of wagons were built to carry iron ore for the Ministry of Munitions. During the mid-1920s these became available and after rebuilding many of them passed into traders' hands. One such was rebuilt by Charles Roberts in 1927 and sold to Baldwin becoming number 3082. Originally fitted with side door and bottom doors it was rebuilt to include an end door. The wagon must have been seen as a success, probably at a reasonable price, to Baldwin and two further batches of ex-MoM wagons were refurbished by Roberts in 1928: 3160-3167 (3161 having originally been built by Hurst, Nelson of Motherwell) and 3170-3179 (again, 3176 & 3179 were originally built by Hurst, Nelson).

A return was made to Gloucester for the next known wagons. In September 1932 there was a flurry of activity when a variety of wagons were taken on five years' simple hire: Fifteen 12-ton wagons to the 1923 RCH specification; twenty-five 'new regulation' 12-ton wagons; five 20-ton all steel wagons; fifty new specification 12-tonners; fifty 12-ton style not specified; and two hundred 12-tonners 'which are to be found'. The latter entry suggests that Gloucester had to scour their hire fleet to find the extra two hundred wagons. It would seem that the wagons purchased from Gloucester back in 1925 were bought out early from their purchase lease in September 1932 with Baldwin redeeming them for a payment of £3,038 12s 2d. 1932 was obviously a very good year for Baldwin.

Gloucester also provided some wagons in 1934 but unfortunately the details of the wagons are unknown due to a gap in the Gloucester records at this period. One wagon was,

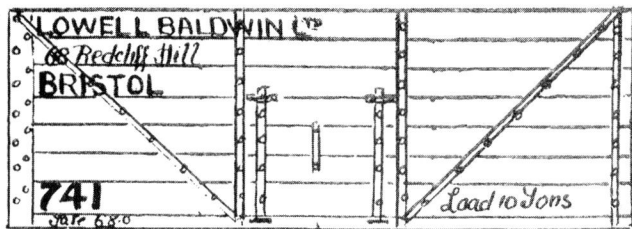

A sketch of 10-ton wagon No. 741 from *The Modeller's Sketch Book of Private Owner Wagons* Volume One by A. G. Thomas. Painted black with small white lettering in the top left corner, this is probably a wartime paint scheme. *A. G. Thomas*

however, photographed and this shows it to have been a coke wagon numbered 3000.

In November 1935 fifty 12-ton wagons were ordered from Gloucester with the instruction that they were to be delivered in January 1936 at a cost of £6,012 10s. In January 1936 there was a further order for the hire of thirty-three 12-ton wagons for 5 years and twenty-five 12-ton wagons were ordered in June 1936 although no details as to whether on hire or purchase were given.

Further hires were taken in December 1936 when a single 10-ton wagon was taken for 5 years and in September 1937 when six 20-ton were hired for 3 years.

BEACHIM & BALMONT

With an address of 38 Queen Square, Bristol and also Raymond Road, Bedminster, Bristol Beachim & Balmont can be found in Kelly's *Bristol Directory* for 1902 as sand and ballast merchants at Redcliff Back and cement merchants at Cheese Lane, St Philip's as well as being coal shippers.

The partners behind the title were Zebedee Beachim and James John Balmont. The 1881 census shows Beachim as being aged 50 and a coal merchant and colliery proprietor living in Abbotsford Road, Westbury on Trym. The reference to colliery proprietorship is interesting in that Beachim had been involved with Darranddu Colliery at Pontypridd between 1871 and 1875. Prior to this Beachim had also been a contractor, timber and coal merchant t/a Beachim Brothers (with Thomas, John, William and Walter) at Vobster and Kilmersdon, Somerset. This partnership was dissolved on the 1st January 1864.

Beachim & Balmont were operating wagons as early as December 1887 when three 10-ton wagons were taken over seven years from the Western Wagon Co. for £123 (presumably the total price for each). The wagons were reportedly sold for cash circa April 1890 to the Midland Railway Co. This would have been in the Midland's attempts to rid their system of privately operated wagons in which they were only partially successful but may explain why in many of the South Gloucestershire and Bristol colliery photographs only Midland Railway wagons are seen. It could be therefore that Beachim & Balmont only operated wagons for a three year period.

The partnership was dissolved in June 1903. Balmont was to continue the business although the services of Beachim were retained until May 1907. When they finally ceased trading is unknown but it seems to have been before the First World War.

BERRIL & Co.

The trading address of Kingsland Road Siding, St. Philips, and the signing up to the 1933 RCH Commuted Charge scheme are the only evidence of wagon ownership by this company. They do not appear to have purchased any new wagons during the grouping period so any wagons owned must have been acquired secondhand.

Not a lot is known of Percy Berril either, In 1912 he was the manager for A. J. Smith (see later) and was also a director of Princess Royal Colliery in the Forest of Dean (see *Private Owner Wagons of the Forest of Dean*). He was also on the board of A. J. Smith Ltd until he resigned in 1931. He then set himself up on his own account and in 1935 was acting as a coal factor at 101-102 St. Thomas Street and at Atlas Wharf, Redcliff Back. The 1938 *Colliery Year Book* lists him as a coal merchant at Atlas Wharf. It would appear that during the Second World War the business address changed a couple of times, first to 28 Garnet Street, then 186 North Street.

BIRD BROTHERS

It was James Charles Bird and Thomas B. Bird who traded as Bird Bros. James, born in 1868, and Thomas in 1869, were the sons of Samuel Bird, a dealer in horses living at 4 Bath Buildings, Bristol. Bird Brothers are recorded as having wagons in 1896 and an office at Montpelier Station in July 1897.

It would appear that the brother's partnership had been dissolved by 1900 when it is recorded in the Great Western & Midland Joint Committee minutes for the Clifton Extension Railway that James C. Bird was trading as the Cannock Coal Co. at Montpelier. He became the new tenant of an office and signboard – had he taken on the site previously used by Bird

```
BIRD BROS. FOR CLEAN COALS.
     As Supplied to Industrial Exhibition,
Best Drawing Room Cobbles, 17s 6d; Best Kitchen
Cobbles, 16s 6d; Best Durable House, 16s 6d; Best Large
Anthracite, 17s 6d; Briquettes, 17s per ton; Oak Chumps,
1s 6d cwt.; Sticks, 1s 9d sack.  Less 6d per ton, 3 or more
tons 1s. cash to carter.—Head Office: 196a, Cheltenham Road
Telephone 375.  Clifton Office: 77, Whiteladies Road.   9421
```

An advertisement for Bird Bros from September 1896 showing that they also traded in firewood.

Brothers? It seems that this business was short-lived as by January 1901 some of the tenancy had been transferred to the Central Coal Co. whilst in October there is mention of a new business, J. C. Bird & Co.

The 1902 Kelly's *Bristol Directory* has both Thomas R. Bird & Co. at 113 Whiteladies Road and Bird & Co. at 196A Cheltenham Road. The latter was actually J. C. Bird & Co. and was probably the only entry for the business as in January 1903 J. C. Bird & Co. were declared bankrupt having been put into receivership by creditors, despite the fact that a new tenancy was signed with the railway for coal stacking ground on the 26th January.

By 1912 there is a partnership of Wetmore & Bird (see page 109) listed in directories at Montpelier Station but it is unknown if the Bird in question was either James or Thomas.

Various wagons for Bird Brothers can be found in the wagon registers of the Midland Railway. On the 11th May 1896 two 10-ton wagons were built and financed by the Midland Railway Carriage & Wagon Co. of Birmingham. They were numbered 23 and 24 (registration numbers 19433/4, Midland owner's numbers 32342/3). Both measured 14ft 6in. x 6ft 11in. x 3ft 2in. with a full height (cut through) side door. Number 23 was recorded also as being rebuilt in 1925 by Wagon Repairs Ltd at Gloucester for H. Ablitt & Co. becoming their number 25. Where the wagon had been between the demise of Bird Bros and 1925 was not recorded.

In February 1897 the Midland Railway registered two more 10-ton wagons built by Midland RC&WCo. These were numbers 125 and 126 (Reg. No's 20390/1, Midland owner's No's 32873/4). Midland RC&WCo. also supplied two 8-ton wagons in March. These were numbered 127 and 128 (21187/8 and 32875/6). Again in the register it is recorded that number 128 was rebuilt by Wagon Repairs in 1924 to become number 10 in the fleet of W. J. Oldacre & Sons of Bishop's Cleeve near Cheltenham.

In February 1898 four 10-ton wagons were acquired from the same builder (their owner's numbers 33662-5). Numbered 129 to 132 they were again registered by the Midland Railway (23319-22). The final registrations were in November 1901 by which time the company was trading as Bird & Co. Again the Midland RC&WCo. were the builders and financiers of two 10-ton wagons numbered 20 and 21. The Midland Railway again registered the wagons, numbers 37087/8. (Midland owner's numbers were 36845/6.)

F. BIRD & Co.

F. Bird & Co. were a widespread coal merchants, originally based in Radstock with at least seventeen retail depots in Wiltshire, Somerset and Dorset including Salisbury, Weymouth, Devizes, Westbury and Trowbridge. The firm was liquidated in 1910 and many branches were sold off to their managers. They are recorded in 1889 with an address of Station Road, Montpelier. How long they operated from here is unknown, it is unlikely that any of their wagons would have been lettered for Bristol although they must have been seen in Montpelier goods yard. Possibly the agency here was taken over by Oliver Gullick who is detailed later.

BRISTOL & WEST OF ENGLAND COAL Co. Ltd

This company traded out of Pylle Hill sidings and was formed as a limited company in July 1892 to take over the business of John Warren. It is not known if Warren operated wagons and the new company had little chance to do so, being wound up in December 1892.

BRISTOL & WEST OF ENGLAND WAGON Co. Ltd

The company was incorporated in 1860 with a share capital of £100,000 divided into £10 shares 'to carry on the general business of a railway rolling stock company', that is to say they would finance and hire out railway rolling stock to both the main line railway companies and to private operators, usually through one of the wagon building companies. Indeed, two of the original shareholders were Messrs Shackleford and Ford, wagon builders of Cheltenham. Others included Handel Cossham, who will be encountered later in these pages and who was also connected with Shackleford & Ford, and John Butt, ironfounder, of Gloucester. By 1863 the capital was increased to £200,000 and the name was changed to the Bristol & South Wales Wagon Co. Ltd. Perhaps it was realised that greater profits could be made from the South Wales coalfield than in the West Country and thus the name was changed to reflect this.

Capital was increased several times over the years, reaching £500,000 in 1885. The half-year report for 1902 stated that the company owned (i.e. was financing) 15,149 carriages and wagons, and thirteen locomotives. Voluntary liquidation took place on the 2nd March 1934 although the remaining business may have been acquired by the Yorkshire Railway Waggon Co. Ltd, they certainly held a large shareholding.

One recorded order for wagons was in January 1875 when the company took twenty wagons on redemption hire from the Swansea Wagon Co. and in March agreed that they would maintain the wagons. Whether these wagons were for their own

A B&SWRWCo. owner's plate.   *courtesy Chris Sambrook*

use or were to be put into the hire stock is unknown.

For a period the company operated a wagon repair depot in Cardiff and may also have had one in the Bristol area. Wagons financed by the company would have been repaired at these depots and would also have carried a Bristol & South Wales Railway Wagon Co. Ltd owner's plate for the duration of the purchase period.

BRISTOL CO-OPERATIVE SOCIETY Ltd

The Bristol & District Co-operative Society was formed in 1884 with a shop at 32 Houlton Street, St. Pauls. In 1916 a merger took place with the Bedminster Co-operative Society at which date the name may have changed to the Bristol Co-operative Society Ltd. Like many other co-operative societies that in Bristol dealt in coal. It is possible that such trading did not start until after 1902 as there is no reference to the society as a coal merchant in the 1902 Kelly's *Directory of Bristol*.

By 1914 there were depots at Montpelier Station, Station Road, Montpelier; Lawrence Hill Station; Stapleton Road Station; Avonmouth; and New Station Road, Fishponds.

In the early part of the twentieth century wagons were provided by the Ince Waggon & Ironworks Co., Wigan, but the number supplied is unknown as no orders survive. Wagon number 12, above, was one supplied by this builder.

It is known that 12-ton wagons No's 1927 to 1966 were built by the Co-operative Wholesale Societies own wagon works at Peterborough in 1927-28 and registered by the LMS. Further 12-ton wagons, numbered 173 to 175, were built by the Bolton Wagon Works in 1936 and registered by the GWR.

Ten 12-ton mineral wagons were built by the C.W.S. wagon works in 1938 and numbered 46-55. Finally No's 36 to 45 and 1967 to 1971 were built in 1939 and rated as 13-ton capacity. All were registered by the LMS.

The Society also acquired wagons secondhand but these are difficult to track down. Only two are known with certainty and details of these are sketchy. Two were first registered by the Great Central Railway in 1904/05 as reconstructed wagons – probably converted from dead buffers to sprung. They both passed through the hands of the British Wagon Co., a wagon finance house based in Rotherham, to become numbers 13 and 15 in the Bristol fleet. They were possibly acquired soon after reconstruction as number 15 is recorded as being broken up in 1928, 13 continued in service until 1947.

BRISTOL MALAGO VALE COLLIERIES Co. Ltd

Malago Vale was a colliery in the Bedminster area to the north-west of the South Liberty Colliery of the Ashton Vale Co. Like South Liberty it was served by sidings off the Bristol & Exeter Railway between Bedminster and Parson Street stations and these were brought into use in August 1879.

The colliery was actually sunk back in 1840 and by 1848 was being run by Samuel Reynolds, Samuel Garratt, John Morgan,

Wagon No. 12 for the Bristol & District Co-operative Society was built by the Ince Waggon & Ironworks Co. in Wigan. A six-plank wagon with side doors only the livery appears to be black with plain white lettering. Unfortunately there is no record of the number of wagons taken at this time nor of the date of the order but it would have been in the first few years of the 20th century.

courtesy HMRS ACA025

An advertisement for the Malago Brick Works dating from 1901.

Malago Colliery & Brick Works
BEDMINSTER, BRISTOL.
Registered Telegraphic Address—MALAGO, BRISTOL.   Telephone No. 233.
CELEBRATED BEDMINSTER GREAT VEIN COAL. MACHINE AND HAND=MADE BRICKS, TILES, SQUARES, DRAIN=PIPES, &c.

James Scull, Henry Williams, and George Challenger trading as the Malago Vale Coal Company. On the 18th January 1848 Morgan and Scull left the partnership, on the 31st January 1849 Williams departed followed on the 24th June 1850 by Challenger. This left Samuel Reynolds and Samuel Garratt who continued to trade. By 1851 the partners were given as Edward Reynolds, Samuel Garratt and John Seaman and on the 31st December 1851 the partnership was dissolved leaving Garratt to continue alone. Garratt went bankrupt in August 1854 when his address was Perran Wharf, Penryn, Cornwall trading there as a contractor and as a coal pit proprietor in Bedminster.

In February 1855 the partners of the Malago Vale Coal Co. were given as Samuel Reynolds, James Sidney and Daniel Seaman together with Edward Sidney who still traded as the Malago Vale Coal Company as coal pit proprietors and vendors of coal. They were also part owners of Guinea Lane Colliery, the North Side Coal Works and Perry Hill Colliery. However, Edward Sidney was then declared bankrupt.

By 1862 Malago Vale was being worked by Steeds & Pilditch. The partners were Stephen Steeds and Richard Pilditch who both had other interests throughout the West Country and were related by marriage. Steeds and Pilditch also traded together as the Somerset Coal Co. at Radstock whilst Steeds was part owner

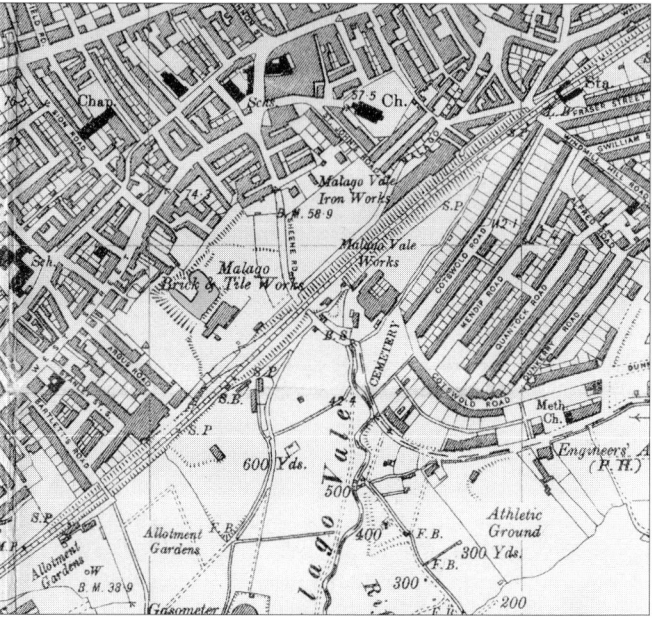

By the date of the Ordnance Survey 1930 6-inch map Malago Colliery was long gone but the brick and tile works with their siding remained. The main Bristol & Exeter line passes by with Bedminster Station in the top right-hand corner.

A cruel enlargement off an excellent quality image of Greyfield Colliery at Clutton, Somerset reveals the top two planks of a Malago Colliery Brick & Tile Works wagon. It is probably of four or five-plank construction with raised ends and what look to be full height (cut through) side doors. Livery would appear to be grey with white lettering but a red body cannot be ruled out. It is likely that the photograph post dates the closure of Malago Colliery and the brick works was now forced to source coal to fire the kilns from elsewhere.
Neil Parkhouse collection

of Vobster Colliery, Radstock and was a major shareholder in the Westbury Iron Co. Ltd at Westbury in Wiltshire. Steeds was also in partnership for a while with Frederick Bird of Radstock who has already been mentioned under F. Bird & Co. Pilditch was also a partner in the Devonshire Coal & Trading Co. based in Plymouth, Barnstaple and Newton Abbot. Perhaps here are some clues as to where Malago Vale coal may have been going.

It would appear that Pilditch left the partnership as by 1868 Malago Vale is recorded as being worked by S. Steeds & Co. It would seem that he invested heavily in the works and formed the Bristol Malago Vale Collieries Co. Ltd circa 1874. It was they who took out a private siding agreement with the Great Western Railway for sidings at Malago Vale.

The only wagons actually listed for Malago Vale were recorded by the Great Western Railway in their Freighter's Register. In September 1879 8-ton wagons numbers 201-225 built by the Bristol Waggon Co. are recorded and in January 1880 numbers 226-250. There are many wagons from several builders recorded for Stephen Steeds but given his wide interests it is impossible to say if any of them were lettered for Malago Vale.

The 1880 List of Mines shows Malago Vale to be worked by the Bristol Colliery Co. The private siding agreement had been transferred to the company in October 1879. The colliery was to close in 1892 by which time a brick works had been established on the site. The brick works continued in use for a period. Bristol Collieries Ltd were in receivership by 1910 and the works were bought by C. Pass & Sons and by 1916 the siding agreement was down to Malago Brick Works. According to the Ordnance Survey the works was still extant in 1930. The exact date of closure is unknown.

BRISTOL RAILWAY COAL ASSOCIATION

This is likely to have been a coal club formed by railwaymen, probably connected with the Midland Railway. A similar association existed in Gloucester as described in *Private Owner Wagons of Gloucestershire*. No address can be put to the association and the only evidence of wagon ownership comes from the Midland Railway wagon registers in which a 10-ton wagon, numbered 1, can be found being registered in July 1901. It was built by S. J. Claye of Long Eaton, Derbyshire and financed by the Lincoln Wagon & Engine Co.

BRISTOL ROLLING STOCK Co. Ltd

This company is mentioned in the Western Wagon Co's ledger (rent and purchase) but only in 1905. Despite the title it appears not to have traded in the city but was an attempt in 1904 to revive the Wheeler & Gregory wagon building business at Radstock. The company was dissolved in 1908.

BRISTOL STEAM NAVIGATION Co. Ltd

The company was registered in 1877 and reconstructed with the same name in December 1917. A Gloucester address was quoted in the RCH *Handbook of Stations* for 1904. However, Lloyd's Register of Shipping for 1894-95 gives 50 Princes Street, Bristol as the office address. The company's fleet at that time comprised eight steamers, ranging from the *Aline* of 1,112 tons to the *Juno* of only 488 tons. In 1914 there was also an office in Bute Street, Cardiff, which dealt with coal exporting.

On the 10th July 1895 the Gloucester RC&WCo. noted a recent agreement with the steamer company for the hire of two secondhand 10-ton wagons on a monthly basis. Apparently satisfied, a month later they agreed to take forty-eight more of the same, this time for a year. The wagons may have been used for hauling bunker coal from a colliery to one of the ports surrounding the Bristol Channel.

BRISTOL WAGGON WORKS Co. Ltd

The works was at Lawrence Hill, on the northwest side of the Midland's Bristol-Birmingham line. The founders of the firm in 1851 were Theodore and Albert Fry who were both Quakers. They set up in Temple Gate and initially probably produced road vehicles and agricultural equipment. With a move into railway rolling stock the business was moved to Lawrence Hill in 1866 where siding accommodation could be obtained. In 1889 the title of the business was changed to the Bristol Wagon & Carriage Works Co. Ltd to better reflect the work now carried out.

The company was acquired by the Leeds Forge Co. Ltd in 1920. The railway rolling stock building part of the business was transferred to Leeds in 1924 and the Bristol company was liquidated.

The works themselves can be seen on this map extract to the north of the goods yard at Lawrence Hill Station and served off the Midland Railway. The line running north-south is the Great Western Bristol & South Wales Union line. North of the wagon works is the site of Easton Colliery. *Ordnance Survey 6-inch 1930*

Another enlargement of a Somerset colliery, this time Norton Hill, reveals a wagon lettered for the Bristol Railway Carriage Works Co. Ltd. The wagon is somewhat elderly and of four-plank construction with dead buffers, raised ends and brakes one side. It is lettered 'Bristol Railway Carriage' along the top two planks with 'Works Co. Ltd' on the next plank down spaced either side of the side door. Unfortunately it is not possible to read the number. It is assumed that the wagon is a product of the works and is in Norton Hill to collect a load of boiler coal. *collection Neil Parkhouse*

BRITISH COAL Co.

The British Coal Co. has connections throughout the coal trade of the whole company in that connected with it were the Smith family – that of Alpheus Smith. Wherever one seems to look the name of Alpheus pops up, together with that of his son, Montague.

The *Bristol Mercury* of the 30th September 1882 carried details of the formation of the The British Coal Co. Ltd with a capital of £10,000 in 2,000 £5 shares. It was set up to acquire and consolidate the business carried on by Messrs Alpheus Smith & Sons as colliery agents at London & Bristol and as coal factors and merchants under the style of the British Coal Co. The company traded at Paddington in London and seem to have been as Montpelier Station in Bristol. Alpheus Smith was to be managing director and his sons, Eustace and Montague, agents. Montague's address was given as 1 Worcester Terrace, Clifton Park, Bristol. The first registered office was in London but moved to 1 Queen Road, Clifton and then to 109 Whiteladies Road.

The company was wound up in November 1893 as it could not continue in business due to its liabilities. The Bristol end of the operation, however, appears to have been taken over as in April 1904 the British Coal Co. renewed a tenancy on coal stacking ground at Montpelier. In April 1907 it was recorded that the Coal Pit Heath Coal Co. were now trading as the British Coal Co. suggesting that they may have been them who bought up the business.

The Midland Railway wagon registers show two wagons put down to the British Coal Co., Bristol in September 1901. Two 10-ton wagons, numbered 101 and 102 are recorded as having been built by S. J. Claye at Long Eaton, Derbyshire.

I. B. BRITTON

Britton was a late-comer into the Bristol coal supply business. On the 1901 census Isaac Benjamin Britton can be found aged 16 with the note 'helps in coal trade'. By 1911 he had set himself up as a coal dealer. He was listed by the RCH in 1926 and 1933 with an office address of 152 Avon Vale Road, Barton Hill and in the 1938 *Colliery Year Book* as a coal merchant at the same address. It is only that he signed up to the two RCH schemes that leads to the belief that he operated his own wagons.

SAMUEL BROOKMAN

Samuel Brookman was born in 1867 and is shown on the 1881 census as living at Warmley Tower, Bitton with his parents. His occupation was a 'salesman in coal yard (dealer)'. His father, Benjamin, was a 'foreman in coal yard'. This was undoubtedly for the Kingswood Colliery as in 1879 he was the manager for them at Bitton and Warmley stations. There may be a deeper connection with the Kingswood Colliery as in October 1900 Samuel Brookman is reported in the GW&Mid Jt Comm. minutes as being the new tenant of wharfage at Montpelier Station, the old tenants being the Kingswood & Parkfield Colliery Ltd. In 1901 Samuel is given in the census as a coal merchant aged 34 whilst his younger brother, Frank, born in 1881, was a coal merchant's clerk.

In 1902 Kelly's *Bristol Directory* gives the trading address as Station Road, Montpelier and this address continues through until at least 1938. In February 1902 Brookman took possession of a 'hut' at Montpelier and in 1903 an office and coal stacking ground.

Little is known of his wagon fleet apart from two orders with the Gloucester Railway Carriage & Wagon Co. and registrations with the Midland Railway. In April 1902 an 8-ton wagon was purchased new for cash. This was to be numbered 30 and he also took a seven year repair contract on it which was renewed in April 1908. His next two wagons were bought from the Midland RC&WCo. of Birmingham. Both were of 8-ton capacity and the first one was numbered 31 and registered in November 1901 (37061), the second, numbered 32 was registered in August 1903 (42360). There is then a gap until June 1913 when Brookman returned to the Gloucester RC&WCo. for a pair of 10-ton wagons, numbered 33 and 34. These were bought new on seven years deferred purchase terms and registered with the Midland Railway. It would appear that at the same time Brookman disposed of his 8-ton wagon number 30 to fellow Bristol merchants W. W. Milton & Co.

Brookman may have obtained a secondhand 10-ton wagon as in November 1915 he took a repair contract with Gloucester on a single wagon.

He signed up to both the 1926 and the 1933 RCH schemes and is listed in the 1938 *Colliery Year Book* trading as a coal merchant at Montpelier Station. It is likely therefore, that his wagons went into the 'pool' in 1939.

An advertisement from 1901 for Brookman shows him to have once been with the Kingswood & Parkfield Collieries Co.

S. BROOKMAN,
Late Kingswood and Parkfield Collieries Company's Depot, MONTPELIER STATION.
All the Best Quality Coals kept in Stock, at Lowest Possible Prices.

8-ton wagon No. 30 was photographed in March 1901 having been bought new for cash together with a seven year repair contract. The five-plank wagon with full height side doors was painted 'light lead colour', with black lettering and red shading separated from the letter by a thin line of body colour. Note the monogram of the intertwined S and B on the side doors. The solebar carries Gloucester builder's and repairer's plates and a Midland Railway registration plate. *GRC&WCo.*

Wagon No. 33 built by Gloucester in 1913 is an extremely attractive example of the art of the signwriter. With the two wagons bought at this time being on deferred purchase No. 33 has the complete set of Gloucester plates on the solebar, builder's, owner's and repairer's plus a registration plate for the Midland Railway. Of seven-plank construction with side doors only, the wagon is also fitted with the 'gap closing' bar between the hinges of the side door. *GRC&WCo.*

Samuel Brookman operated out of Montpelier Station on the Clifton Extension Railway which can be found centre right on this 6-inch to the mile map extract dating from 1930. The well laid-out sweeping roads on the hills of Montpelier, Redland and Clifton contrast with the more compact dwellings of the area to the bottom right of the extract in St. Paul's. All of the houses would however, have had many open fireplaces with a demand for coal keeping merchants such as Brookman busy with deliveries.

Ordnance Survey 6-inch, 1930

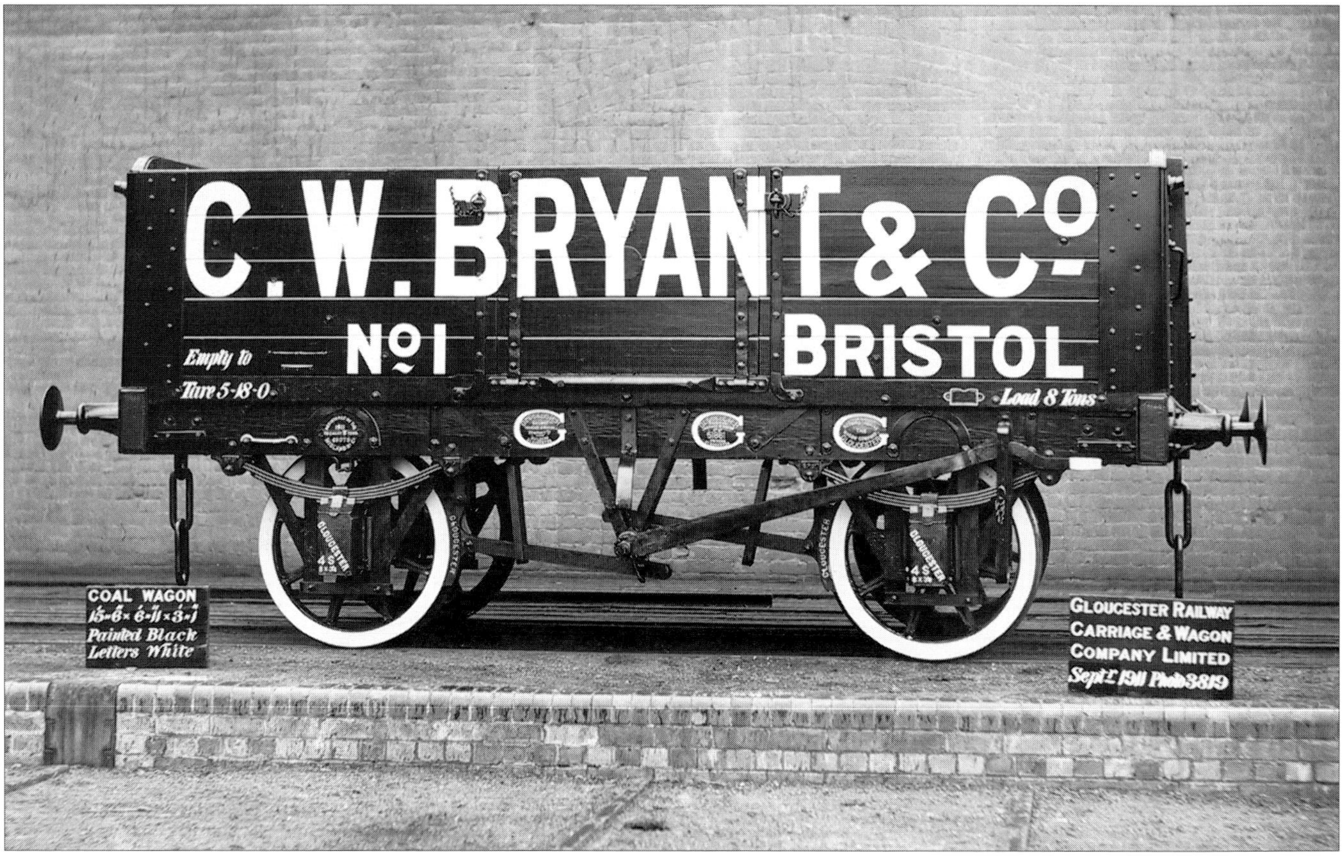

Bryant's wagon No. 1 was photographed by Gloucester in September 1911. It was one of two five-plank 8-ton wagons taken at the time on seven years deferred purchase terms. Fitted with side doors only and brakes one side there is also an angled commode handle at the right-hand end. As already mentioned these were used to allow the merchant, or one of his coalmen, to pull themselves up to check that the wagon was empty and that no 'foreign bodies' had been thrown in. They also served as a useful, although dangerous, handhold from which to gain extra purchase on the brake lever should it be sticking in the guide or stiff to move. Registration of the wagons was with the Midland Railway. The wagons were painted black with plain white lettering. *GRC&WCo.*

C. W. BRYANT & Co.

Little can be found of this business. It is believed that the proprietor was Charles William Bryant who is shown in the Kelly's *Bristol Directory* for 1914 at 88 Kennington Avenue, Ashley Down Road and at the Upper Railway Wharf, Midland Road, St. Philip's.

His only known wagons were obtained from the GRC&WCo. in October 1911 with two 8-ton wagons, numbered 1 and 2 being taken new on seven years deferred purchase at £12 per wagon per annum. Gloucester were to do the repairs. The two wagons were registered by the Midland Railway (68075-6). There is no evidence of any further wagons being obtained and Bryant can not be found listed in any other directories. He was also not listed among Coal Merchants in the 1938 *Colliery Year Book*.

W. BUTLER & Co. (BRISTOL) Ltd

Butlers were covered in *Private Owner Wagons of Gloucestershire* in connection with their works on the River Severn at Upper Parting near Gloucester but are included again here for the sake of completeness of this volume.

The main works of the company was on the River Avon at Crew's Hole to the east of Bristol. Neither of their works were rail connected and they relied on barges to transship cargoes. Core products were tar, rosin and oil which they both distilled and imported. The works at Crew's Hole were set up in 1843 mainly to provide preservative for the sleepers and longitudinal baulks of Brunel's Great Western Railway. Brunel chose as his manager of the works one William Butler. Financial backing came from Messrs Roberts and Daines who were iron masters at St. Philips. By 1863 Butler was operating the works in his own name.

In 1872 management was in the hands of William Butler,

An impression of the company's offices and stores in Silverthorne Lane, St. Philips from a publication of 1892, probably with a degree of artistic licence. Note the Feeder Canal alongside, the nearest rail would have been the Kingsland Road Sidings.

A rectangular tar tank built for Butler by Charles Roberts of Wakefield in 1932 and one of two taken at this time. A further batch was built in 1941 of which No. 73 can be seen on page 97 of *Oil on the Rails* by Alan Coppin. The wagons were insulated and fitted with heating coils to allow the tar to be warmed up for discharge. *courtesy HMRS AAR024*

William Henry Butler, Joseph B. Butler and Thomas Butler. As well as Crew's Hole the company now had a depot at St. Philips where as well as offices there was a storage facility for all of the company's products which was convenient for transfer to rail, indeed the Kingsland Road Sidings were just across Silverthorn Lane. William Butler retired from the works in 1889 and died in October 1900.

Originally creosote and pitch were the saleable products from Bristol, the pitch going to South Wales for the manufacture of patent fuel briquettes and such was the trade that Butler ended up buying out the Crown Preserved Coal Co. of Cardiff when it ran into financial difficulties rather than see it close. The crude tar from which all of the products were made was sourced from far and wide, mainly from gas works, some as far away as Reading whose tar was brought by narrow boat along the Kennett & Avon Canal. More came from Bath along the Avon, from Portishead and from the Stapleton Road Gas Works in Bristol – transferred in rail tanks from the gas works to St. Philips and then by barge to Crew's Hole. Gas works remained the main source of tar until the advent of natural gas in the 1970s after which tar came in from coke ovens in South Wales. Crew's Hole continued in use until 1981.

Over the years other by-products came to be of importance, particularly during the two World Wars. One was motor benzole and William Butler & Co. were quick into the market place through a subsidiary, The British Refined Motor Spirit Co.

As would be expected Butler's had a large tank wagon fleet, at one time it is believed that there were fifty-three in use. These were used for both spirits and tar, the former carried in cylindrical tanks, the latter in both cylindrical and rectangular vehicles. A number of open wagons were also in the fleet as shown by number 29 below. Some of these were fitted with coke crates, a portion of one being seen in a view of Bristol Docks reproduced in *The Bristol & Gloucester Railway* by Colin Maggs (page 39).

A 10-ton open wagon built by the Gloucester RC&WCo. in 1904. It may have been used for bringing coal into the works or for collecting tar in barrels from gas works. The wagon is more fully described in *Private Owner Wagons of Gloucestershire*.
GRC&WCo.

Two postcard views of the Cattybrook works with the Great Western main line to South Wales via the Severn Tunnel passing by. Unfortunately no Cattybrook wagons are visible although in the upper view a line of coal wagons stands in the sidings seen above the row of cottages. Here also were the private sidings belonging to the brick works. The row of cottages no longer stands but a footbridge is still at this location. The scene is typical of large brick works anywhere with a forest of chimneys dominating the landscape. Today not a chimney is to be seen. *both Neil Parkhouse collection*

CATTYBROOK BRICK Co. Ltd

It was the building of the Great Western Railway's Severn Tunnel line which led to the foundation of this company. In digging a cutting on the approach to the tunnel at Pilning a good bed of clay was found by the resident engineer, Charles Richardson. As the tunnel had a huge appetite for bricks a local works would save on shipping charges and so he established the works at Cattybrook. 19,125,440 bricks were supplied by Cattybrook for use in the Severn Tunnel which was about a quarter of the total used.

The title Cattybrook Brick Co. Ltd was in use by 1880 when *Slater's Directory* showed an office address of 9 Berkeley Square, Bristol whilst the manager was one Ernest Street. Street was still there in 1905 at which time the secretary was W. H. L. Durnsford.

Once the Severn Tunnel contract was over the brick works turned to selling its output to the general building and contracting trade. Many bricks were exported through Bristol

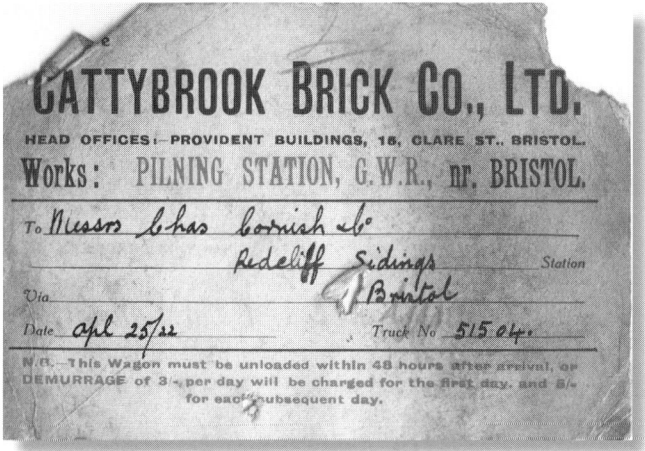

A wagon label from Cattybrook dating from April 1922 for a local delivery to Redcliff Sidings in what was probably a Great Western open wagon. *courtesy Steve Grudgings*

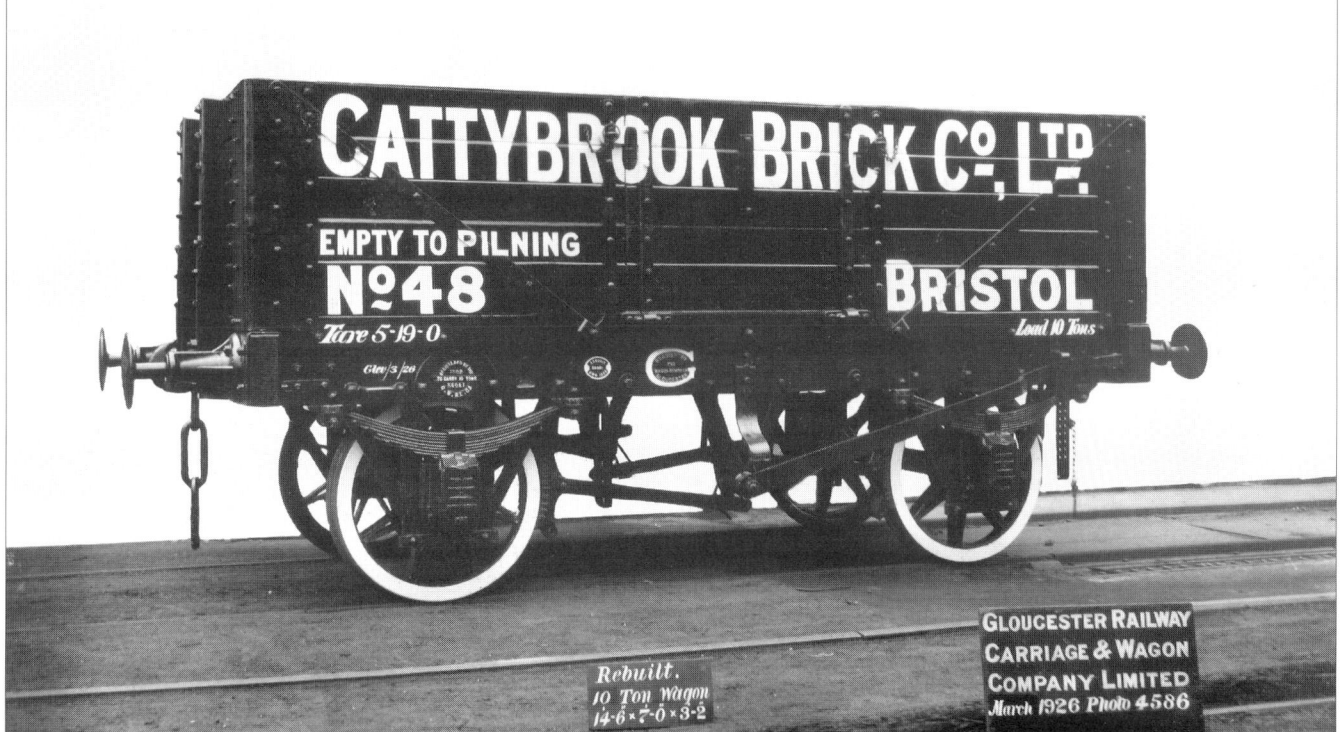

All of the wagons supplied to the Cattybrook Brick Co. by the Gloucester RC&WCo. in 1926 were secondhand. They date from 1902 and registration was with the Great Western but without that company's registers who they originally belonged to cannot be said. No. 48 was picked out of the line of 48-50 for individual attention. *both GRC&WCo.*

No. 92 was photographed in February 1926 and this time it is possible to read the axlebox covers which show that the wagon was originally built by the Midland RC&WCo. in 1902. The solebar has a large Gloucester G plate showing that they had rebuilt the wagon, together with a small oval GWR rebuilt plate indicating that the railway company's inspector had inspected the wagon after its rebuild. Livery looks to be black with plain white lettering. *GRC&WCo.*

Docks to South Wales whilst many of Bristol's fine red-brick buildings are built of Cattybrook products.

The works were served by a siding off the GWR which was extant pre 1881 and for which a private siding agreement was taken out in April 1881. About 1903 the Cattybrook company took over the works of the Shortwood Brick & Tile Co. at Shortwood to the east of Bristol, together with a siding off the Midland Railway Yate to Bath line.

Very few records of wagons for the brick works survive. The earliest are possibly those ordered by Charles Richardson from the Cheltenham & Swansea Wagon Co. in November 1870 when four broad gauge wagons were taken on a six year purchase lease at £18 per wagon per annum. Financing was done via the Bristol Waggon Co. – probably the Bristol & South Wales Wagon Co. Four wagons, gauge not specified so presumed to be standard gauge, were ordered from the Cheltenham & Swansea in March 1872 in the name of the Cattybrook Brick Works on six year redemption hire at £20 per wagon per annum.

The Great Western Railway Freighter's Register shows 10-ton wagons numbered 7 to 24 being registered in January 1873 having been built by the Bristol Waggon Works Co. The same builder provided 10-ton wagons 25 to 30 in April 1882.

In 1926 the Railway Clearing House gave the office address of the company as Provident Buildings, 15 Clare Street, Bristol. It was in that year also that four secondhand wagons, numbered 92 and 48-50, were photographed by the Gloucester Railway Carriage & Wagon Co. Number 92 was photographed in February 1926 and had first been registered by the GWR in 1902. 40 to 50 were photographed the following month. There is, however, no record of the orders so it is impossible to say how many wagons were taken at this time.

CENTRAL COAL Co.

The Central Coal Co. had an address of Blackboy Hill, Bristol, and later at 9 Charnwood Road, Fishponds. The business was extant in the late 1890s and was a partnership between two brothers Robert Henning and Wilfred Wharton Parr, together with one Henry Coles. The brothers were the sons of Robert H. Parr who in 1881 was the vicar of St. Martins, Scarborough, Yorkshire. Robert junior had been born in Scarborough in 1872 whilst Wilfred had been born in Clifton in 1873. What made them both come to Clifton and set up in business as coal merchants is unknown. Possibly the link is Henry Stratton Coles who was born in Clifton and who was described on the 1901 census as a retired banker aged 36.

In January 1901 a minute of the Great Western & Midland Joint Committee's Clifton Down Extension Railway refers to a new tenancy for the site of an office at Montpelier with the Central Coal Co. taking over from J. C. Bird trading as the Cannock Coal Co. In January 1902 they were renewing the tenancy on the hut but in July the tenancy passed to C. E. Shirley, both for the office and for coal storage space. It may

CENTRAL COAL CO.,
18, Victoria Street,
CLIFTON,

Depots & Branch Offices: CLIFTON DOWN STATION.
MONTPELIER STATION.

R. H. PARR,
W. W. PARR, } Proprietors.

TELEGRAMS—
"CENTRAL, BRISTOL"

TELEPHONE 5667.

ALL COALS KEPT IN STOCK.
Special Advantages to Large Consumers.
TRUCK LOADS OF ANY COAL QUOTED FOR TO ANY STATION.

An advertisement for the Central Coal Co. dating from 1901 and giving fairly good details of the business, certainly having the proprietors listed is extremely helpful.

have been at this date that they moved to Clifton Down Station. Certainly Kelly's *Bristol Directory* of 1902 shows them at Clifton Down Station as well as at 18 Victoria Street, Clifton.

The business was also trading at Bath and Corsham when in December 1910 Henry Coles left the partnership, interestingly there was no mention of any Bristol address. By March 1936 another member of the Coles family was back with the company as at that date the partnership between Robert Henning Parr and Denys Francis Parr Coles was dissolved with Parr to continue. The addresses given at this time were Lansdown Road, Clifton and 1 Bladud Buildings, Bath. Denys Coles later had a connection with T. Paul (see page 69).

The 1914 edition of *Kelly's* lists the business at 5 Grove Buildings, Whiteladies Road, Redland with depots at Clifton Down Station and Canon's Road Station and agencies at 17 Victoria Street, Clifton and 67 Henleaze Road, Westbury-on-Trym. The 1923 *Colliery Year Book* has them as coal contractors and factors at 87 Alma Road, Clifton whilst the Central Coal Co. appear in Kelly's *Directory of Bristol* for 1935 with an address of 'Colliery Chambers, Lansdown Road, Clifton 8' and at Clifton Down Station, the same address appears in the 1938 *Colliery Year Book*.

The first wagons for the Central Coal Co. were five 10-ton wagons built and financed by the Midland Railway Carriage & Wagon Co. and registered by the Midland Railway in December 1898. They were numbered 1 to 5. In December 1902 10-tonners numbered 16 to 20 were acquired from the same source.

In March 1909 the Central Coal Co. makes an appearance in the Gloucester RC&WCo's records when they took a secondhand 10-ton wagon on five years deferred purchase terms and with a twelve year repairing contract. The wagon had actually been sold by Gloucester in February 1907 to the Western Coal Co. of Bristol.

At the end of 1909 a further twenty Midland RC&WCo. 10-ton wagons were taken. They were registered in two batches, numbers 90 to 99 in December 1909 and 100 to 109 in January 1910. 90 to 99 were put down to Bath and may have been lettered as such.

There may have been a renumbering of the fleet at some point as the Midland Register added notes to wagons 1 to 5 built in 1902 to the effect that number 1 was rebuilt as number 332 by Derbyshire C&WCo., New Whittington; number two became 333 on rebuilding by Wagon Repairs, Radstock, in 1925. Number 3 was rebuilt as number 334 by Derbyshire C&WCo., Chesterfield, and became 1 inch wider. Number 4 became 335 at Wagon Repairs, Radstock in 1924 and number 5 was rebuilt as 336 at Wagon Repairs, Gloucester, in 1925.

CLEEVE COAL Co.

Very little can be found on this business. In 1926 they were listed by the RCH with an address of 9 Charminster Road, Fishponds. This is repeated in 1933 and in Kelly's 1935 *Bristol Directory* where they can be found listed as coal factors.

A wagon of the Cleeve Coal Co. caught in a snapshot of Clifton Down. The wagon number appears to be three-figure, possibly 260. The wagon appears to be of five- or six-plank construction and painted black with plain white lettering. *collection K. Darke*

CLIFTON COAL Co.

Listed by the Railway Clearing House in 1933 at Clifton Down Station it would appear that Walter William Porch & Son were behind the business and appear as such in Kelly's 1935 *Bristol Directory*. This also gave them as having a depot in Kingsland Road, St. Philips. The company went into voluntary receivership in June 1937 when W. W. Porch was given an address of 2 Hartington Park, Redland together with depots at Clifton Down and 23 Kingsland Road.

There are, however, references to a much earlier Clifton Coal Co. who were advertising in 1876 (overleaf) as colliery proprietors and coal merchants both wholesale and retail with offices at 1 West Clifton Terrace, Whiteladies Road and depots at Clifton Down, Montpelier and other stations. They were also trading in stone and sand as witnessed by advertisements in the *Bristol Mercury* in 1883 when details could be had of a Mr Wookey of Rowberrow. Somerset. John Snow (page 00) also traded as the Clifton Coal Co. for a period.

Walter Porch can be found aged 32 on the 1901 census working as a coal merchant's manager and it is tempting to wonder if he took over the Clifton Coal Co. from previous owners.

CLIFTON COAL COMPANY
Colliery Proprietors
AND
COAL MERCHANTS
Wholesale and Retail.

CHIEF OFFICES:

1, West Clifton Terrace,

White Ladies' Road,

CLIFTON.

DEPOTS:

CLIFTON DOWN,

Montpelier & other Railway Stations

PRICE LISTS, POST FREE, ON APPLICATION.

Left: An 1876 advertisement for the Clifton Coal Co. which, unfortunately, gives no clues as to the owners of the business but does grandly state that they were also colliery proprietors.

COAL AGENCIES Ltd

The Princess Royal Colliery Co. Ltd from the Forest of Dean (see *Private Owner Wagons of the Forest of Dean*) had a retail branch in Bristol which opened in Cheese Lane in 1906. In 1910 the agency was taken over by the directors of A. J. Smith Ltd (see page 95) and in 1920 it was formed into a limited company, Coal Agencies Ltd which in 1935 was trading at Passage Street and from the GWR Sidings, Canons Marsh. It is possible that having seen what could be achieved by an agency for a single colliery company that the formation of Coal Agencies Ltd allowed the taking on of the sole sales agency for more collieries all over the country as would be suggested by the company title. It would certainly give a better impression than a single coal merchant applying for an exclusive sales agency for an area.

This company in turn took over its parent, A. J. Smith Ltd in December 1948 the 'directors and shareholders of the two companies the same'. Coal Agencies Ltd continued trading until June 1959 when it amalgamated with Renwick, Wilton & Dobson who were one of the largest West Country coal factors.

Several batches of wagons can be put down to the company, two from the Gloucester RC&WCo. and one to Marcroft

Below: Coal Agencies number 413 was photographed by Gloucester RC&WCo. in October 1935. Of seven-plank construction with side and end doors it was painted black with plain white lettering. As will be seen the main title on an arc is almost identical to that of sister company Alfred J. Smith Ltd. *GRC&WCo.*

TELEGRAMS :— BRISTOL 23271 TELEPHONE :— 23271 PTE. BCH. EX.

ALL SALES ARE SUBJECT TO WAR, STRIKES OR OTHER STOPPAGES BEYOND OUR CONTROL AND TO EXPORT DUTY OR TAX OR INCREASED RAILWAY OR DOCK CHARGES IMPOSED DURING CONTRACT PERIOD. COLLIERY WEIGHTS TO BE CONCLUSIVE FOR INLAND TRADE AND DOCK WEIGHTS FOR SHIPMENT, QUOTATIONS ARE SUBJECT TO MARKET FLUCTUATIONS AND TO REPLY BY RETURN OF POST.

ALL COMMUNICATIONS TO BE ADDRESSED TO THE COMPANY

COAL AGENCIES LIMITED
COAL AND COKE MERCHANTS AND FACTORS
ST. PHILIP'S BRIDGE
BRISTOL 2

DEPOTS
PYLLE HILL RAILWAY SIDING
CANONS MARSH RLY. SIDING

CONTRACTORS TO H.M.
GOVT., CORPORATION OF
BRISTOL. ETC. ETC.

One of the two 13-ton wagons built by Gloucester in 1943 and lettered in the utility style. The seven-plank wagon has a steel underframe and three-hole disc wheels. The livery was again black with plain white lettering and with a white stripe along the diagonal to denote the opening end.
GRC&WCo.

Wagons Ltd, Coalville, Leicestershire but not until the 1930s. This suggests that previously if wagons were operated then they were acquired secondhand.

It was in November 1935 that an order for fifteen 12-ton wagons was recorded with Gloucester followed in May 1936 by a further twenty similar wagons. The 1935 wagons were registered by the LMS and were numbered 401 to 415. There is no further trace of the 1936 batch. Also in 1936 fifteen 12-ton wagons, 416 to 430, were built by Marcroft.

No more wagons were registered until 1943 when two 13-ton wagons were bought from Gloucester and numbered 431 and 432.

COALPIT HEATH COAL Co.

The Coalpit Heath Company was covered in *Private Owner Wagons of Gloucestershire* as the colliery they operated was actually to the north of Bristol in south Gloucestershire. However, a couple of images of their wagons have now been discovered together with some more documentary evidence of wagon ownership and this, coupled with the fact that they operated a sales business in the city, allows for the company to be revisited. Historically the Coalpit Heath collieries were some of the first to be directly connected to Bristol by rail via the Bristol & Gloucestershire Railway which terminated at Avon Wharf. The connection with Avon Wharf was retained through 1902 when they appear in Kelly's *Bristol Directory* with addresses of Avon Street, St. Philips and Station Road, Montpelier. Another connection here is that the coal yard at Avon Wharf was originally known as Hewitt's Yard. Whilst originally being coal merchants, from around 1820, the family later became concerned with the management of the Coalpit

Heath collieries, retaining this interest until the First World War period.

At some point between 1904 and 1914 they seem to have moved their sales depot from Avon Wharf to the Upper Railway Wharf in the Midland Yard at St. Philips. In 1914 their offices were given as Albion Chambers, Broad Street whilst they had depots at St. Philips as already noted and at Montpelier Railway Station.

The depot at Montpelier may have come about as a take over of the British Coal Company as the Great Western & Midland Joint Railways minutes record in April 1907 the transfer of 140 yards of coal stacking ground at Montpelier.

The first details of wagons come from the records of the Midland Waggon Co. in October 1857 which show that the Coalpit Heath Coal Co. had thirty wagons on hire and that the manager, Mr Hewitt, wanted them to be fitted with side chains at a cost of 10s each.

In October 1861 ten 6-ton wagons were taken over five years at £9 per wagon per annum. June 1866 saw a further fifty 7-

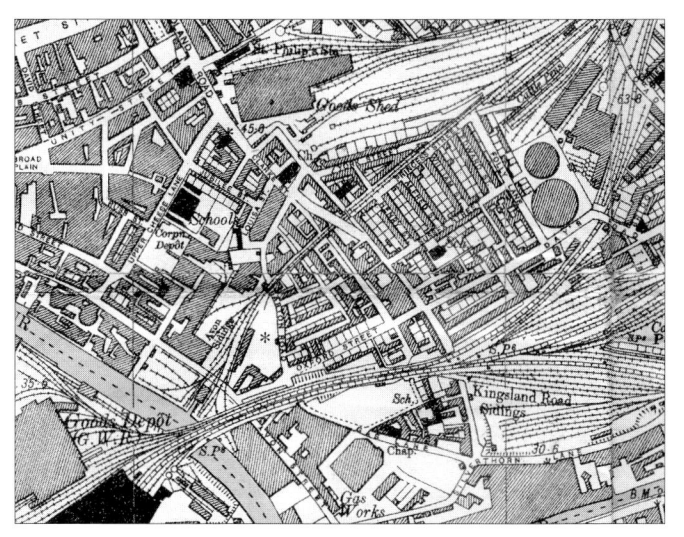

The Avon Wharf, bottom left, terminated alongside the River Avon. The blank space marked * was Hewitt's Yard and later the Coalpit Heath depot before they moved to St. Philips, top.

Mr Eames, colliery manager at Coalpit Heath, stands by wagon No. 36 built by the Midland RC&WCo. Unfortunately no further details of the wagon, such as date of building, are known. The livery would appear to be black with plain white lettering. Italic lettering on the side rail shows that repairs were to be carried out by Wheeler & Gregory Ltd at Radstock. In the view on the opposite page the Midland RC&WCo's owner's number can be read as 34735 showing the wagon to have been on hire or deferred purchase. It is a pity the registration plate cannot be seen! *both courtesy Frampton Cotterell & District Local History Society*

ton wagons being taken at £9 pwpa but this time over ten years. Finally in December 1869 twenty 7-ton wagons were acquired at £8 pwpa over seven years. It is assumed that all of these orders with the Midland Waggon Co. were deferred purchases.

As recorded in *Private Owner Wagons of Gloucestershire* there were orders with the Gloucester RC&WCo. during the 1890s.

The advertisement reproduced here shows that the Coalpit Heath Coal Co. also operated as coal factors bringing coal from other coalfields into Bristol. This opens up the fact that wagons for the company may have been seen in various collieries in Derbyshire, Staffordshire and Warwickshire as well as collecting anthracite from South Wales.

HERBERT S. COLBORN

Colborn took a single secondhand 10-ton wagon from the Gloucester RC&WCo. in May 1917. It was paid for in cash and a repair contract for seven years was taken at the same time.

Herbert Samuel Colborn was born in 1873 the son of Richard Colborn who was an iron merchant's clerk. By 1901 Herbert was the manager for a coal factor in Bristol and he still held this position in 1911. *Kelly's* directory for 1914 shows him living at 80 Downend Road, Fishponds.

Unfortunately Colborn does not appear in the 1928 *Colliery Year Book* either as a coal factor or merchant, nor does he have a listing in the 1935 edition of *Kelly's*. All that we can do is surmise that he set himself up in business around 1917, probably in the Fishponds area. He may, as was often the case, have taken over the business for which he had once been manager. As no further wagon purchases can be found it may also have been the case that his trading was short-lived.

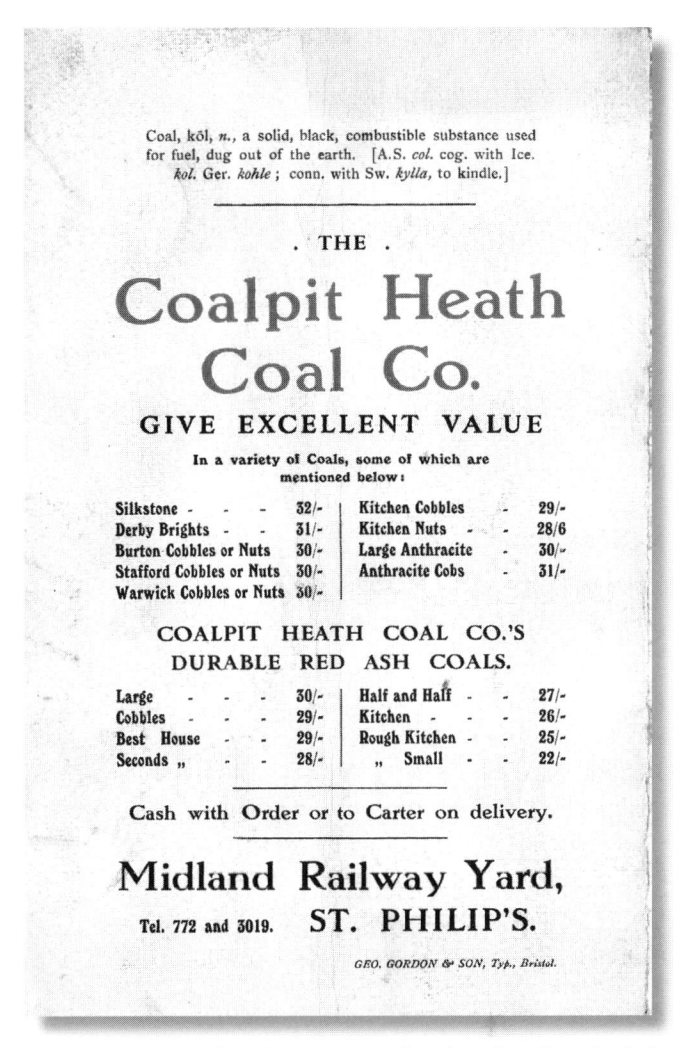

An advertisement for the company showing that they dealt in coals other than those won at Coalpit Heath in their capacity of coal factors. The various grades of coal are of interest, as is the fact that they could supply coal from Derbyshire at virtually the same price as coal from Coalpit Heath, this probably reflecting the fact that coal could be won more cheaply from a large colliery as the railway carriage charge would be commensurately larger for the greater distance travelled. *Author's collection*

H. E. COOLE & Co.

When signing up to both the 1926 and 1933 RCH agreements the address of the business was given as Lawrence Hill Wharf, Bristol. Coole was in business at least as early as 1914 when *Kelly's* shows Coole & Co. at Lawrence Hill Station. The 1911 census shows him to be Herbert Edward Coole, born in Bristol in 1886. The 1935 edition of *Kelly's* still lists H. E. Coole & Co. but with Reginald Dymock as proprietor with an address of Lawrence Hill Station and 46 The Greenway, Fishponds. The business was listed in the 1938 *Colliery Year Book*.

Apart from the 1926 and 1933 RCH lists there is no evidence that Coole had wagons, certainly no new ones were registered post 1924 so it is assumed any that were operated were bought secondhand.

There is a reference to a Cool (sic) & Williams at Bryants Hill Road, St. George, in the 1902 *Kelly's* but no connection can be established.

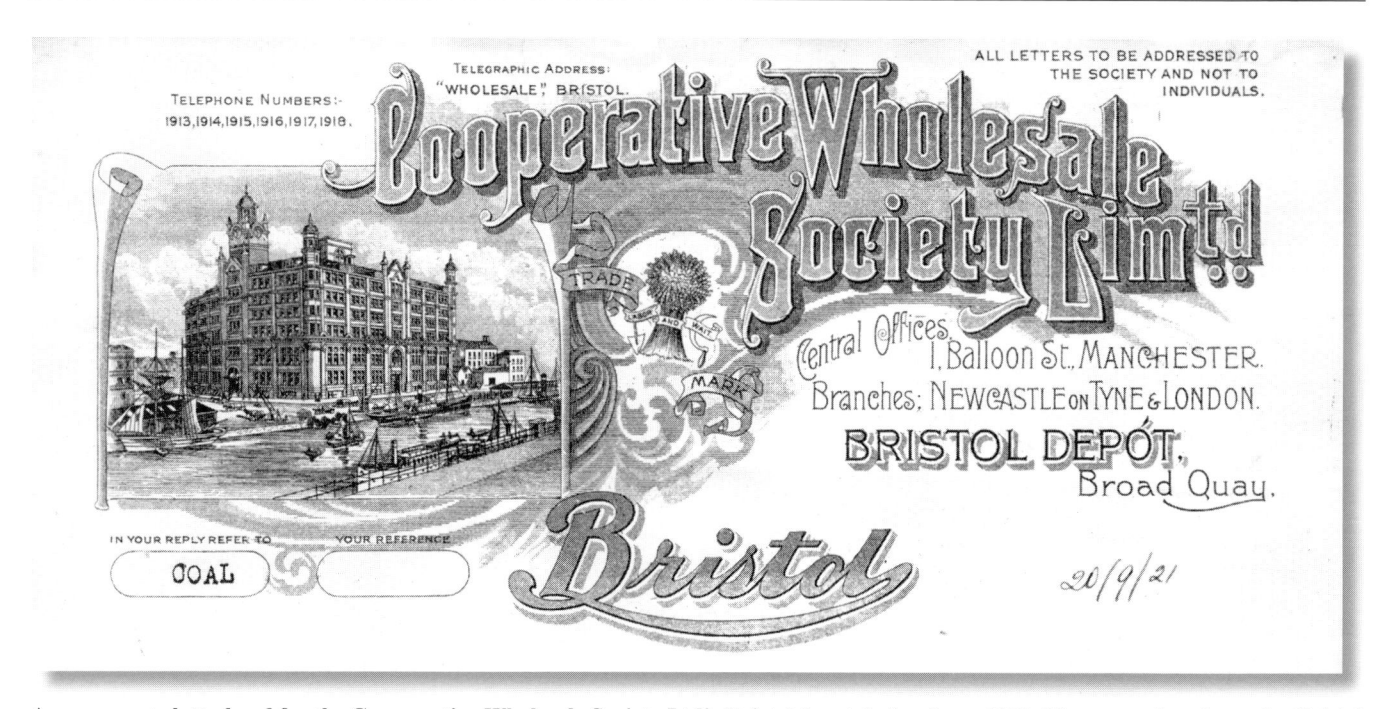

A very ornate letterhead for the Co-operative Wholesale Society Ltd's Bristol depot dating from 1921. The engraving shows the Bristol offices on Broad Quay whilst the relevant department from which the communication originated was typed into one of the ovals on the left.
Author's collection

CO-OPERATIVE WHOLESALE SOCIETY Ltd

The C.W.S. was the body that supplied many of the independent co-operative societies with many of their requirements and to that end operated their own collieries in Northumberland, together with flour mills etc. and also a railway wagon works at Peterborough.

It would seem that they also operated as coal merchants in Bristol – which would have been in direct competition with the local society – and in 1914 could be found dealing from an address at Broad Quay. They were not listed as such in 1935. Possibly the C.W.S. dealt with larger customers leaving the housecoal trade to the loyal customers of the local society's shops.

It was from the Peterborough wagon works that one known batch of wagons came. Numbers 46 to 55 were registered by the LMS in January 1939.

Wagon number 326 from an unknown builder, possibly the C.W.S. works at Peterborough. The livery would have been the C.W.S. standard of red body with white lettering shaded black.
courtesy Paul Karau

A product of the C.W.S. Wagon Works photographed when outshopped at Peterborough which shows a different lettering layout to that on number 326. The lettering here also includes the words 'Broad Quay' above 'Bristol'. It is a pity that the proud group of wagon builders have mostly obscured the fleet number although it could be 866.
courtesy Gordon Griffin

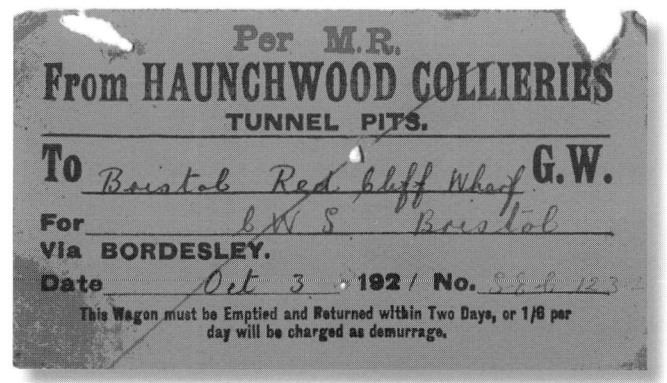

Above: A wagon label for coal from the Haunchwood Collieries at Nuneaton for the C.W.S. Bristol delivering to Redcliff Wharf.
courtesy Keith Ettle

Wagon 401 was photographed at Gloucester in November 1902. The seven-plank 10-ton wagon was painted black with plain white lettering. The oval plate to the right of the 'V' hanger shows the owner to be A. E. Gibson. Note the wooden doorstops which appear to be fitted on both sides and the 'gap filler' at the bottom of the side door. *GRC&WCo.*

DUDLEY & GIBSON

The partnership between William Morgan Gibson and Thomas Clifford Dudley commenced in 1854 trading in coal at the Clifton Coal Wharf. It was Dudley who had experience of the coal trade having previously worked for almost eighteen years for J. Poole. An advertisement in the *Bristol Mercury* on the 7th October 1854 solicited trade with orders to be placed at the wharf or by post or a visit to various agents who were mainly in the Clifton area. William Gibson's background was in journalism being on the staff of various local newspapers before joining Dudley (who was related via marriage) in the coal business.

Probably one of the first advertisements for Dudley & Gibson appeared in the *Bristol Mercury* on the 7th October 1854.

Dudley died in the first half of 1863 leaving Gibson to carry on the business. By 1872 Dudley & Gibson were listed as coal and gravel merchants, described as having 'a high reputation for punctuality, integrity, and excellent business principles' led, no doubt, by Gibson's strong Baptist beliefs. They were

A Dudley & Gibson wagon was captured on film passing through Cheltenham Lansdown Station in the early 1900s. Seemingly fresh out of the paint shop, four-plank dead buffered wagon number 421 carries a Gloucester plate on its side and is probably one of those wagons for which repair contracts were taken in 1898 and 1899. The lettering layout varies from the other wagons seen here with Dudley & Gibson filling the top two planks and having an enlarged 'D' and 'G'. On the third plank down is 'Clifton Down' spaced either side of the side door and with enlarged initial letters. 'Bristol' is centred on the bottom plank of the side door.

courtesy Richard Kelham

An advertisement from 1901 showing that the company traded in gravel.

Telephone 743. DUDLEY & GIBSON, Telephone 743.
COAL AND GRAVEL MERCHANTS,
CLIFTON DOWN STATION & FLOATING DOCK, HOTWELLS.
COALS OBTAINED FROM ANY DISTRICT.
Quality Good.   Prices Low.   Delivery Prompt.   Price Lists on application.

The five wagons purchased in July 1909 lined up outside the wagon works in Gloucester behind Gloucester RC&WCo's shunter. *Henry Wright* was an 0-4-0 saddle tank built by Manning Wardle in 1900 (works number 1501). It served the works until being sold for scrap in 1937. The wagons were numbered 403 to 407 of which the first was picked out for an individual portrait as seen below. All of the wagons are facing the same way with the single-sided brake facing the camera. *GRC&WCo.*

All of the wagons in this batch, paid for in cash, were of five-plank construction with raised ends. They were painted 'chocolate' and lettered in white with black shading and ironwork picked out in black. An angled commode handle is fitted on the right-hand end and there would have been one on the opposite corner as well. *GRC&WCo.*

dealing in anthracite, silkstone, Derby, Welsh, Forest of Dean, Somerset and other coals. They also had a large trade in gravel brought from Jersey, the Bristol Channel and Black Rock Quarry near Portishead. Spar for rockery work was also stocked. The business was still based at Clifton Wharf, Hotwells, with offices at 239 Hotwell Road and a depot at Clifton Down Station.

William Gibson died in May 1895 aged 67 after which the business was run by his widow, Selina, and one of his five sons, Arthur Edward, until Selina's death in July 1903. In 1911 it would seem that Arthur and his sister Kate Mortimer Gibson were in charge. In 1914 Kelly's *Bristol Directory* it would seem that the office had moved to 70 Alma Road, Clifton with an agency at 217 Hotwell Road and the depot at Clifton Down.

When signing up to the RCH 1926 and 1933 schemes the address of 70 Alma Road, Clifton, is given. 1935 has a firm of Dowding, Dudley & Gibson Ltd listed in *Kelly's* with an address of 111a Whiteladies Road and Clifton Down Station. It is assumed, as mentioned in *Private Owner Wagons of Gloucestershire*, that Dudley & Gibson had merged with the business of G. E. Dowding. However, no evidence of the company can be found apart from the fact that it was struck from the company lists in 1936 so was obviously fairly short-lived.

The first evidence of wagons for Dudley & Gibson comes in 1875 when four wagons 401 to 404, built by the Somerset Engineering Co. of Bridgwater and financed by the Western Wagon Co., were registered by the Great Western. In November 1889 four secondhand 7-ton wagons were purchased on five years deferred terms at £6 17s 6d pwpa from the Midland RC&WCo. A further wagon came from Midland in June 1892. Of 10-ton capacity it was numbered 433 and was registered by the Midland Railway.

Dudley & Gibson then appear to have moved to the Gloucester RC&WCo. Initially the contracts with them were for repairs and these may give some idea of the wagon fleet at the end of the 1890s. In October 1898 a repair contract on two 10-ton wagons was taken for seven years. Obviously satisfied with the service the following year a seven year contract on five 7-ton, seventeen 8-ton and three 10-ton wagons was signed. This was renewed in October 1906.

The first wagons purchased from Gloucester were put down in the books to A. E. Gibson in December 1902 when two 10-ton wagons, possibly numbered 400 and 401, were bought for cash together with a repair contract to run for fourteen years and one month. The repair contract appears to have been renewed in January 1917. In January 1905 Arthur also bought one secondhand 10-ton wagon for cash together with another fourteen year and one month repair contract.

In July 1909 it was Dudley & Gibson who ordered five new 10-ton wagons paying £302 10s cash. At the same time a seven year repair contract was taken on three 8-ton and three 10-ton wagons (this was renewed in September 1916) and one for fourteen years on five 10-ton wagons. In July 1916 two 10-ton wagons were bought for £91 cash together with a seven year repair lease. October 1917 saw two secondhand 8-ton wagons bought for cash together with a seven year repair contract.

The final order with Gloucester was in December 1923 when two 12-ton wagons were bought for cash.

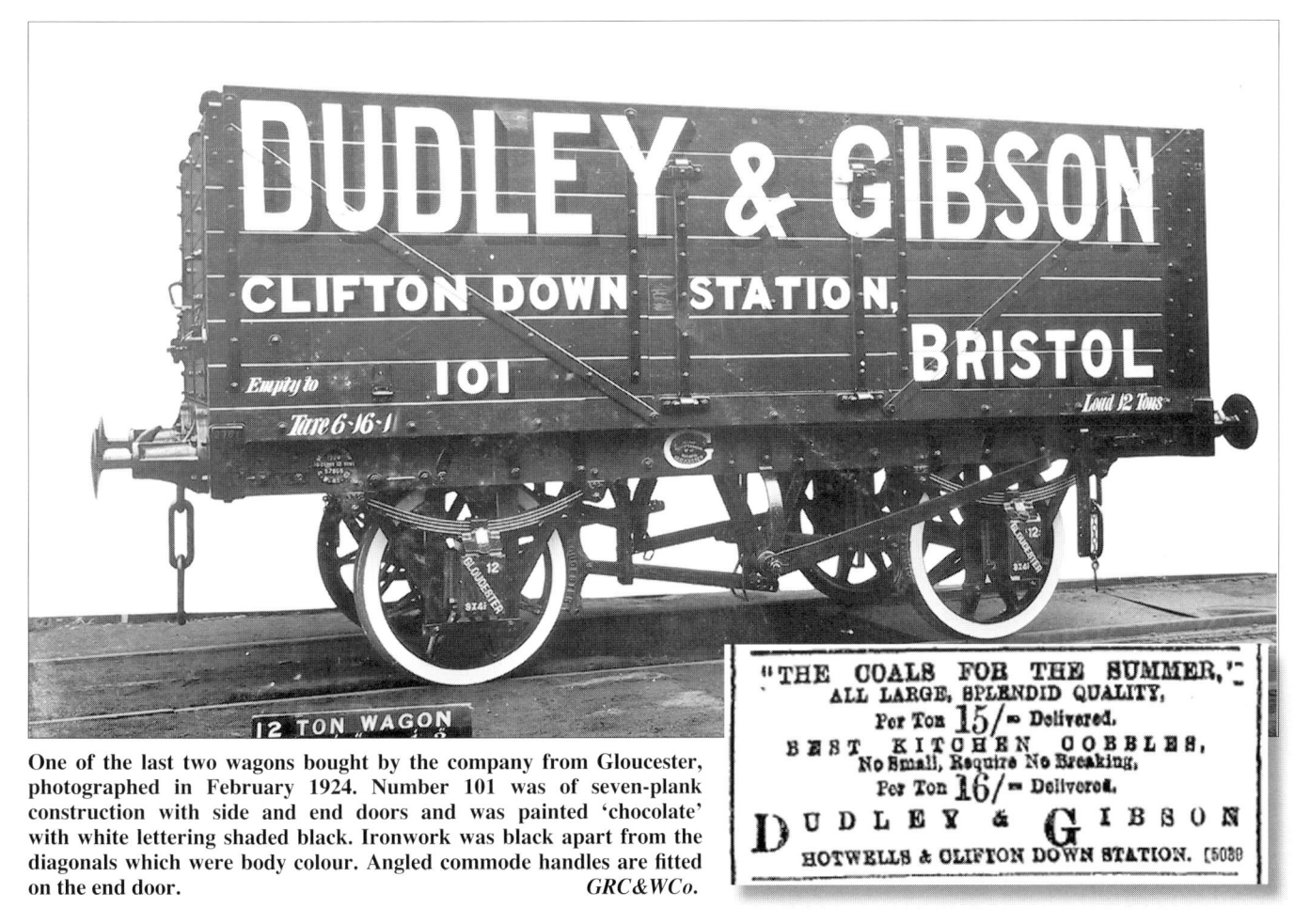

One of the last two wagons bought by the company from Gloucester, photographed in February 1924. Number 101 was of seven-plank construction with side and end doors and was painted 'chocolate' with white lettering shaded black. Ironwork was black apart from the diagonals which were body colour. Angled commode handles are fitted on the end door. *GRC&WCo.*

JAMES DURNFORD & SON Ltd

It is possible that the business dates back to at least the late 1870s as wagons for a J. Durnford & Son were supplied by the Midland Waggon Co. in both November 1879 and April 1880. Both of the orders, for four 8-ton wagons on a weekly basis in 1879 and for four ballast wagons on a weekly basis in 1880, suggest that Durnford was a contractor and was taking old wagons for spoil movement and ballast carrying. There is even the possibility that the wagons were of the side-tipping contractors type. This assumption is borne out by an entry in *Slater's* 1880 trade directory for James Durnford & Son, railway contractors, based in Totterdown.

The '& Son' is likely to be one John James Durnford, 26, who can be found on the 1881 census living at Martock House, Bedminster, with the occupation of 'contractor'.

In 1885 John James Durnford was living at Weston super Mare when he was executor to the will of George Bishop, another contractor. By 1901 Durnford was living at Westbury-on-Trym with the occupation of 'building contractor'. He died at Stoke Bishop in October 1911.

There was also a Maton Durnford, a builder and contractor, timber merchant and operator of a steam saw mills living in Penn Street. In 1902 it was said his business had been established 'upwards of 100 years'. Both John and Maton were born in Somerset, John in Martock and Maton in Taunton, were they related?

In the period immediately preceding the First World War the business of James Durnford & Son came to be based in the GWR yard at Wapping Wharf. In Kelly's *Bristol Directory* of 1914 it was listed as coal merchants, contractors, white & brown lime works, at Wapping Wharf, Cumberland Road. An agreement was taken with the Great Western Railway to lease buildings at Wapping in 1914 also. Being in the contracting business they apparently shipped a great deal of material by rail and not having their own siding at Wapping obviously used those of the railway company and were thus not able to determine exactly where in the yard their wagons would end up. To facilitate the loading and unloading they constructed a moveable gangway which could be moved over the sidings and for which they took out an agreement in 1921.

However, in August 1926 the gangway was in use to discharge a wagon load of lime from a motor lorry into a railway wagon. Whilst the lorry was on the gangway (which was obviously of a substantial nature) some other wagons were shunted down the

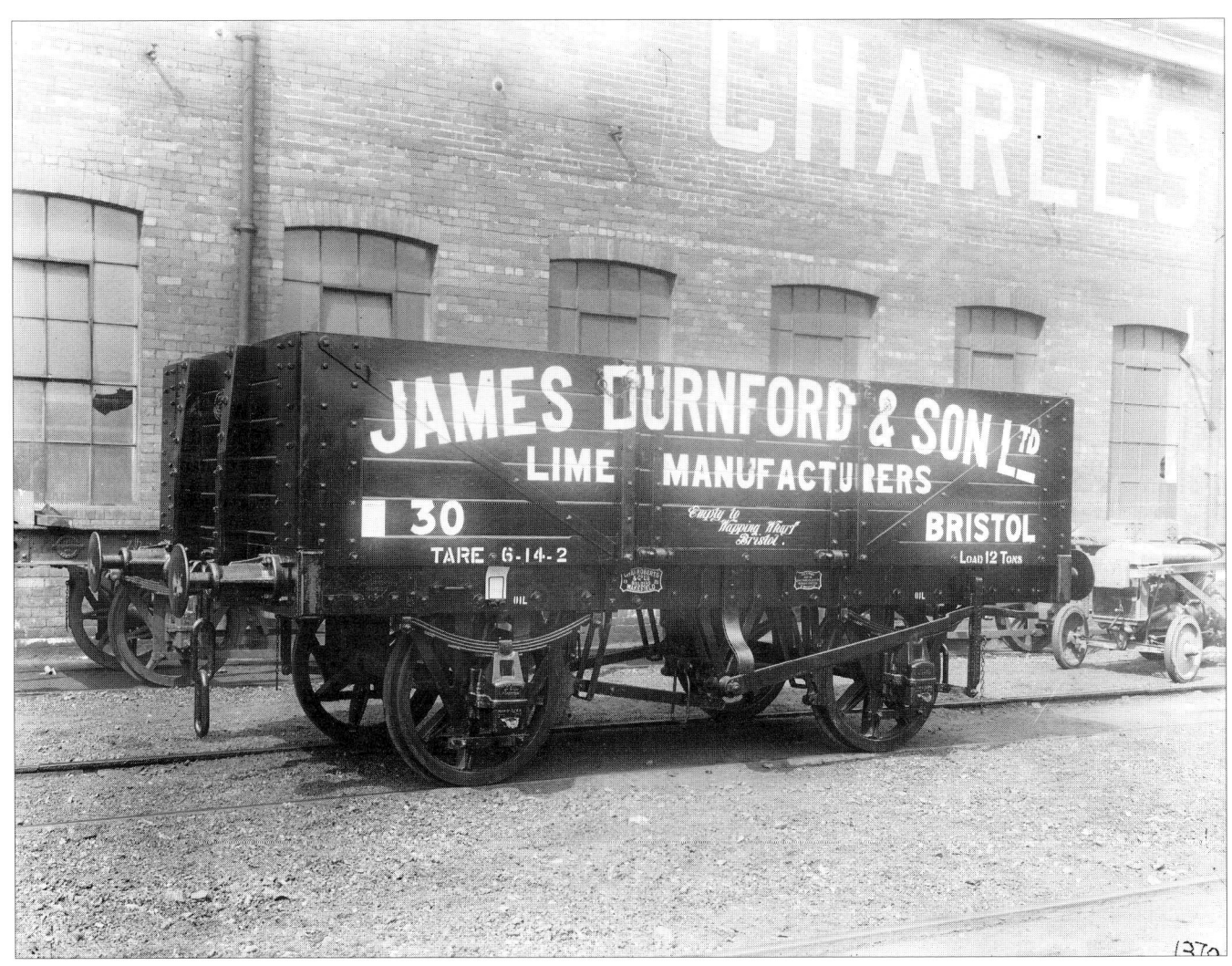

Charles Roberts of Wakefield supplied six 12-ton open goods wagons numbered 30 to 35 in 1928. Of five-plank construction with full height side doors this batch advertised the fact that part of Durnford's business was the manufacture of lime. *courtesy HMRS AAR403*

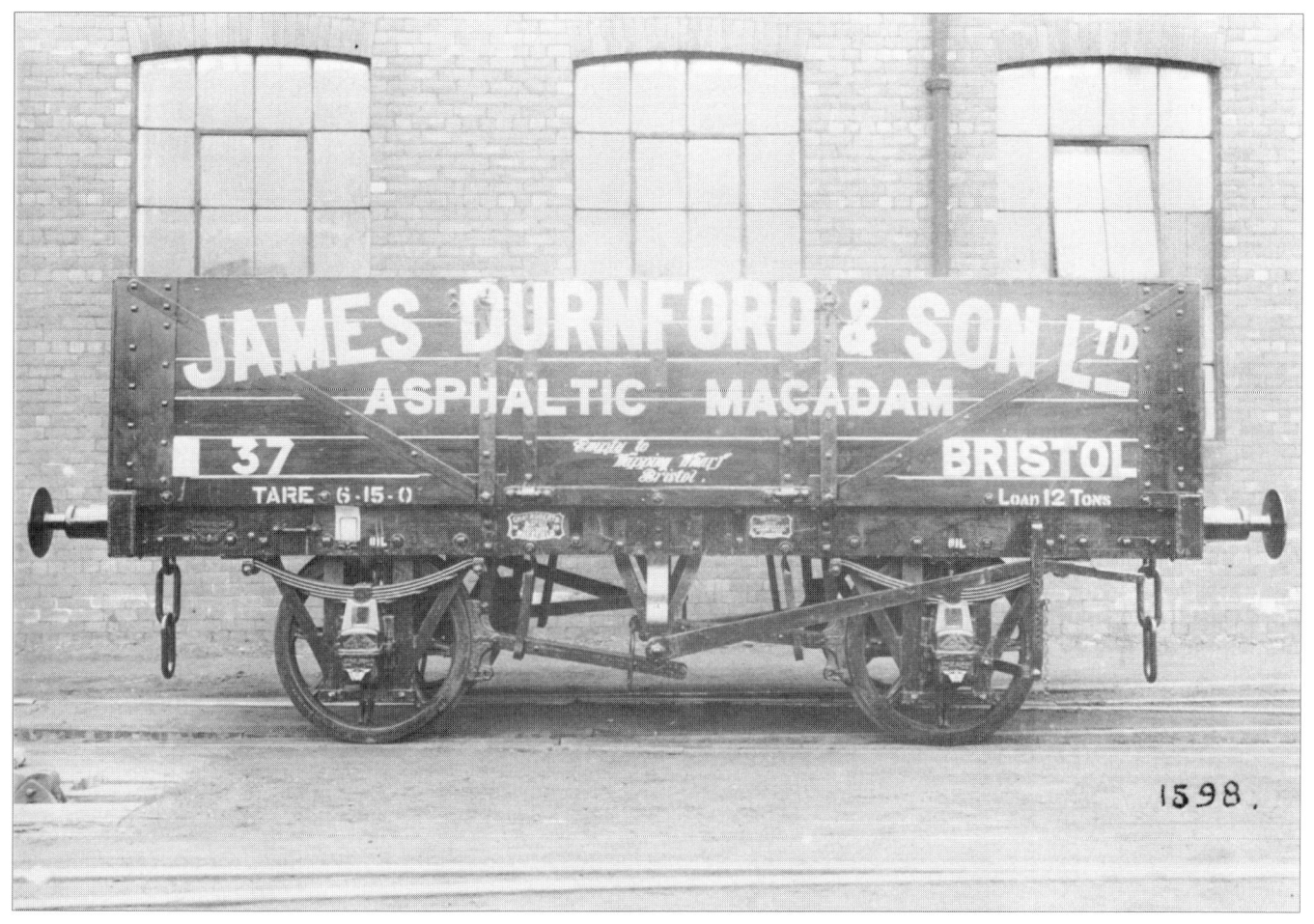

12-ton wagons numbered 37 to 47 were built by Roberts in 1929. The lettering this time proclaims that Durnford were in the business of asphaltic macadam. All of the wagons were registered by the LMS and all were branded as emptying to Wapping Wharf. Durnfords had their depot here and later an asphalt plant stood there.
courtesy HMRSAAR521

siding over which it stood. The resulting collision destroyed the gangway and badly damaged the lorry. The whole matter ended up in the courts with Durnfords claiming damages against the railway company but as is usual with such matters it all hinged on the small print in the agreement – even the appeal judges were split on a decision!

In 1935 the company was listed as also being quarry owners and dealers in sand and gravel. Whilst the quarry they operated cannot be traced with certainty there was a Durnford Quarry on the Ashton Court Estate. There was no mention of them as coal merchants at this date and it is likely that dealing in coal was always a very small part of the business.

The known wagons for Durnford were built by Charles Roberts of Wakefield in 1928 and 1929. In 1928 six five-plank 12-ton wagons, numbered 30 to 35, were supplied followed by eleven more, 37 to 47, in 1929. No other wagons were acquired new between 1923 and 1939.

EDWARD EDWARDS

With an office address of 41 Oldbury Court Road, Fishponds, Edwards appears in both the 1926 and 1933 RCH lists but cannot be found in the 1928 *Colliery Year Book*. There is the possibility that he was the E. Edwards connected with Pepler, Edwards & Co. who are covered later in this volume.

FIELD

The records of the Oldbury Carriage & Wagon Co., of Oldbury, Staffordshire, record a quotation given to Field of Bristol on the 16th December 1865 for 6-ton wagons. No further details were given, nor has it proved possible to find out who the mysterious enquirer was.

FISHPONDS COAL Co.

A business trading as The Fishponds Coal Co. can be found as early as 1901 when two 8-ton wagons were acquired from the Midland RC&WCo. Numbered 30 and 31 they were registered by the Midland Railway. In June 1910 the two wagons were refinanced by Midland for the sum of £64.

It would seem that the company took over a business run by Edward Monks (see later) whose siding agreement at Fishponds was taken over in 1902. The proprietor of the Fishponds Coal Co. was George Webb and in 1914 the *Kelly's* listing gave him as trading from 1 Guinea Lane, Fishponds. By 1926 the trading address was Wharf Road, Fishponds.

George Webb, born in Pucklechurch circa 1855, was trading in co-partnership with William John Mills in 1902 when they petitioned as creditors for the winding up of the British Collieries Syndicate Ltd. Who Mills was has yet to be discovered although a William Mills, 29, born in Penzance, Cornwall, is listed on the 1901 census as a coal merchant in Bristol (see later).

The business appears to have been taken over by Arthur Pepler in 1937 although the trading name was retained and the business can be found as such in the 1938 *Colliery Year Book* at the Wharf Road address. In 1940 the siding agreement was taken on by T. W. Ward Ltd of Sheffield who continued to trade here as the Fishponds Coal Co. The siding agreement was not terminated until September 1965.

The two wagons from the Midland RC&WCo. are the only ones that can be found for the business but that does not preclude the acquisition of wagons secondhand. Indeed, it is possible that they took wagons from E. Monks if his business was acquired.

JOHN G. FOSTER

John G. Foster traded as a coal merchant at Montpelier Station and can be found in *Slater's* 1880 trade directory listed as trading both as John G. Foster and Sampson, Foster & Co. and living at Hatfield Villa, Cromwell Road, Montpelier. The Sampson half of the business was Martin Shickell Sampson who was also carrying on business as a coal merchant at Bullo Wharf, St. Philips whilst residing at Tyne Villa, North Road. In March 1880 Sampson was recorded as a bankrupt, followed in May by the bankruptcy of Foster. The latter revealed that he was also trading at Poole Station, Poole, Dorset. The 1881 census shows John G. Foster (there is some confusion as to whether the G stood for Godwin or George) as a coal merchant, aged 31, living at 64 North Road with his wife and four sons. By 1901 he was working as a timber salesman in Essex.

The only references to wagons are from the Great Western Railway Freighter's Register where four coal wagons, numbered 1, 2, 8 and 9 were registered in October 1874. Numbers 1 and 2 were built and financed by the Bristol Wagon Works and 8 and 9 by the Birmingham RC&WCo.

ALFRED J. FUDGE

In 1926 the address given by the Railway Clearing House was 210 Fishponds Road. This was also his address in Kelly's 1914 *Bristol Directory* but no occupation was listed. On the 1901 census Alfred John Fudge is found aged 37 with the occupation of coal agent.

He was buying from the Midland RC&WCo. in January 1905 when three 10-ton wagons numbered 1 to 3 were registered by the Midland Railway. His next new wagons were six 8-tonners bought in 1912 of which numbers 6 to 8 came from the Midland RC&WCo. and numbers 9 to 11 from the Gloucester RC&WCo. All were registered by the Midland Railway in August and October respectively. One is left to wonder if the gap in the sequence, numbers 4 and 5, was filled by secondhand wagons. There was certainly an isolated repair contract taken out with Gloucester in May 1916 for a single 8-ton wagon.

Alfred Fudge, as mentioned above, signed up to the RCH 1926 scheme but not to that in 1933. He was not listed in the 1928 *Colliery Year Book* but that is probably no surprise as he does not seem to have had himself listed in any directories. Fudge may have deceased by February 1934.

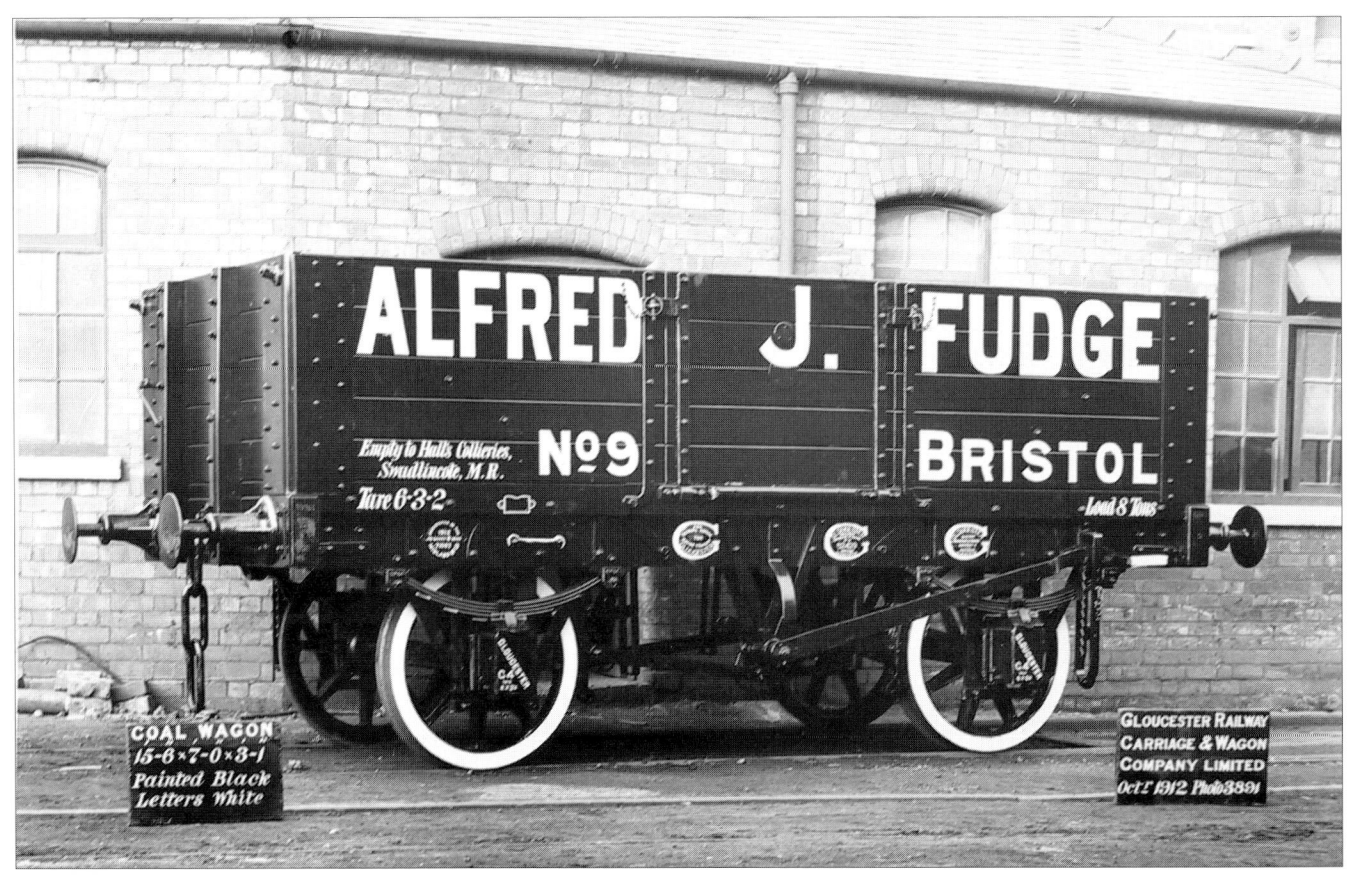

Three wagons, numbers 9 to 11, were built by the Gloucester RC&WCo. in 1912 for Alfred Fudge. Of 8-ton capacity they had side doors only and were fitted with angled commode handles on opposite corners handy for the brake lever. *GRC&WCo.*

HERBERT J. FUDGE

From 1914 through to between 1926 and 1933 Herbert Fudge can be found as a coal dealer at 28 Morley Street, Barton Hill. The only evidence of wagon ownership is that he signed up to the 1926 RCH scheme. He did not partake of that in 1933 nor is he listed in the 1928 *Colliery Year Book*. He is found, however, in the 1935 edition of Kelly's *Bristol Directory* as a coal dealer at the same address. It is also unknown if there was any family connection between Alfred and Herbert Fudge.

S. M. GAEL & Co.

Stuart M. Gael was born in Bromley, Kent circa 1878 but had moved to Falmouth in Cornwall by 1881 with his family. By 1901 he was in Bristol and trading as a coal merchant. Kelly's 1902 *Bristol Directory* has him with an address of 77 Whiteladies Road, Clifton. By 1914 the address was 41 Whiteladies Road. The same address was used for an entry in the 1928 *Colliery Year Book* but no trace can be found after that date.

Wagons were acquired in 1902 from the Midland RC&WCo., four 10-ton wagons numbered 41, 44, 50 and 66 being registered by the Midland Railway in October.

W. T. GARLICK & Co.

William Tanner Garlick had an address of 62 Old Market Street and can be found on the 1881 census aged 45 living at Clare House, Springfield Road. He was a coal merchant in partnership with Tom Lathey and William Powell trading as W. T. Garlick & Co. at Lawrence Hill Station and the Upper Railway Wharf, St. Philips. On the 1st December 1881 Garlick left the partnership by mutual consent. The other partners were to continue the business under the style of Lathey & Powell.

Garlick continued on as a haulier on his own account but in October 1883 he was reported as going into liquidation by arrangement with creditors. He obviously bounced back as in the 1902 Kelly's *Bristol Directory* he was still trading as a haulier and coal merchant and still in Old Market Street. Garlick died in late 1902 aged 67.

In March 1880 the Great Western registered four 10-ton wagons, numbered 1 to 4, built and financed by the Bristol Wagon Works Co. In October of the same year six 8-ton wagons were taken on a seven year purchase lease from the Western Wagon Co. at £35 each. A note was appended in the ledger that the contract was sold in 1882. It is unclear whether this refers to Garlick moving the wagons on or to the Western Wagon Co. selling the finance to another wagon financier but it is possible the wagons were transferred to Lathey & Powell.

Lathey & Powell did not trade for long as in July 1883 they too were going into liquidation. Tom Lathey was living at Barrow Hill House, Stafford Street, and Powell at 6 Prince Street, St. Philip's.

GOULD & BAKER

Gould & Baker were listed in the 1926 RCH list as being coal merchants in Bristol but with the note 'see J. D. Pounsberry, Bristol'. This suggests that the business had been taken over but was still trading under its own name. No trace can be found of Gould & Baker.

GRANVILLE, SMITH & Co.

Trading with an office address of 30 Baldwin Street, little can be found on the company. They signed up to both the 1926 and 1933 RCH schemes and in 1924 can be found taking twenty-two wagons from the Butterley Company at Codnor Park, Derbyshire. These were built to the 1923 RCH standard and were numbered 450 to 471 being registered by the LMS.

The company was not listed among coal merchants in the 1938 *Colliery Year Book*.

GREGORY & Co. Ltd

Gregory & Co. signed up to both the 1926 and 1933 RCH schemes but do not appear in any trade directories. However, there is the possibility that it was a wagon agency, owning and hiring wagons to other operators. There is also the possibility that behind the company was Tom Canvin Gregory who was previously a partner with Frederick Wheeler as railway wagon builders in Radstock, Somerset. Their business, trading as Wheeler & Gregory, was wound up in 1904 although Wheeler had left the concern considerably earlier. The 1911 census shows Tom Gregory and his wife Sarah Ann to be in Brentford, Middlesex with Tom being 63. The 1914 Kelly's *Bristol Directory* shows a Tom Gregory living at 104 Hampstead Road, Brislington but in 1935 it is a Sarah Ann Gregory there, suggesting that Tom had deceased. It is the fact that it was a Tom and Sarah Ann Gregory living there which leads to the belief that it was Tom Canvin Gregory. The Hampstead Road address was also that supplied to the Railway Clearing House by Gregory & Co. Ltd.

There are various references in the records of R. Y. Pickering of Wishaw between November 1919 and August 1921 to wagons supplied to 'Gregory, Bristol'. All were secondhand wagons from Scottish owners and not necessarily built by Pickerings themselves.

15 November 1919	Bought of Jas. Lamont & Co., 140 West George St., Glasgow, ten 10-ton oak frame wagons No's 109-118, built by Pickering 1904.
10 December 1919	Bought of A. Jack & Son, Barrhead four 12-ton wagons No's 72-75, built by Pickering 1905.
30 January 1920	Bought of Jas. Lamont & Co., 140 West George St., Glasgow, six 10-ton oak frame wagons No's 103-108, built by Pickering 1901.
9 April 1920	Bought from Wm. Forbes, Glasgow, wagons No's 15-17 built by Pickering 1902 and wagons No's 18-20 built by Hurst, Nelson.
9 April 1920	Bought from Geo. Will Ltd., Dundee, ten 10-ton wagon No's 126-135, built Pickering 1901.
9 April 1920	Bought from J. W. Reid, Ladybank, one 10-ton wagon No. 1 built Hurst, Nelson, 1903.
9 April 1920	Bought from Lamont, Glasgow, two 9-ton wagons No's 101-102, built Pickering 1898. Sold to Gregory, Bristol.
3 June 1920	Bought from Edinburgh Collieries, 150 twelve-ton wagons No's 1726-1825, built Moy 1908, and No's 1826-1875 built Ince 1908.

7 July 1920	Bought from Ormiston Coal Co., ten 12-ton wagons No's 59-68, built Pickering 1917.
15 July 1920	Bought from Wishaw Coal Co., fifty 12-ton wagons No's 2036-2085 built Pickering 1915.
18 August 1921	Sold, twenty-five 12-ton wagons No's 265-289 (built Pickering) late Gemmell. Re-lettered for City of Birmingham, Electrical Supply Dept. No's 3201-3225. To order of Gregory & Co., Bristol.

That several of these orders were for substantial numbers of wagons supports the theory that Gregory was dealing in wagons rather than operating them in a business such as a coal merchants. The last recorded order tends to confirm that Gregory was also hiring wagons out as, whilst they were bought by him, they were lettered for the City of Birmingham Electrical Supply Department.

OLIVER J. GULLICK

In 1881 a George Gullick can be found as a colliery bailiff in Writhlington, Somerset. His son, Oliver J., aged 20, was a salesman in the coal trade. He may well have been working for F. Bird & Co. of Radstock and it might well have been with this firm that Gullick came to Bristol.

Indeed, it would appear that by 1902 he had become an integral part of F. Bird & Co. as it was Charles William Pearce, Oliver James Gullick and William Redwood who were the vendors when several of Bird's former depots were transferred to F. Bird & Co. Ltd. Most of these were in Wiltshire and no mention was made of Montpelier. At the same time Gullick and the others transferred interests in the Clandown Colliery and Old Welton Brick Works to the Clandown Colliery Co.

Gullick was in fact trading on his own account by April 1899 when he took a lease on the site of an office at Clifton Down Station from the Great Western & Midland Joint Railways. He was also leasing 209 Cheltenham Road.

The 1902 Kelly's *Bristol Directory* records Gullick as being a coal merchant at Station Road, Montpelier, the Railway Wharf, Lawrence Hill and Clifton Down Station.

There were a number of leases with the Great Western & Midland Joint Railways. In April 1903 some coal stacking ground at Clifton Down and an office; in October 1903 a brick office at Montpelier and 414 1/9 yards of coal stacking ground; July 1904 a tool shed at Clifton Down; April 1906 379 4/9 yards of coal stacking ground at Clifton Down; and in January 1916 some land at Montpelier.

The 1914 edition of *Kelly's* has Gullick at the Upper Railway Wharf, Midland Road, St Philip's and at 17 Kingsland Road, St Philip's with 'Gullick's Coal Depots' at Station Road, Montpelier, Clifton Down Station, and St Philip's Station. The use of the term 'Gullick's Coal Depots' appears to have been a marketing move on behalf of Gullick.

Gullick signed up to the 1926 RCH scheme but not that of 1933. In the 1928 *Colliery Year Book* he is found as a coal merchant at Montpelier Station only. By this time, however, he was more than just a local coal merchant. Possibly he had always had far wider interests than just the Clifton and Montpelier area and perhaps his connection with F. Bird & Co. paid off for him with customer contacts. By 1926 he was listing himself as a coal factor and his wagons can be found delivering coal right down into the west country.

It would seem that it was around the early 1930s that Gullick

Wagon number 116 belonging to Oliver Gullick of Bristol is seen at Minehead in January 1923. Gullick must have had a trade customer in the town for one of his wagons to have strayed this far. It may have been a regular contract in which case wagons would often be seen in the yard.
Great Western Railway

Two pieces of Gullick ephemera. On the right a postcard which would have been sent out to customers either with order advice on or with an offer on. This one is for the Bishopston Office where orders for coal could be placed. It is difficult to imagine today that a postcard sent off one day could well result in a coal delivery the following day.

Below right is a very graphic advert for Gullick's Coal dating from just after the First World War as they are stating that they have gone back to their regular pre-war suppliers to guarantee quality of supply. Four depots are also listed, Clifton Down; Montpelier; St. Philips; and Coalpit Heath. Trade supplies were dealt with through the main Montpelier office.

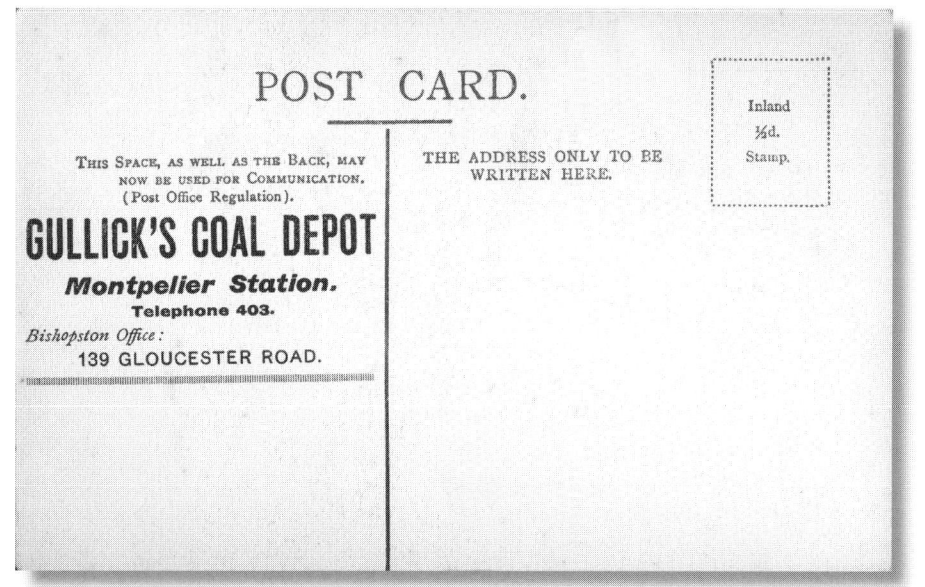

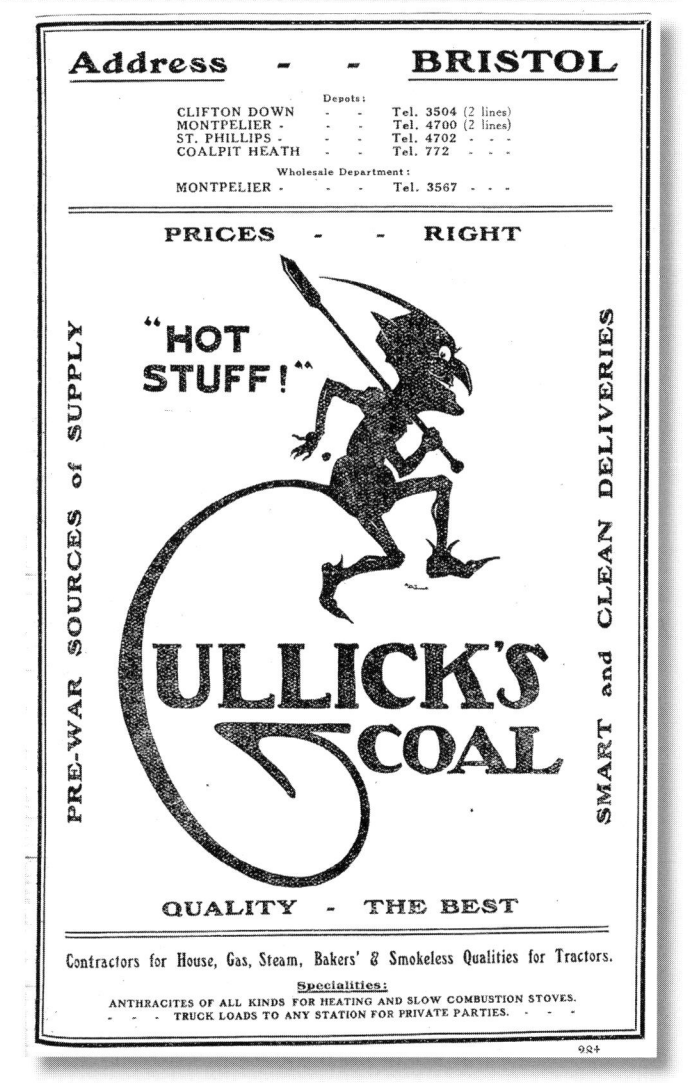

gave up his interest in coal dealing. *Kelly's* 1935 directory lists Gullick's Coal Depot at Clifton Down Station but in brackets has 'Frederick William Elsworthy, proprietor'.

On the wagon front a number of references can be found. The Midland RC&WCo. supplied three 10-ton wagons in 1903, numbered 60 to 62 and these were registered by the Midland Railway in October. Gullick used the Gloucester RC&WCo. for some repairs, a contract being signed in June 1915 for seven years repairs on ten 10-ton wagons.

Gullick, like Tom Gregory, also traded with R. Y. Pickering of Wishaw near Glasgow, seemingly in Gullick's case via the British Wagon Co. of Rotherham. In 1920 fifteen secondhand 8-ton wagons ex A. & G. Anderson of Barblues Colliery and built by Pickering between 1894 and 1896 were taken by Gullick. They were originally registered by the North British Railway. All were dead-buffered when new being converted to sprung buffers by Anderson at various dates between 1911 and 1919. They were sold to the British Wagon Co. in March 1920.

NBR Reg.	Gullick No.	Anderson No.	Built
5857	304	170	11.1894
5862	209	175	11.1894
5863	319	176	11.1894
5866	313	179	11.1894
7523	325	201	6.1896
7525	327	203	6.1896
7531	333	209	6.1896
7532	334	210	6.1896
7535	315	213	6.1896
7540	338	218	6.1896
7655	345	221	10.1896
7656	346	222	10.1896
7657	347	223	10.1896
7658	307	224	10.1896
7659	349	225	10.1896

All were withdrawn in September 1930 and the registration plates were destroyed. This suggests that the wagons were on hire from the British Wagon Co. Does this date tie in with when Gullick gave up some of his business?

Pickering's records also show the supply of replacement axleboxes for wagons belonging to Gullick which suggests that they were held on hire from the wagon company. Pickering

A snapshot taken at Crosshill and Codnor Station in Derbyshire. The station was on a Midland Railway branch opened in 1890 but closed temporarily in 1917 for three years as a wartime economy measure. It is believed to be seen here at the time of the 1921 miners strike in use for wagon storage. Included in the long line of wagons are four for Gullick, the two nearest the camera being 297 and 289 both of which, plus one of those inset on the left, appear to be ex Scottish wagons. *Author's collection*

obviously did not have repair depots and did not deal with Wagon Repairs Ltd (Pickering joined the latter in 1925) so contracted the work out to Thomas Hunter, a Rugby wagon builder. The surviving orders are:

5 June 1922	T. Hunter's depot at Kingsland Rd. sidings, Bristol for Gullick No. 189A
25 July 1922	T. Hunter's depot at Tyseley for Gullick No. 298
7 August 1922	T. Hunter's depot at Brent sidings, for Gullick No. 344
1 November 1922	T. Hunter's depot at Tyseley for O. J. Gullick No. 264
23 November 1922	T. Hunter's for Gullick No. 267
06 December 1922	T. Hunter's for Gullick No. 334
15 December 1922	T. Hunter's for Gullick No. 344
10 January 1923	T. Hunter's for Gullick No. 291

H. HECTOR HALL

With an address of 42 Alma Vale Road, Clifton, Hall signed up to both the 1926 and 1933 RCH schemes which suggests that he was operating wagons. However, no further evidence can be found. He appears at the same address as a coal merchant in the 1928 *Colliery Year Book*. But in *Kelly's* for 1935 the business is listed as 'Hall, H. Hector (Exors. of) with the same office address and a depot at Clifton Down Station. H. Hector Hall (Exors. of) at the same address were also listed as coal merchants in the 1938 *Colliery Year Book*.

How long Hall's business was continued after this is unknown.

An unusual rectangular tank wagon photographed by the builders, the Gloucester RC&WCo., in November 1901. The plate on the side states that Hare & Co. were tar distillers so the presumption has to be that this was the trade for which the tank was built. It is the construction of the wagon which is unusual with the two diagonal restraining bars attached to angle-irons across the top of the tank ends. The end staunchions are continued across the top of the tank. There appears to be a filler on the top with a screw down lid, there are two emptying points on this side of the tank and probably the same on the far side. A chain hanging below the wagon suggests an emptying point underneath as well. The wagon solebars look to be painted grey with black ironwork. The tare weight was 7-12-2. *GRC&WCo.*

JOHN HARE & Co.

Hare & Co. was a long-established business in Bristol. The founder, John Hare, although born in Taunton in the early to mid 1750s came to Bristol to set up in business. In this he was extremely successful and made a sizeable fortune based around the production of floorcloth, oils, white lead, paints and colours. The offices were at Temple Gate opposite Temple Meads Station and nearby were the floorcloth, oil and colour works. Other factories were petroleum cellars in Arnos Vale, a flax mill in St. Philip's Marsh and the white lead mills in Avon Street, St. Philip's close to the Avonside sidings and wharf. It would seem that they also dealt in tar, possibly collected from a nearby gas works. Hares also had a colour and oil works at 8 Redcross Street in London.

The production of white lead – an unpleasant occupation involving the grinding of lead into a powder – was closely linked to the colour industry acting as a base for many paints which with the additions of oils and ochres or chemicals, including arsenic, could be produced in a number of colours. Floorcloth, or linoleum, was made by coating a canvas with layers of colour which could then be stamped with a pattern or left plain. All of the processes consumed vast amounts of oil, especially linseed oil (hence the flax mills) which was stored in barrels in the basement of the works. Thus not only did the workers have to inhale and handle noxious chemicals and materials, they also had to be careful about handling the inflammable oils and the history of the works is littered with small fires and several major blazes.

Despite having such a large business little can be traced of a wagon fleet. In July 1879 the Great Western registered an 8-ton wagon numbered 2, built by the Bristol Wagon Works Co. In September 1901 a tank wagon numbered 3 was built by the Gloucester RC&WCo. for £117 10s cash.

The business survived into the latter half of the twentieth century.

ALFRED G. HARRIS & Co.

This company, based at St. Philip's Railway Station, can be found in the 1880 *Slater's Directory* under 'coal proprietors and merchants'. However, they obviously date further back as they were taking wagons from the Midland Waggon Co. in August 1861. Sadly, no other details of the business can be found, Alfred Harris is not obvious in the 1881 census nor can references be found in the *London Gazette*.

What is known is that in August 1861 two secondhand 6-ton wagons were taken on yearly hire. In April 1866 two secondhand 7-ton wagons were bought at £10 10s pwpa over three years. There is the possibility that Harris was buying the two wagons that he had previously had on hire and that they had been refurbished and uprated to 7-ton capacity.

There are several other entries in the Midland Waggon books which may refer to A. G. Harris, all of which date to 1879 and all were for secondhand 6-ton wagons on hire. In March three were taken for a year, in April one for a year, in October two for a year and in November one for a year.

Photographed in November 1892, wagon No. 57 was purchased outright by Hendy & Co. together with nine others, No's 50-56 and 58-59. It was still to be registered by a main line company and this was done on the 11th November by the Midland Railway together with wagon No. 58. The rest of the batch had been registered the previous day and the registration numbers were 9469-9478. Of 5-plank construction it was painted black with white lettering. This particular wagon survived until broken up in 1944. *GRC&WCo.*

HENDY & COMPANY

The Hendy family appear to have been engaged in the coal trade around Bitton and Mangotsfield for a number of years. The 1881 census gives an Enoch Hendy, aged 40, living with his widower father George at Lodge Causeway, Stapleton. Enoch's occupation was 'coal dealer' and he had the same occupation twenty years later in 1901. The 1881 census also shows an Edwin Hendy, 38, born in Bitton and married to Eliza with a son George. Again, Edwin's occupation was 'coal dealer' but in 1901 he is shown as a 'retired coal merchant'. By this date George had become a coal merchant, probably taking over from his father. It was Enoch and Edwin who were to form Hendy & Co.

However, Enoch and Edwin appear to have been in business earlier trading together with Thomas Silvey as Hendy, Silvey & Hendy as coal merchants and salesmen at St. Philips and at Fishponds. On the 30th June 1880 the partnership was dissolved with Silvey leaving – moving on to greater things on his own account as will be seen. Enoch and Edwin were to continue the existing business but now under the name of Hendy & Company.

The 1889 and 1902 *Kelly's* directories show the business to have been based at 17 Kingsland Road and the Upper Railway Wharf in Midland Road. With Edwin being retired by 1901 and son George in the business the next reference to Hendy & Company comes with the bankruptcy of George Edward Hendy (trading as Hendy & Co.) in July 1904. He was at the time living at Purview, Fishponds Road, Fishponds and carrying on business at Fishponds Railway Wharf. Note that there was no reference to the business being at Kingsland Road or the Upper Railway Wharf, St. Philips. Enoch Hendy, who may still have been in partnership with George, died on the 2nd May 1910 at Fishponds and was still described as a coal merchant.

It would seem that the business may have been sold off or taken over as in December 1913 one Arthur Henry Poole was trading as Hendy & Co. when he went into bankruptcy. He was living at Normal Villa, Victoria Street, Staple Hill, and carrying on business at 17 Kingsland Road, St. Philips. Thus until at least 1913 Hendy & Co. were still in business in St. Philips but there was no mention of Fishponds. The final bankruptcy meeting for Poole was not until 1922.

This might have been the end of Hendy & Co. as there is no mention in the 1914 Kelly's *Directory of Bristol*, nor did Hendy & Co. sign up to the 1926 RCH scheme.

The earliest found reference to wagons is from the Gloucester RC&WCo. in September 1883 when twenty secondhand 10-ton wagons were taken on six months simple hire. In August 1884 a further twenty secondhand wagons were taken on six months hire but this time the wagons were of 7-ton capacity. The fact that Gloucester recorded the hires as for six months only means that this was six months certain with the possibility to renew the hire. These hire renewals often were not recorded in the books of the wagon company. This is the case here as at a stocktaking of hired wagons conducted in the middle of 1885

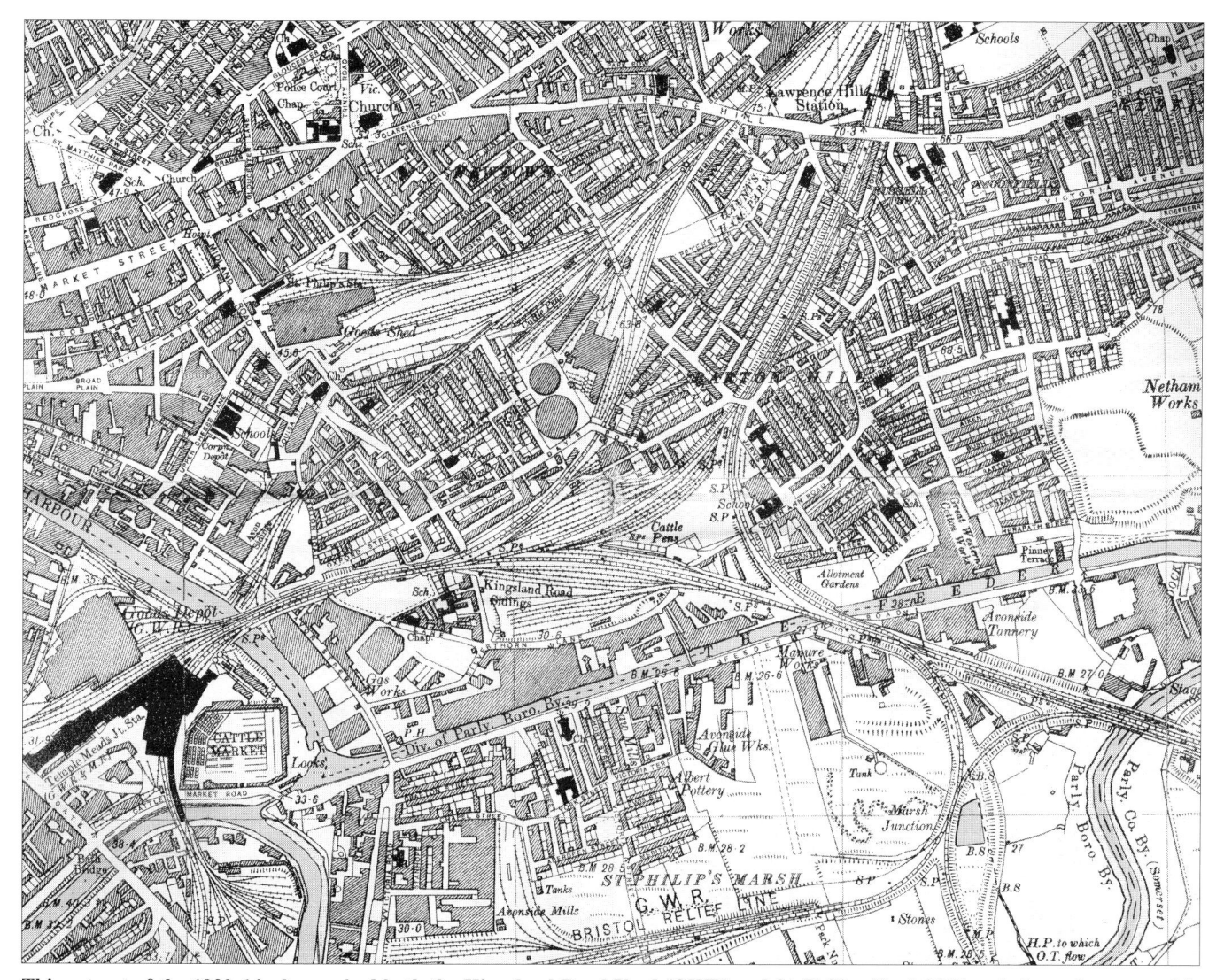

This extract of the 1930 6-inch map had both the Kingsland Road Yard (GWR) and St. Philips Yard (MR) and shows the reasonable proximity of the two facilities to the city centre. Temple Meads Station is on the left. Notice the amount of industry clustered around The Feeder, the stretch of water running across the extract.
Ordnance Survey 6-inch, 1930

two batches were recorded for Hendy & Co., wagons numbered 53 to 72 were the twenty 10-tonners and 41 to 60 the 7-tonners. How long the hire actually continued for is unknown.

It is possible that the hire of the 10-tonners may have continued until 1892 as in November of that year the Midland Railway registered ten 8-ton wagons for Hendy & Co. numbered 50 to 59. They had been built by the Gloucester RC&WCo. who noted the sale of the wagons as being new for cash at £58 each in October. A repair contract was taken on them at the same time together with a similar contract on twenty-six 7-ton wagons. Where the latter were from is unknown but the contract for all of the wagons was renewed in October 1899 for a further seven years.

A batch of registrations with the Midland Railway in November was put down to 'E. Hendy' but it is likely that they were for Hendy & Co. The six 8-ton wagons were built by the Bristol Waggon Co. and numbered 101 to 106.

It was back to Hendy & Co, in June 1903 when the Midland registered three 10-ton wagons, 51 to 53, built by Wheeler & Gregory of Radstock. Notice that the numbers duplicate those of the 1892 Gloucester-built wagons. This could be due to several reasons; one, that some of the Gloucester wagons were renumbered; two, that the wagons replaced some that had been lost, possibly through accident; or three, simple clerical error in the register and they were not numbers 51 to 53 at all.

A return to the Gloucester RC&WCo. was made in October 1905 when a further ten 8-ton wagons were ordered for cash at £56 10s each – note that they were actually cheaper than similar wagons ordered thirteen years earlier. They were not registered by the Midland Railway until March 1906 when the numbers were recorded as being 60 to 69.

It would be interesting to have had more recorded details of the order as it might have helped sort out who was running Hendy & Company at this time. It was after George had gone bankrupt so was Enoch running the business?

In November 1906 comes another slight mystery as ten 8-ton wagons were taken on simple hire for seven years from the Gloucester RC&WCo. with the addition of 'renewal' after the order. However, no earlier hire can be found around the 1899 period. Again this would not be unusual for the wagon company's records. Thus the Hendy fleet may have been ten wagons larger for a period.

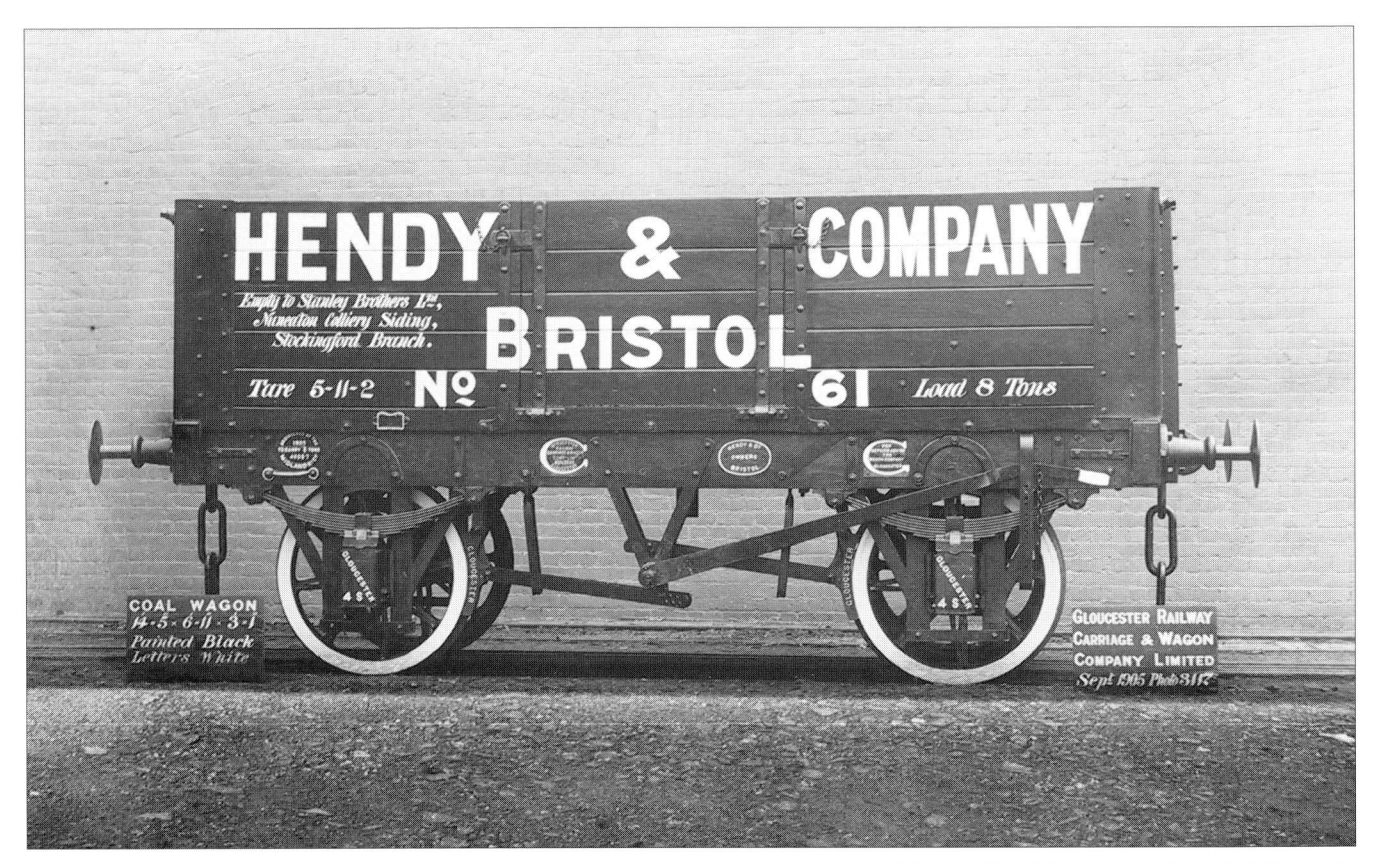

No. 61 was photographed in September 1905 and was another 5-plank 8-ton wagon painted black with white lettering. Branded 'Empty to Stanley Brothers Ltd, Nuneaton Colliery Siding, Stockingford Branch.' it was registered by the Midland Railway. *GRC&WCo.*

Hendy & Co. may also have acquired some wagons from an unknown source in June 1910 as they took over a repair contract for the remaining three years and seven months on ten 8-tonners.

The last order for wagons comes after Enoch's death and was placed with the Midland RC&WCo., five 8-ton wagons, numbered 70 to 74, being registered by the Midland Railway in December 1911. Adding up the number of wagons bought the Hendy & Company fleet appears to have been around the sixty wagon mark. With hired wagons it could well have been between seventy and eighty.

C. H. & J. HEWITT

As mentioned under the Coalpit Heath Coal Co. the Hewitt family were coal merchants originally based at Avon Wharf. Charles Hardwick Hewitt and John Hewitt were born in Suffolk in the early years of the nineteenth century. By 1851 they were trading at the Lower Railway Wharf, St Philips and Limekiln Lane. It is likely that a connection with Coalpit Heath Colliery was forged early on and the family later became shareholders in the concern. There is no evidence at present that they operated wagons apart from having a rail connected coal yard.

ALICK GRANT HEYWARD

Heyward was another of the many merchants based at both Clifton Down and, for a while, Montpelier stations. Heyward was born in Launceston, Cornwall in 1871 the son of a bank manager. By 1901 he was working as a coal merchant in Bristol. He was in fact operating at least as early as the end of 1900 and in the minutes of the Great Western & Midland Joint Railways he can be found taking over the tenancy of an office at Clifton Down from Milton & Co.

In 1902 Kelly's *Bristol Directory* lists Heyward at Station Road. Montpelier and in October 1903 he can be found in the GW&Mid minutes renewing the tenancy on an office here plus 336 yards of coal stacking ground, at the same time he renewed the lease on the Clifton Down office and 171 yards of coal stacking ground. In January 1906 Heyward's office at Montpelier was taken over by Milton & Co.

By 1914 the business name had become A. G. Heyward & Co. with an address of Clifton Down Station. That address then remains constant through the 1926 RCH list and the 1928 *Colliery Year Book*.

In September 1928, however, Alick Grant, then living at 18 Downs Park East, filed for bankruptcy. He did not sign up to the 1933 RCH scheme so it is suggested that the business finished or was taken over, at or soon after his bankruptcy. He was not discharged from bankruptcy until 1933.

Ten-ton wagons 10 and 11 were built by the Midland RC&WCo. and registered by the Midland Railway in 1901. The owner's location was recorded as 'Montpelier and Clifton'. When two more 10-tonners came from the Midland RC&WCo. later in 1901 they were numbered 12-13 and noted as 'Clifton Down'.

Wagon 4, also to carry 10 tons, was built by Claye and registered in 1904 with a location of 'Montpelier'.

Wagons 28 to 31 were supplied by Thomas Hunter of Rugby in 1924.

HUNTLEY & COCKRAM

This would appear to be a partnership between William Huntley and Thomas Cockram but when they commenced trading is uncertain but they were in business by 1889. An advertisement from 1894 (*above*) shows them as coal factors at Lawrence Hill Railway Wharf. An advert from two years earlier shows them to have also been dealing in fencing posts etc, both at Lawrence Hill Railway Station and at St. Georges Steam Saw Mills, joinery and packing case works, Easton Road.

Kelly's 1902 *Bristol Directory* shows them trading in coal and as furniture removers at the Railway Wharf, Lawrence Hill; 56 West Street and Easton Road. It also shows Richard Cockram as a furniture broker. Possibly Cockram was moving more into furniture, although the 1901 census shows him aged 52, 'living on own means', as early in the 1900s the partnership appears to have been dissolved with the business re-emerging as Huntley & Co.

HUNTLEY & Co. Ltd

William Huntley, aged 45 in 1901, remained in the business of coal and furniture removals at Lawrence Hill Wharf and set up trading as Huntley & Co. Ltd, possibly in 1904. He also expanded to Montpelier Station and had coal stacking ground and an office there by 1906. *Kelly's* directory for 1914 shows them at Lawrence Hill Station; 182 Easton Road; l96a Cheltenham Road; Station Road Montpelier; 351 Gloucester Road, Horfield and Wapping. The latter location suggesting that the business had expanded further to a presence in the yard at Wapping Wharf.

Huntley & Co. signed up to the 1926 and 1933 RCH schemes but unfortunately no details whatsoever can be found on any wagons operated, nor any images. The business at this time might have been in the hands of Albert Huntley, probably William's son. In 1935 Huntley & Co. Ltd are listed only at Lawrence Hill and Montpelier stations with offices at 196a Cheltenham Road. The 1938 *Colliery Year Book* lists them both as 'Coal Exporters and Shippers' at 196a, Cheltenham Road, and as 'Coal Merchants' at Lawrence Hill Station. When the business ceased trading is unknown.

GEORGE WILLIAM IMBER & Co.

George William Imber can be found on the 1881 census living at Westbury-on-Trym with the occupation of accountant. Aged 42 he had been born in Shaftesbury, Dorset. He had two sons, Leopold G., aged 10 and born in London, and Horace S., aged 8, born in Southampton. Visting the family was one George Eaton a brick merchant. This might not have been a chance visit as Imber had been involved with bricks whilst living in Southampton.

The *London Gazette* of the 11th January 1876 shows that Imber had been in partnership with one Edwin Saint Aubyn Angove trading as Imber & Angove, builders factors.

He was trading as a coal merchant in Bristol by April 1894 and in Kelly's *Bristol Directory* for 1902 George William Imber & Co. can be found trading as coal merchants at the Upper Railway Wharf, Midland Road, St. Philips. This listing continues through both the 1914 and 1935 directories.

What cannot be found is any evidence of wagon ownership despite trading out of the Midland yard at St. Philips.

W. F. JONES & Co.

This coal merchant only appears in the 1902 Kelly's *Bristol Directory* trading at the Redcliff Railway Wharf, Pump Lane, Cathay. There is, so far, no evidence of wagon ownership. He was also proprietor of the Star Coal Company which was advertising in December 1900 as also trading out of Redcliff Wharf and may well have been connected with several other trading names.

Wagon No. 4 belonging to Huntley & Cockram was photographed at Greyfield Colliery. Of four-plank construction with raised ends, dead buffers, what looks like wooden brake blocks and side doors only, the wagon is obviously of some antiquity. Livery appears to be black with plain white lettering. **courtesy Alastair Warrington**

B. G. KING

With an address of 51 Broad Street the only hint that he may have had wagons is the fact that he appears in the 1926 RCH Commuted Charge list. However, 51 Broad Street appears to be the registered office, probably a solicitor or accountant's office. He did not subscribe to the 1933 RCH scheme, nor is there any sign of him in *Kelly's* 1935 directory.

A sketch by A. G. Thomas of wagon number 615 operated by Kitson. He recorded the livery as being black with plain white lettering. *A. G. Thomas*

GEORGE STONE KITSON

Kitson was a coal merchant trading from 76 Robertson Road, Eastville. He is another merchant whose only evidence of wagon ownership comes from signing up to the 1926 and 1933 RCH schemes and a personal recollection that his wagons were black with plain white lettering. On the 1911 census he can be found aged 30 and in the coal business but earlier, as shown on the previous census, he was a tinplate worker. He was listed in the 1935 *Kelly's* Directory as a resident at the above address but there was no business entry. Kitson died on the 7th November 1940.

KNEE & Co.

Apart from being based at Lawrence Hill Station in 1914 there is no evidence of wagon ownership. It is also unknown if there was a connection with Knee Bros of Clifton, a long-established removal firm who, in 1844, were one of the first to use a container that could be lifted from a set of road wheels and put onto a railway truck.

ROBERT LEWIS

Listed in Kelly's 1902 *Bristol Directory* with an address of Railway Wharf, Lawrence Hill there is no evidence so far of his having owned wagons.

HENRY LITTLE & SON

In 1880 given in a trade directory as trading at Lawrence Hill Station. No evidence of wagon ownership.

WILLIAM LOVE & Co.

Again listed in *Kelly's* in 1902 Love & Co. had an address of Redcliff Railway Wharf, Pump Lane, Cathay. Once more there is no record of wagon ownership so far. The company was not listed in the 1914 edition.

LUCAS & Co.

With an office address of Midland Road, St. Philip's, Lucas & Co. were trading out of the Midland yard. The company looks to have been founded by Marshall Henry Lucas, born in Pontypool, Monmouthshire, circa 1849. He was in Bristol by 1881 living in St. Nicholas Road and occupied as a colliery clerk. By 1901 he was a colliery book keeper and perhaps this gave him a good insight and grounding in the coal trade and within the next three years he felt confident enough to set up as a coal merchant in a city already well endowed with many such. With him may well have been one of his sons, Graham, who was certainly listed as a coal merchant in 1911.

The first record of wagons comes in November 1904 when two 10-ton wagons, numbered 20 and 21, were supplied by the Midland RC&WCo. and registered by the Midland Railway. It was not until December 1911 that the next two wagons, this time 8-tonners appear in the registers. Again, they were built by Midland RC&WCo. and were numbered 30 and 31. In March 1916 a single repair contract was taken with the Gloucester RC&WCo. on one 10-ton wagon. Being for seven years any renewal would have been with Wagon Repairs Ltd.

Lucas & Co. appear with the same address right through to the 1938 *Colliery Year Book* albeit they do not appear in the 1935 edition of *Kelly's*.

T. LUCAS & SONS

It is unknown if there was a connection between T. Lucas & Sons and Lucas & Co. Lucas & Sons were trading out of the Great Western Yard, Mead Street (Pylle Hill). The only evidence of them trading is an advertisement from an 1894 trade directory. They were also hauliers, contractors and house removers but there is no evidence of wagon ownership.

The advertisement for Lucas & Sons shows that they traded in coals from the Forest of Dean, Derbyshire and Leicestershire.

JOHN LYSAGHT Ltd

Lysaghts were makers of galvanised and black iron and steel sheet at Bristol, Wolverhampton and Newport. In 1910 they began building their integrated steel works at Normanby Park, Scunthorpe, in order to produce their own material. A controlling interest was acquired by Guest, Keen & Nettlefolds in February 1920. Lysaghts ran their own wagon fleet but it is unknown if any of these were lettered up for the Bristol operation.

MILES MAUDSLEY

Born in Kettlewell, Yorkshire, Maudsley first had a career on the Midland Railway based in Bradford, Burton-upon-Trent and then Bristol where he finished as a railway inspector. The 1881 census shows him with such rank living at 9 Meyrick Street aged 39. At some point between then and 1901 he switched to trading in coal and can be found on the census of that year as a coal merchant. In 1902 Kelly's has him trading at the Redcliff Railway Wharf, Pump Lane, Cathay. Maudsley died towards the end of 1909 aged 68. There is no evidence thus far of him having had wagons.

MIDLAND COAL Co.

There are several companies with the same name trading in the city, which confusion is added to by the number of businesses with the name 'Midland Coal Company' across the whole county.

The earliest found in Bristol advertised in 1876 as the Midland Coal Co., 'Coal, Coke & Cannel Merchants, Upper Railway Wharf, St. Philips, Bristol, Henry H. Wright, manager. Office 24 Lower Arcade'. This may be the same company as can be found operated by John Bird and George Williams (see also Williams & Bird) who were described as being in co-partnership and as 'late of the Midland Railway Wharf, West Street and afterwards of Midland Railway Wharf trading as the Midland Coal Co.' They went into bankruptcy as the latter in July 1879.

This may also be the Midland Coal Co. who were taking wagons from the Midland Waggon Co. in March 1876 when six 6-ton wagons were bought on a seven year deferred purchase at £10 2s 6d pwpa.

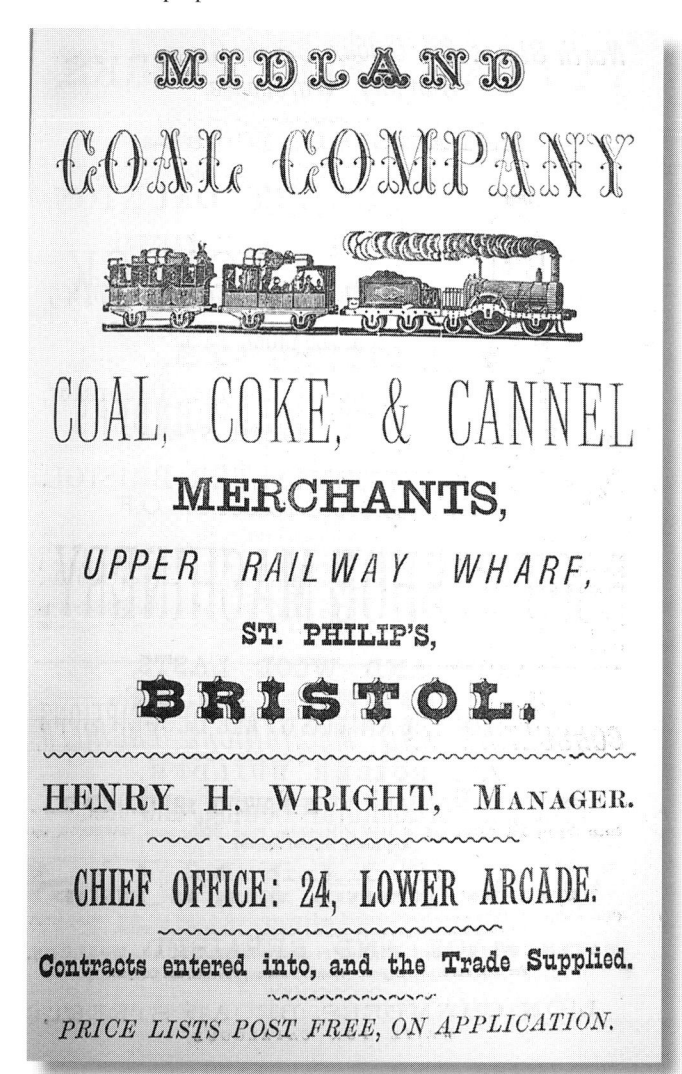

The 1876 advertisement for the Midland Coal Company.

The next reference comes in April 1883 when a Francis Richard Henry Protheroe, trading as the Midland Coal Co. at the St. Philip's Coal Wharf went bankrupt. Protheroe, living at 2 Moreton Villa, Stapleton, was also trading at the Pennywell Road Brick Works and the St. Philip's Brick Works, The Marsh as a brick and tile manufacturer. Had Protheroe bought the residue of the Williams & Bird operation to go with his brick interests?

MIDLAND COAL Co.

The next instance of a Midland Coal Co. is found in Kelly's 1902 *Bristol Directory*. Again it was based in the Upper Railway Wharf at St. Philips and was listed as 'Geo. Critchie, proprietor'. Critchie can be found on the 1901 census aged 60 but apart from that he is a bit of a mystery. His place of birth was given as 'UK' but no other references in the usual family history resources can be found for him at an earlier date. The company did not appear in the 1889 *Kelly's* directory but that is not to say that it was not in existence. There also appears to be a bit of a puzzle over the company name. *Kelly's* had it as the Midland Coal Co. but upon Critchie's bankruptcy in August 1910 he was said to be trading as the Midland Coal Supply Co.

It is known that this business ordered wagons from the Midland RC&WCo. In January 1902 a single 8-ton wagon numbered 2 was registered by the Midland Railway to the Midland Coal Supply Co. A year later another 8-ton wagon, numbered 3 was put down to the Midland Coal Co. There is then a gap until August 1909 when 10-ton wagon number 10 was registered, again to the Midland Coal Supply Co.

Critchie may also have dealt with the Gloucester RC&WCo. as several orders are recorded for the Midland Coal Co. In March 1906 four secondhand 10-ton wagons were hired for one year. In October the same year six secondhand 10-ton wagons were purchased (which wagons would fit between those supplied by the Midland RC&WCo. if numbered 4 to 9) on ten years deferred purchase lease. At the same time a further six 10-ton wagons were hired for 15 months. That the wagons bought in 1906 went to the Bristol Midland Coal Co. is in part confirmed by the fact that they were back with Gloucester for resale in 1911 which would tie in with Critchie's bankruptcy and subsequent exit from the Bristol coal trade.

MIDLAND COAL Co.

The exit of Critchie left a gap in the market for another Midland Coal Co. in Bristol and this was filled by 1935 by the Midland Coal Co. (Bristol). Behind this concern were A. E. Frape & E. N. Dry who traded from 78 Alma Road. There is no evidence of any wagon ownership.

WILLIAM J. MILLS

In 1902 *Kelly's* has Mills trading at the Railway Depot, Lawrence Hill and at 308 Gloucester Road. The 1901 census shows William John Mills aged 29, born in Penzance and trading as a coal merchant. In 1914 only Lawrence Hill Station is given as Mills' address.

The RCH 1926 and 1933 schemes give an E. E. Mills at Lawrence Hill Wharf trading as a coal merchant. This, it is assumed, is likely to be a son of William who has taken on the business. E. E. Mills was still trading in 1938.

Seven-plank wagon No. 6 was photographed by Gloucester in January 1910. Despite the order stating that cash was paid by Wilfred Milton the wagon carries a Gloucester owner's plate (number 49936). It also has builder's and repairer's plates and a Great Western registration plate. Livery was 'dark lead colour' with white lettering, shaded black and with black ironwork. The block lettered W and M superimposed over each other on the side door echoes the design used by Samuel Brookman at Montpelier nine years earlier. Notice the axlebox covers with the cast G, these 4N boxes do not appear often on Gloucester wagons apart from between 1897 and 1898 and 1907 and 1910. The study of such features and the period each pattern was in use would make a book on its own! *GRC&WCo.*

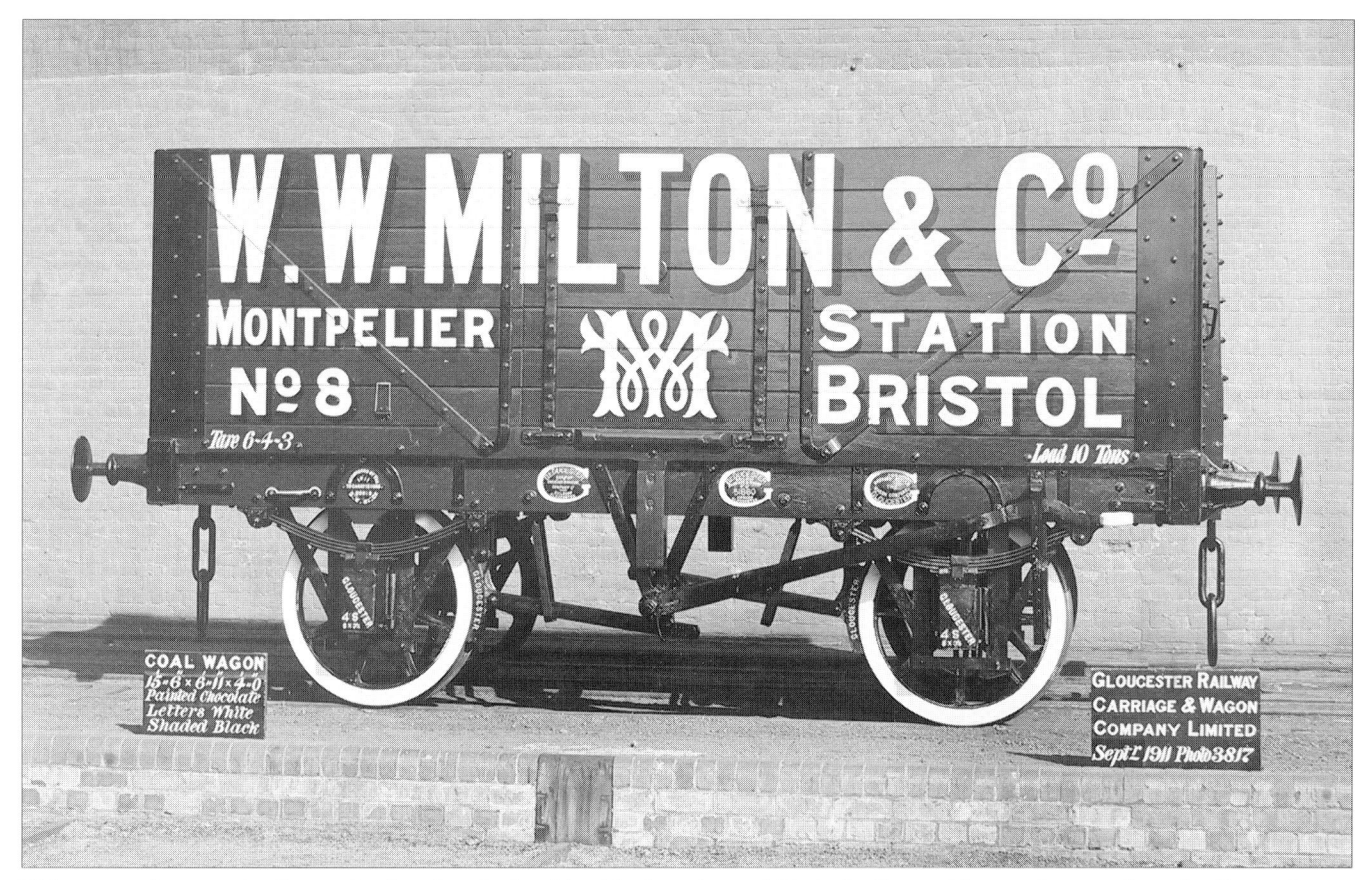

This extremely attractive livery of a chocolate body with white lettering and black shading and ironwork, apart from the diagonals, was applied to wagon No. 8 in September 1911. The intertwined WM on the side door has now been altered to a particularly ornate style. It carries all three Gloucester plates, builders, owners and repairers and was registered by the GWR. *GRC&WCo.*

A. H. MILTON & Co.

In 1889 Alfred H. Milton & Co. can be found trading at the Redcliff Railway Wharf, Pump Lane, Cathay and at 105 Whiteladies Road, Clifton. How long the business had been established for has not yet been ascertained but at that date Milton would have been in his late twenties. He had been born in Bath and in 1881, aged 21, he was a clerk in the chocolate trade living at 99 City Road.

By 1902 a move had been made away from the Redcliff Railway Wharf to Clifton Down Station with a depot at St. Andrews Road, Montpelier. This move may have been made as early as 1900 as in October the office occupied by Milton at Clifton Down was taken over by A. G. Heyward. The office address was still 105 Whiteladies Road whilst Alfred Milton was living at 205 Cheltenham Road.

The 1914 *Kelly's* directory shows that the business had once again relocated, this time to Station Road, Montpelier with an office address of 91 Cotham Brow. The name of the business changed to W. W. Milton & Co. prior to 1910. Wilfred W. Milton was the son of Alfred but he had not gone straight into the coal business. In 1901, when aged 18, he was a railway clerk but by 1911 had joined the family business. Indeed, there is the possibility that Alfred had retired as he can be found at Fylde in Lancashire in 1911 but could have been taking a holiday or travelling on business. Interestingly Alfred's older sons, Alfred and Harold, do not appear to have been involved with the business.

Despite having been in business since the 1880s the first written reference to wagons does not appear until 1910 in the records of the GRC&WCo. In January Wilfred purchased one new 10-ton wagon for cash, together with a seven year repair lease. In August 1911 he purchased another new 10-ton wagon, this time on five years deferred purchase. Only three months later he was back ordering two more 10-tonners on the same basis. These were numbered 10 and 12 and were registered by the Midland Railway in December. As already seen Milton took over one of Samuel Brookman's wagons in June 1913. Perhaps Brookman was struggling with the repayments and sold the wagon off to Milton at a price the latter could not refuse. Milton took over the remainder of the original purchase lease and renewed it for a further seven years in April 1915.

There are no other references to wagons. It would seem that Milton's numbered their wagon fleet using only even numbers, the four wagons taken from Gloucester being 6, 8, 10 and 12. Does this mean that prior to 1910 they were operating two secondhand wagons numbered 2 and 4? Perhaps also the wagon bought from Brookman was renumbered 14 in Milton's fleet.

The business was still trading at Montpelier Station in 1938 with an office address of 17 Whiteladies Gate and with a depot at Clifton Down Station. Soon after they would have lost their wagons into the pool. How long they continued to trade as coal merchants is unknown.

Three months after the purchase of number 8 Milton was buying two more wagons from Gloucester of which No. 10 was photographed in December 1911. It was painted in the same colour scheme as number 8 but this time with just MILTON along the top four planks. It is interesting that in the time between the two orders that the idea of a much more 'punchy' title on the wagon should have come about. One wonders if the customer received any guidance from the wagon company concerning lettering styles or if current design fashion had caught up with Milton.
GRC&WCo.

EDWARD WILLIAM BOULT MONKS

Monks was trading as a coal merchant by 1869 and in 1889 was at Snowdon Road, Fishponds. However, there was far more to Monks than just being a coal merchant. He was part of a family whose history was intertwined with coal mining in the Bristol area. The inclusion of the name Boult suggests strong family ties with the Boult family who were connected with Easton and Hanham collieries whilst the Boult Monks themselves were connected with collieries at Yate and Easton. Indeed, the 1881 census shows Edward Monks to have been aged 38, born in Stapleton and a 'colliery proprietor and coal merchant'. He was living at The Grange, Stapleton with his wife and elderly members of both the Monks and Boult families.

Monks took out a private siding agreement in January 1869 for a siding at Fishponds which, as already noted, was taken over in 1902 by George Webb trading as the Fishponds Coal Co. Perhaps this gives an indication as to the span of Monks' trading. Certainly the 1901 census lists him as 'retired coal merchant'. He died early in 1911 aged 68.

Monks can be found taking four secondhand 10-ton wagons on simple hire for one year in 1894 from the Gloucester RC&WCo. No other references to wagons can be found suggesting that any others run would have been bought secondhand.

MONTPELIER COAL Co.

As suggested by the title the Montpelier Coal Co. were to be found trading out of Montpelier Station prior to 1877. The *London Gazette* for the 26th June 1877 records that one Albert Weston, of the Montpelier Railway Station, coal merchant, trading as the Montpelier Coal Company had gone bankrupt. Once again, apart from trading out of the station yard, there is no evidence that he operated wagons, nor can any trace of him be found in trade directories.

THOMAS MULFORD

The *London Gazette* of the 31st October 1876 records the bankruptcy of Thomas Mulford trading as a coal merchant at Clifton Down Station coal depot and at 77 Philip Street, Bedminster. However, there is no evidence of wagon ownership, only the fact that he worked out of Clifton Down Station suggests that he may have done so.

That a number of coal merchants are included in these pages for which at present there is no evidence of wagon ownership is based on the fact that in previous volumes it has been proved that most merchants who advertised a railway address turn out to have wagons – the proof has yet to be found !

F. G. MULLIS & SONS

Frederick George Mullis was a contemporary of Alfred Milton, both being born in 1854. Fred was born in Bristol as were his sons, Frederick in 1891 and Montague in 1893. Frederick senior does not appear as a coal merchant in 1889 but was listed as such on the 1901 census. *Kelly's* for 1902 and 1914 show him trading at Clifton Down Station with offices at 25a Oakfield Grove, Clifton.

Mullis did a lot of business with the Gloucester RC&WCo. but did not exclusively use that company. The first order recorded was in April 1901 when two 8-ton wagons costing £63 10s each were bought for cash, together with a seven year repair contract which was renewed in May 1908 and again in May 1915. The next two wagons were bought from the Midland RC&WCo. and were of 10-ton capacity, numbered 25 and 26. Registration was with the Midland Railway in April 1903. Two 10-ton wagons were then bought from Gloucester in October 1903 at a cost of £59 10s each, cash plus a seven year repair contract which was renewed in November 1910. Of these number 28 was photographed and it is suggested that the other was numbered 27 as a month later numbers 29 and 30 were registered by the Midland Railway. These two 10-tonners had been built by Midland.

In August 1906 a return was made to Gloucester for two 8-ton at £62 each, cash plus a seven year repair contract which was renewed in December 1913. It was then almost six years before two new 10-ton wagons were bought in March 1912 at £66 10s each, plus the usual seven year repair contract. In March 1915 two more 10-ton wagons at £79 2s 6d each were bought for cash together with a repair contract for ten years.

In June 1916 a change to his buying policy was made when two secondhand 8-ton wagons were bought from Gloucester although they were still paid for in cash, together with the seven year repair contract.

There is then a gap again until April 1920 when two 12-ton wagons at £272 each were bought followed by five more 12-tonners in April 1924 at £166 each. This batch were numbered 60 to 64 and were registered by the GWR. There were no more new registrations after this for Mullis & Sons.

It would seem that Mullis was reasonably consistent in his wagon numbering policy between 1901 and 1916. Buying in twos, wagons numbered 23 to 32 and 35 to 38 can be accounted for and it is likely that 33 and 34 were either bought secondhand or from an unknown builder, they certainly fit in the period 1906 to 1912 when no other wagons were bought. It is possible that Mullis began his fleet numbering at 20 or 21 as it is unlikely he was running a fleet as large as twenty wagons by 1901. His last wagons, 60 to 64, might also be a change in numbering policy as 41 to 59 are missing but, again, could have been bought secondhand or from other builders.

Mullis & Sons signed up to both the 1926 and 1933 RCH schemes. In 1935 they are listed as still being at the Oakfield Grove address and at Clifton Down Station as well as an address in Princess Victoria Street. The business was still active at the start of the Second World War so all of the wagons would have been taken into the pool.

It was in April 1901 that Gloucester photographed wagon number 22 for F. G. Mullis. Two 8-ton wagons were bought at this time, each costing £63 10s. For that amount you got a five-plank wagon with full height side doors and brakes one side. The wagons were painted black with plain white lettering. *GRC&WCo.*

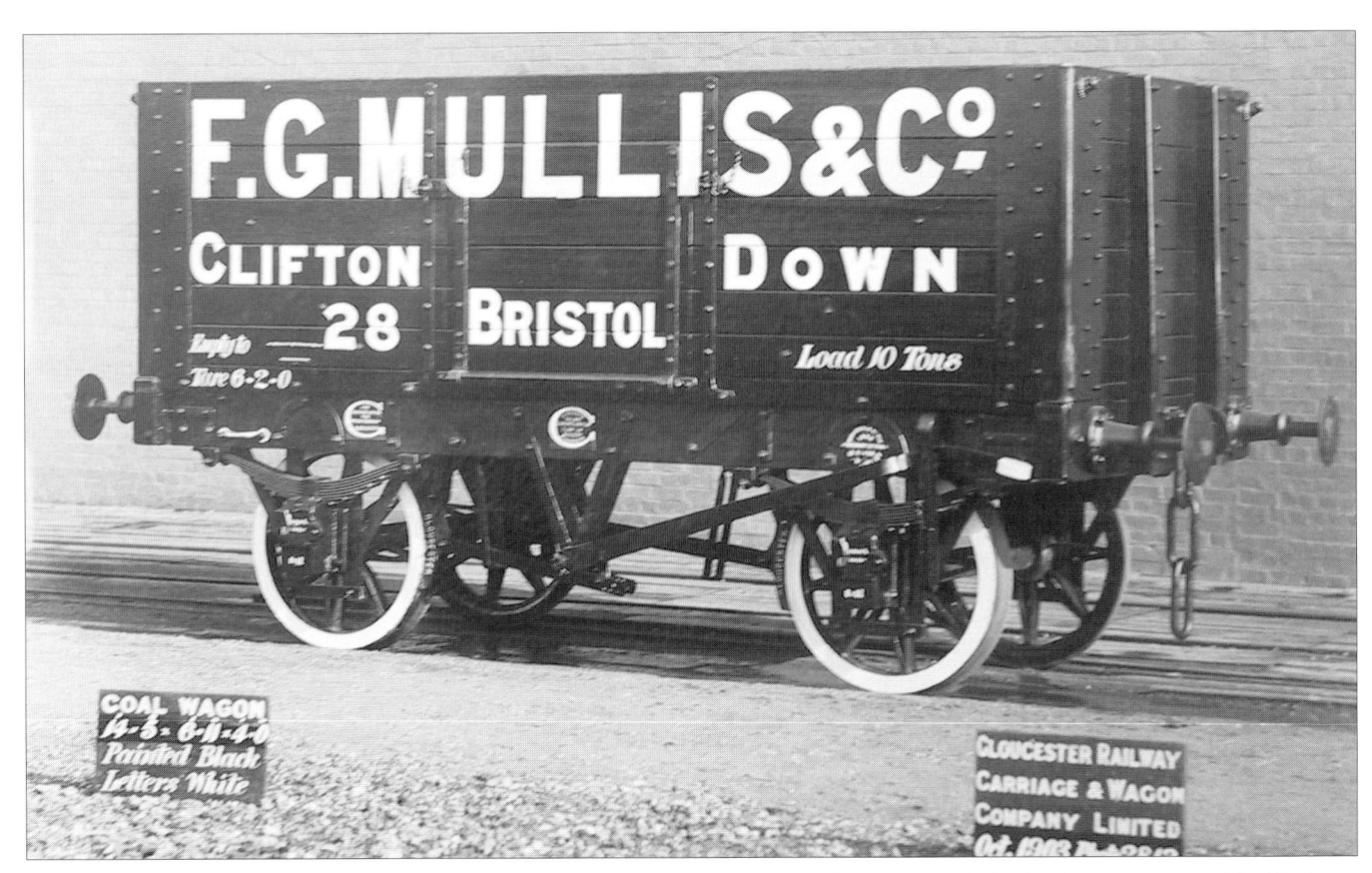

The next wagon photographed for Mullis was in October 1903. Number 28 was a 10-ton wagon of six-plank construction with side doors only and brakes one side only. Again two wagons were bought coming in at £59 10s each – £4 cheaper than the smaller wagons bought two years earlier. Again they were painted black with plain white lettering. *GRC&WCo.*

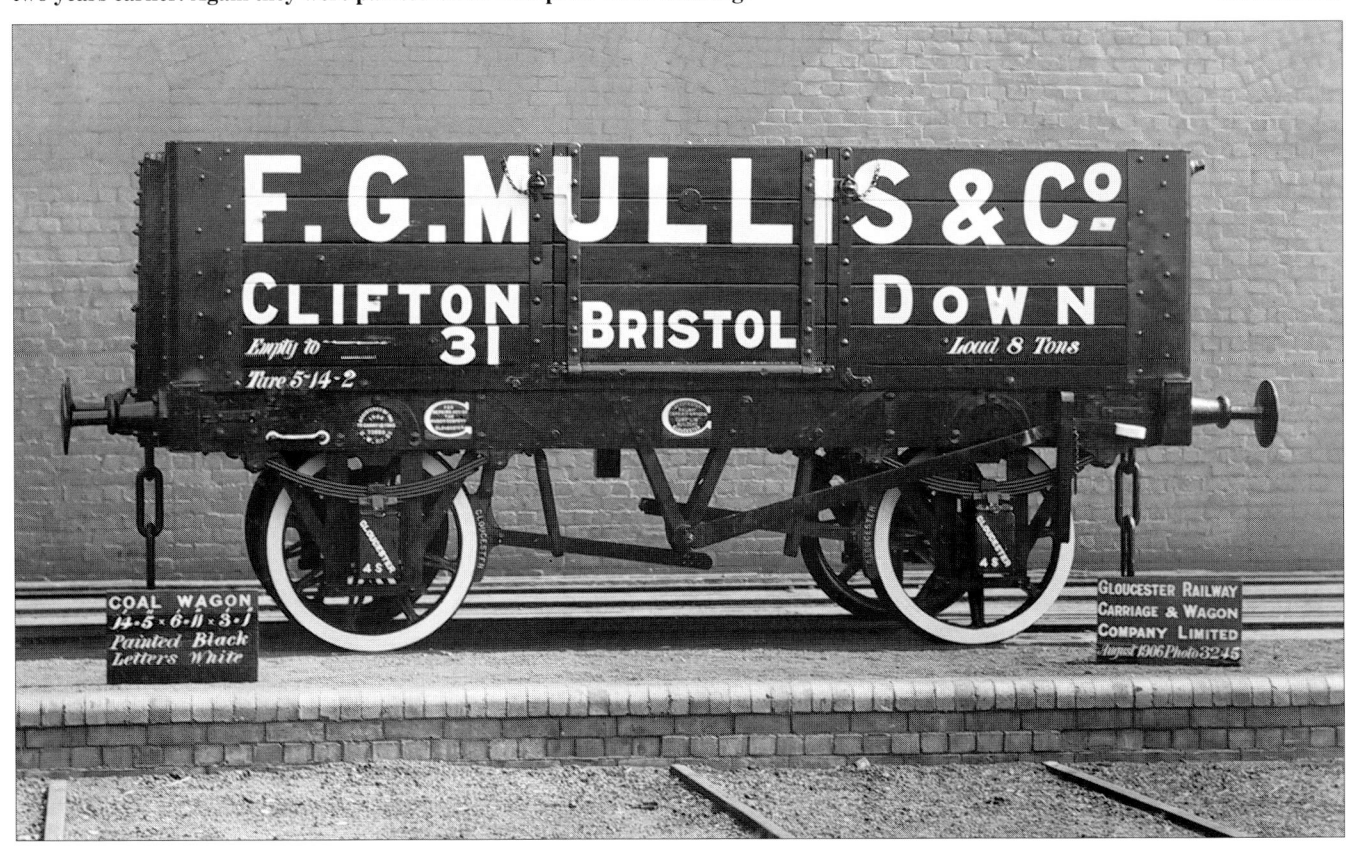

The 10-ton wagons bought in 1903 represented something of a bargain as the price for an 8-ton wagon in August 1906 was £62. Mullis again paid for two wagons in cash. There is a slight variation in the lettering to the ones bought in 1901 in that the initial letters for Clifton Down have been enlarged, Notice also the large wooden doorstop fitted on the far side. *GRC&WCo.*

A more significant change in lettering came with two 10-ton wagons bought in September 1912. The business title has now become F. G. Mullis & Sons. These seven-plank wagons, fitted with brakes both sides, came in at £66 10s each. *GRC&WCo.*

Two more 10-ton wagons were bought in March 1915 and apart from a few minor variations in the lettering – probably down to the individual signwriter – they were identical to those above. One difference, however, probably due to the difficult conditions now prevailing was that the price had increased to £79 2s 6d each. *GRC&WCo.*

One feature of the post First War period was the much greater cost of wagons. The two 12-ton examples bought in May 1920 cost £272 each – more than three times the cost of a wagon in 1915. The trading title has now been shortened to Mullis & Sons and for some reason wagons fitted with both side and end doors have been taken. Possibly Mullis now had an industrial customer who used a tippler to discharge the load.
GRC&WCo.

A wagon belonging to Mullis just managed to make it into the edge of a view of Camerton Station, Somerset. More remarkably the number can be made out, No. 29, which was one of the two wagons supplied by the Midland RC&WCo. in December 1910. The view probably dates from the 1930s with the wagon collecting coal from one of the nearby collieries.
collection John Alsop

The bottom soon dropped out of the coal wagon market and by September 1924 a new wagon could be obtained for £166. As can be seen from the view above Mullis acquired five 12-ton wagons at this time, which, as was usual for the business, were paid for in cash. It is likely that it was these wagons that brought about a totally new look to the wagon fleet being simply lettered with the large Mullis on the side of a lead grey body. Ironwork, excepting the diagonals, was picked out in black. As seen in the view at the bottom of the previous page the style was also applied to older wagons in the fleet, probably at the time of their next due repaint. The batch of wagons bought in 1924 was numbered 60 to 64 of which 64 was singled out for individual attention and is seen below. There is little remarkable about the wagon with the large style of title sitting easier upon the smaller, older, wagons. *GRC&WCo.*

NEWPORT COAL & COKE Co. Ltd

The Newport Coal & Coke Co. appears to have a long history being extant prior to 1862. Behind the business at that time were John Selwyn Payne and John Llewellyn Vining and they were trading at Countess Slip, Bristol. On the 12th August 1862 the partnership was dissolved by mutual consent. John Payne appears to have kept the business on until his death on the 23rd March 1881 when living at 8 Queen's Parade, Bath. The business was then run by his widow Ellen, and solicitor Edward Harwood as executors and then from the 18th March 1881 by Ellen Harriette Payne on her own. At this date the business was trading from Bristol Wharf. In 1889 Frank Reed was the manager for the Newport Coal & Coke Co. with offices in Passage Street, St. Philips.

Alfred John Smith (see later) bought the business in 1893 and turned it into a limited company in 1897. With a capital of £5,000 in 500 £10 shares the subscribers included Alfred John Smith, coal merchant, 9 Queens Square, Alfred Sidney Livingstone Smith of 'Highgrove', Wells Road, a coal manager, and William Davies Huxtable, a coal exporter from Cardiff.

In 1902 the company was still at Passage Street but now with a depot in the Great Western Railway Yard, Mead Street, Bath Parade. *Kelly's* 1914 reveals that the office was at 13 Passage Street. With the interest of Smith in the business it is interesting to note that Passage Street was also the address of Coal Agencies Ltd, another of Smith's companies.

The company signed up to both the 1926 and 1933 RCH schemes but this is the only suggestion that they operated any wagons.

In 1935 the trading addresses were the Passage Street offices with depots at Lawrence Hill Station; the Great Western Yard, Mead Street near Bath Bridge; Canon's Marsh GWR Siding; and Goods Yard, Postview Road, Avonmouth.

The company was wound up voluntarily in December 1938 at which date Alfred Sidney Livingstone Smith was chairman and held all of the shares. Having discharged all the debts of the company the remaining assets were sold to Coal Agencies Ltd for the sum of £4,000 which included the 'lorries, wagons, crane gantry and weighbridges'. Can 'wagons' in this instance be taken to mean railway wagons? Unfortunately the company file did not expand upon this.

T. NICHOLS & SONS Ltd

With an office address of 11 Dean Street, St. Pauls, this company signed up to the 1926 RCH scheme in May 1927 and to that of 1933 in February 1934. Kelly's *Bristol Directory* of 1935 gives 106 Wilder Street and the Midland Railway Station, St. Philips as the business addresses. They were not listed amongst coal merchants in the 1938 *Colliery Year Book*. The only evidence for wagon ownership is that the company signed up to the RCH schemes.

C. W. ORCHARD

A letterhead seen for this business was the first clue that Orchard operated wagons. Dating to 1918 it prompted a check through the records where a C. W. Orchard was found, with no address attached, taking a repair contract on five 10-ton wagons for seven years with the Gloucester RC&WCo.

The letterhead showed Orchard to be operating as a coal merchant and factor, removal contractor and break proprietor from 163 Stapleton Road. He had branch offices, probably for taking orders only, in Warwick Road, Fishponds Road and Gloucester Road. That he arrived on the wagon scene for a repair contract on five wagons suggests that he had either taken over an existing business or purchased secondhand. He does not appear in the 1928 *Colliery Year Book* or the 1935 edition of *Kelly's*, suggesting maybe that the business was quite short lived.

The 1901 census showed Charles W. Orchard to have been born in Wotton under Edge, Gloucestershire in 1877. His occupation on the census was given as coal dealer.

Osborn & Wallis operated their coal business in Bristol from the old Hotwell Dry Dock with a siding off the GWR Canon's Marsh Branch. The rails alongside the dock were used by cranes for unloading the ships and barges.

Two wagons belonging to London coal factors Ricketts being unloaded at Hotwells into an Osborn & Wallis delivery lorry. This seems to confirm that the company did have coal brought in from other coalfields by rail rather than just from South Wales by sea. Two yard workers stand in the wagon shovelling the coal over the top of the sides into the high sided lorry, as the load in the railway wagon got lower so this task became harder.

OSBORN & WALLIS

Osborn & Wallis were mainly involved in shipping and are best known for their colliers which took coal between South Wales and the power station at Portishead, Somerset. The business was started in 1880 when cousins William Osborn and Humphrey Wallis, both already shipowners, came together mainly to better handle imports of copper ore to the United Alkali plant at Netham in Bristol. Osborn was the half of the partnership based in Bristol, at Queen Square and in Hotwells and he soon realised that bringing coal into the city for use by several industrial customers would be profitable. The full history of the company and its ships has been published in *The Portishead Coal Boats* by Mike Winter.

Bringing in coal meant that private customers could also be supplied from the wharf at Hotwells and so Osborn & Wallis also became coal merchants.

They also ran a fleet of railway wagons but whether in connection with the coal merchant's business bringing coal from other coalfields or loading coal transshipped at Hotwells for onward transmission to customers is unknown. There is also the possibility that the wagons may have been used in conjunction with bunkering the company's ships in South Wales ports. The earliest reference was for the hire of six wagons in 1882 from the Swansea Wagon Co. but this may have been on a very short-term basis. In January 1888 the hire of sixteen 8-ton wagons from the Gloucester RC&WCo. for one year is recorded. That sixteen 8-ton wagons were still recorded as on hire in November 1888, September 1893 and December 1895 suggests that the hire might have been continuous. In February 1888 fifteen 10-ton wagons were hired from Gloucester for three months and these were still on hire in November when a further twenty 10-ton wagons were hired for one year. The thirty-five 10-ton wagons were still on hire in September 1893 when the hire was extended for a further year. They do not appear after that date but that is not to say that any renewals of the hire did not take place, they may just not have been recorded.

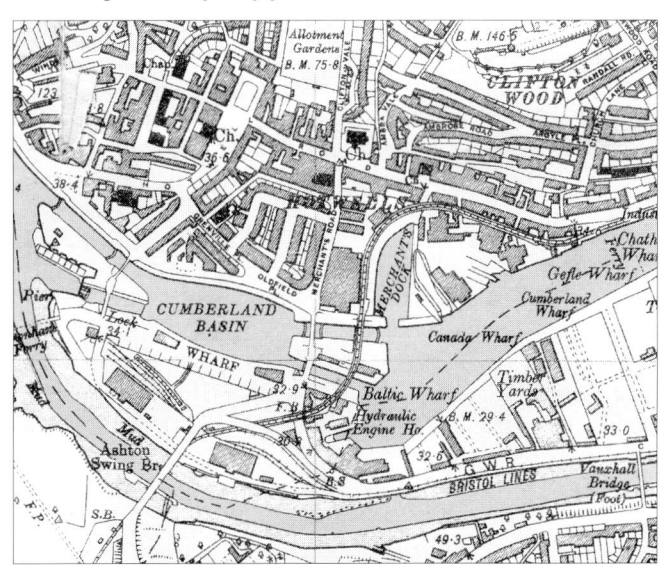

A further extract from the 1930 OS 6-inch shows the location of Osborn & Wallis's dock immediately alongside Merchants Dock (the Hotwells Dock has not been filled with a tint). The GWR's Canon's Marsh Branch curves round the top of Merchants Dock and W. Galbraith had a siding off the top of the curve. Poole Brothers Wharf was where the railway came back alongside the Floating Harbour on the right-hand edge of the extract.

In January 1912 five 10-ton wagons were obtained from the Gloucester RC&WCo. by T, Paul & Co. Of seven-plank construction with side door, folding top planks and brakes both sides, they were painted black with plain white lettering. The folding top planks enabled the opening up of the entire height of wagon side if required for ease of discharge. The A. M. M. across the top two planks stands for Audley Montague Miller, one of the partners in the firm at this time.

GRC&WCo.

Three 10-ton wagons were purchased from Gloucester in July 1914 and were similar in specification to those supplied earlier apart from apparently being half-an-inch less in height. As with the earlier wagons there is a 'gap filler' at the base of the side doors. Miller was still a partner at this date but his initials do not now appear on the wagon side. *GRC&WCo.*

T. PAUL & Co.

Thomas Paul was trading in coal by 1879 and is described in the 1881 census as a wine and coal merchant, as well as being a Captain in the 1st Gloucestershire Regiment which would then have been a volunteer batallion. He was single and forty years of age. In 1889 he was trading at Royal Arcade, Whiteladies Road and at Clifton Down Station. Editions of Kelly's *Bristol Directory* for both 1902 and 1914 give the address as 111 Whiteladies Road, Clifton and Clifton Down Station.

By 1912 an Audley Montague Miller had become involved in the business, possibly as an investment, and when railway wagons were purchased in that year they had the initials A. M. M. above the main title. It is possible that Thomas Paul died in early 1913 aged 73 and by 1917 T. Paul & Co. was being run by a partnership consisting of Thomas Miller, Audley Miller and Elizabeth Theodosia Paul, at 111 Whiteladies Road. On the 7th April Thomas Miller left leaving the other two to continue. By 1924 they were trading at 87 Alma Road, Clifton until the partnership was dissolved on the 31st October leaving Miller to continue alone using the same trading name. By 1938 he had taken Denys Francis Parr Coles (previously encountered in connection with the Cental Coal Co.) into the partnership until he retired in March 1944 leaving Miller on his own again. How long the business was continued after this is unknown. It is likely that the interest of the Miller family was a financial one and that managers probably ran the business itself.

One interesting fact about Audley Montague Miller is that he played one Test Match for England in South Africa in 1895/6 despite never having played for a first class county.

He captained Wiltshire for 25 years and in 1901 was living in Lacock, Wiltshire. The Thomas Miller connected with the business may well have been his nephew who played first class cricket for Gloucestershire.

In terms of wagons the first references come in the books of the Midland Waggon Co. in February 1879 when four secondhand 8-ton wagons were taken on simple hire for one year at £7 pwpa. The following month two more 8-ton wagons were taken on a year's simple hire at £6 pwpa. Towards the end of the year four 6-ton wagons were taken on the same terms at £4 15s pwpa. This may well have been the period in which Paul was starting up the business and hiring wagons as trade expanded. That the wagons were only hired for one year is not unusual and undoubtedly those hires were extended. Indeed there are no further mentions in the Midland RC&WCo's books until September 1889 when the hire of four wagons was renewed. In February 1890 the hire of two more wagons was again renewed followed by that for eight wagons in August.

The next references to new wagons come from the Gloucester RC&WCo. and may result from input from the Miller family into the business. In July 1912 five new 10-ton wagons were bought on a ten year deferred purchase lease at £10 pwpa plus a repair contract. That other wagons were being run by the business is shown by a repair contract being taken with Gloucester in January 1914 on three 10-ton wagons for seven years. In July 1914 three 10-ton wagons were purchased over ten years with Gloucester to do the repairs.

A change was then made to obtaining wagons from the Midland RC&WCo. As well as three wagons from Gloucester

One of the two 12-ton wagons supplied by Gloucester in March 1924. Numbers 41 and 42 were seven-plank wagons with side doors only and were black with plain white lettering. *GRC&WCo.*

in July 1914 three were taken from Midland and numbered 7, 8 and 10. All were 10-ton and financed by the wagon company. Whether Midland's terms were better is unknown but four more 10-ton wagons, 16 to 19, were bought on finance in March 1915, three more, 20 to 22 in April and three more, 23 to 25 in July. In April 1916 three more 10-tonners were bought, numbered 26 to 28 and in September that year two further 10-ton wagons, 29 and 30 were registered. A significant number of the Midland built wagons had folding top planks above the side doors.

No further registrations can be found and the final order that can be traced was with the Gloucester RC&WCo, in March 1924 when two 12-ton wagons were purchased over seven years.

Quite what the number system employed by the company was is unknown. All of the wagons from Midland, apart from the first three follow in sequence 16 to 30. However, the earlier Gloucester-built wagons were numbered in the fifties and the final two in the forties. Sadly, with the Great Western Railway registration books missing we shall never be able to fill in the gaps.

PEPLER, EDWARDS & Co. Ltd

Pepler, Edwards & Co. was in existence by 1902 when it can be found trading out of Lawrence Hill with offices at 272 Stapleton Road. The Pepler of the title was Arthur Albert Charles Pepler, born in 1868 and the son of a grocer. In 1901 Arthur was described on the census as a coal merchant. The Edwards was Edward John Edwards, born in 1872 at Baptist Mills, Bristol and also described as a coal merchant in 1901. How long Pepler and Edwards had been in partnership is unknown but on the 22nd May 1902 the partnership was dissolved. Pepler, of 37 Belgrave Terrace, Fishponds and Edwards of Church Road, St. George, were trading as coal merchants and colliery agents at 272 Stapleton Road and Lawrence Hill Station. After the dissolution Pepler was to continue the business.

In February 1904 a limited company was formed to take over the existing business of coal merchants and tailors belonging to Arthur and Frank Pepler and trading as A. Pepler, Edwards & Co. The mix of coal merchants and tailors seems odd but three of Arthur's brothers, William, Frank and Walter, were all

All Quotations subject to Strike and Accident Clause.

PEPLER, EDWARDS & CO., LTD.

Colliery Agents.
TEL. 2101.

Fox Road.
Bristol.

connected with the latter trade. Also listed under the business interests were 'railway wagon builders and repairers'; 'mineral water and chocolate manufacturers' and 'tailors and outfitters' – a diverse business indeed!

The subscribers to the new company included Arthur Pepler and his wife Florence; Frank Pepler, Arthur's youngest brother; Walter Hancock, a colliery secretary from Braysdown, Somerset and his wife; Clarence Hancock; and Charles Bartlett Bartlett from Frome, Somerset. The authorized capital was £2,000 in £1 shares. Arthur Pepler and Walter Hancock were to be directors with Arthur as general manager and Frank Pepler as assistant manager. The registered office was still 272 Stapleton Road.

In *Kelly's* for 1914 Pepler, Edwards & Co. Limited were listed at 272 Stapleton Road and 258 Gloucester Road, Horfield with a depot at Fox Road off Stapleton Road.

In January 1926 the registered office was moved to Fox Road, with Frank Pepler as secretary. On the 5th March 1929 a liquidator was appointed as the company was to be wound up voluntarily, another victim at a time when many coal merchants were going under.

The only evidence of wagon ownership is the postcard view of a rake of wagons at Sherwood Colliery. No trace can be found of any wagons ordered, nor were any new wagons bought after 1924.

ARTHUR PEPLER

Arthur was not finished with the coal business after the liquidation of Pepler, Edwards & Co. He signed up on his own account to the 1926 RCH Commuted Charge scheme at a time when Pepler, Edwards & Co. were still in existence, they were listed separately in the same scheme. Arthur Pepler did not sign up to the 1933 scheme. In 1926 Pepler's address was 'Maycliffe', Mayfield Park, Fishponds and this was also given in the 1935 Kelly's *Bristol Directory* which lists him as a coal factor.

By 1937 he had taken over the Fishponds Coal Co. from George Webb including the private siding agreement for a siding at Fishponds Station. This acquisition might have been a step too far as in June 1939 Pepler, trading as A. Pepler at Mayfield Park and as the Fishponds Coal Company, Wharf Road, Fishponds, filed a petition for bankruptcy. He was released from this in 1942.

Although signing up to the 1926 RCH scheme no further evidence of wagon ownership can be found.

H. PEPLER & SON

It has to be assumed that H. Pepler was in some way related to the Peplers mentioned above. Possibly it is Sidney Hubert who was a brother of Arthur. He appears on the 1901 census as 'Herbert', aged 30, and was a provision merchants clerk.

An advertising postcard for Pepler, Edwards & Co. Ltd showing that they were sole sale agents in the West of England for the Sherwood Colliery, Mansfield. It is also the only known image of wagons for Pepler, Edwards & Co. Ltd and was obviously 'stage-managed' to get so many of their wagons into the colliery yard at the same time. Only two wagons can be identified, those nearest the camera being numbers 37 and 27. At least twelve wagons are present of varying dimensions but unfortunately the origins of all of Pepler's wagons remain lost to us.

John Ryan collection

The only known image of a wagon belonging to H. Pepler & Son is this one taken at Eastern United Colliery circa 1934 and previously used in *Private Owner Wagons of the Forest of Dean* but included again here for the sake of completeness. The wagon has side and end doors together with hinged planks above the side doors. It looks to be freshly painted although it is not a new wagon. The bottom left-hand corner is obscured but at bottom right is 'Bristol'.
Author's collection

When he set out in the coal trade is unknown. There was no listing in 1914 but he signed up to both the 1926 and 1933 RCH schemes with an address of 12 Lodore Road, Fishponds. In Kelly's 1935 *Bristol Directory* the business is listed as coal merchants trading at 12 Lodore Road and 370 Fishponds Road, Eastville. The business did not appear among coal merchants in the 1938 *Colliery Year Book*.

The only evidence of wagon ownership is the partial image of a wagon in the empty roads at Eastern United Colliery in the Forest of Dean.

POOLE BROTHERS

Poole Brothers were trading from Poole's Coal Wharf in Hotwell Road from at least the 1790s with coal being brought in by sea. They were also shipping agents arranging freights out of Bristol. By the 1890s they were specialising in bringing in Welsh smokeless steam coals both for industrial use and ships bunkering.

At some point Pooles joined forces with the neighbouring builder and stone and gravel contractor, William Galbraith to form Poole Bros, Galbraith & Co. Ltd. The Galbraith business moved to Poole's Wharf where extensive yards and workshops were set out.

In 1905 a private siding agreement was taken out with the Great Western Railway for a siding off the Canons Marsh Branch for W. Galbraith called Merchants Siding. There were already rail facilities into Poole's Wharf.

The company signed up to both the 1926 and 1933 RCH schemes and in 1935 were advertising themselves as coal, cement, gravel, and sand merchants at Poole's Wharf, 139 Hotwell Road.

The only evidence of Poole Bros, Galbraith & Co. Ltd wagon operation is this part view of a seven-plank wagon fitted with a coke crate. What the lettering to the left of 'Contractors' might have been is unknown. Bottom right is 'Bristol & Cardiff'.
courtesy Gerry Nichols

There was no evidence of wagon ownership, apart from the RCH listings until a partial image of a coke wagon lettered for the business was discovered, Sadly, no other wagon material can be found.

Photographed in February 1896 at Gloucester is No. 1 in Pounsbery's smallish fleet of wagons. For the flagship of his business he spared little, having it painted green with cream lettering, shaded red and with black ironwork. Being bought for cash it carries an oval owner's plate for Pounsbery between the legs of the 'V' hanger. *GRC&WCo.*

JAMES DILLON POUNSBERY

Pounsbery was born in 1850 in Bedminster. The 1881 census shows him living at 13 Heburn Road, St. Pauls and working as a coal merchants agent. He was not listed in *Kelly's* 1889 directory as trading in his own right but by 1896 had set himself up dealing in coal and trading at the Upper Railway Wharf, Midland Road and at 116 Kennington Avenue, Ashley Down Road. These addresses remain through to 1928 when he is listed in the *Colliery Year Book*. He did not sign up to the 1933 RCH scheme and can only be found in the 1935 *Kelly's* directory as a private resident at the Kennington Avenue address, presumably enjoying retirement at the age of 85.

Pounsbery seems to have used the Gloucester RC&WCo. exclusively for his wagon requirements. His wagon No. 1, of 8-ton capacity, was bought in February 1896 at a cost of £52 cash plus a seven year repair contract. No's 2 and 3, both 8-ton wagons, were added to the fleet in May 1902 at a cost of £56 10s each together with a seven year repair contract. The final 8-ton wagon, No. 4 cost £56 in November 1902 and, again, a seven year repair contract was also taken. The repair contracts were regularly renewed at seven year intervals with Gloucester right up until they passed into the hand of Wagon Repairs Ltd in 1918.

Left top: Pounsbery's second wagons, photographed in May 1902, reverted to a more typical – and cheaper – paint scheme of black with plain white lettering. It is likely that at the time of its first repaint that No. 1 was turned out in this style also.

Left bottom: No. 4 was purchased in November 1902 and was again a five-plank 8-ton wagon and is also fitted with a substantial wooden doorstop to protect the brake gear. An owner's plate for Pounsbery is on the solebar and reads 'J. D. Pounsbery No. 4 Bristol'. Livery is again black with plain white lettering. *both GRC&WCo.*

The first wagon known to have been bought by Pountney's came from Gloucester in November 1906. It was a 10-ton wagon of seven-plank construction with side doors only, brakes one side and a large wooden doorstop on the far side. Livery was black with plain white lettering. Wagon No. 2 was photographed in May 1912 and differs in having the diagonal side braces on the outside, brakes both sides and sprung steel doorstops
both GRC&WCo.

POUNTNEY & Co. Ltd

Pottery production in Bristol has a long and distinguished history, the first pottery in the city being opened in 1683 at Temple Back. Many others then starting up around Redcliff Back. Whilst having been the second most important pottery producing area in the country the industry in the city was hit by the growth of the Staffordshire potteries and by 1777 only the oldest established works at Temple Back remained.

The pottery went through a number of changes of ownership over the years, one name connected to it being the Ring family who will be encountered later in these pages. The most notable name came on the scene in 1813 when one John Decimus Pountney was taken into the business and he was to be the biggest partner for a number of years.

Pountney died in 1852 and the pottery was then run by his widow until 1872. Eventually it came into the hands of Patrick Johnston and Mr Rogers. They were soon joined by T. B. Johnston, a far-seeing young man. In 1887 he formed Pountney & Co. with Charles Burn having already moved the pottery to better premises in Feeder Road but these were only seen as being temporary. Young Johnston had ideas of building the most modern pottery in the country.

This was achieved by 1905 when the new factory at Lodge Causeway, Fishponds opened. Here were used the most up-to-date methods, the factory production area being on a single floor with raw materials entering at one end and the finished items dispatched from the other. The pottery was, however, still being fired in coal burning bottle kilns. These started to be replaced in 1938 when a continuous kiln fired by gas produced from anthracite was introduced.

The business continued in Bristol until 1969 when it moved to Pool in Cornwall. This was not a great success and the company went into receivership in 1971.

Originally the pottery would have been supplied by coal brought in by sea to Temple Back but with the move to Fishponds coal would have to have been brought in by rail. There are only records of two wagons owned by the company, both provided by the Gloucester RC&WCo. No. 1 was bought new in 1906 and No. 2 in 1912. It is thought unlikely that these two could have satisfied the entire coal requirements of the factory so one of the larger Bristol factors may also have supplied coal.

PRINCESS ROYAL COLLIERY Co. Ltd

As already mentioned under Coal Agencies Ltd, the Princess Royal Colliery Co. Ltd had a sales office in Cheese Lane, St. Philips and a depot at Wapping. With both A. S. Smith and Percy Berril having interests both in the colliery and coal selling in Bristol it is no surprise that they took over the running of the sales office out of which grew the formation of Coal Agencies Ltd.

Princess Royal were not the only colliery to maintain a sales office address in the city. A number can be found, especially in earlier trade directories, before the take over of such trade by some of the larger coal factors such as Renwick, Wilton. The viability of a colliery retaining an office was probably shown to be marginal by the take over of this office by Coal Agencies Ltd who obviously operated on behalf of a number of colliery concerns.

A. PRITCHARD

This is likely to be Alfred Pritchard who can be found on the 1901 census aged 45, born in Llanduing working as a foreman in a coal business. Is this another example of the business being taken on by an employee? Four 10-ton wagons, numbered 11 to 15, were registered by the Midland Railway in January 1903. They had been built by the Midland RC&WCo. Where the business was based is unknown and no other references to it can be found.

REDCLIFF COAL Co.

The Redcliff Coal Co. were listed in a trade directory of 1889 when Frederick Wm Jones was stated to be the manager. The business traded out of Redcliff Railway Wharf, Pump Lane, Cathay but so far there is no evidence of wagon ownership. One possibility is that this is the W. F. Jones already encountered in these pages who traded out of Redcliff Wharf under his own name and that of the Star Coal Co.

RICHARD CHARLES RING

The Ring family were trading in coal in the Bristol area from at least the first part of the 1800s. The first of the family trading as such was Richard Frank Ring who was a clay pipe maker and traded from the Pottery Coal Wharf in Temple Back. Next door was Pountney of the Bristol pottery who was also trading in coal. The coal would have been brought in by sea for burning in the pottery kilns and for which only larger coal would have been required. The remaining small coal was then sold off locally. By 1840 Ring had a second wharf, Penylln Coal Wharf also in Temple Back. In 1850 Richard Frank Ring took his son, Richard Charles into the business trading as Ring & Son. By 1862 it had become Richard Charles Ring & Co.

Richard Charles Ring, born in 1819, was to introduce Alfred John Smith into the coal business. In 1874 an agreement was signed between A. J. Smith of Totterdown, then described as an accountant and Richard C. Ring, coal merchant, under which Smith would serve Ring for two years at a salary of £225 and a % of the profits. The partnership was dissolved by mutual consent in November 1884 with Smith then setting up on his own (see later). This may also have been the time at which Richard C. Ring ceased trading.

An invoice from the Princess Royal Colliery Co. Ltd's office in Cheese Lane. The interest of A. J. Smith in the colliery is explained in the text and is undoubtedly why another of his companies, Coal Agencies Ltd, took over the sales interests for Princess Royal.
Author's collection

The only reference to him operating wagons was an agreement with the Western Wagon Co. in February 1882 for twenty-four 10-ton wagons over five years. The cost of the wagons was £700 and the numbers 169 to 192 were given but it is unsure if they were the numbers allocated by Ring or if they were the Western Wagon Co's fleet numbers. A note in the file states that the wagons were sold for cash to Wheeler & Gregory, wagon builders of Radstock, Somerset circa 1885.

F. ROBINS & Co.

Frederick Robins, aged 38, was listed on the 1911 census as a coal merchant in Fishponds. Ten years earlier he was recorded as a tinplate box maker. *Kelly's* 1914 directory gives an address of 99 Staple Hill Road, Fishponds. He is recorded as having wagons in 1910 when two 10-tonners numbered 201 and 202 were supplied by the British Wagon Co., probably from the old Wheeler & Gregory works at Radstock. How long Robins remained in business is unknown. He was not listed in the 1935 edition of *Kelly's*.

John Robinson's tank wagon No. 1 was photographed by the builders, Hurst, Nelson of Motherwell, circa 1904. The 10-ton tank wagon was obviously used for delivering oil to a destination requiring the use of the hand operated pump mounted on the frame which has a canvas hose coiled against it. There is also a bottom discharge pipe, the end of which can be seen just below the '0' of the tare weight with its stopper attached to the solebar by a chain. It would appear that this bottom outlet was only provided on one side. The tank is held down in a cradle by the wire ropes. The livery is unknown, the tank may be red oxide with black framing and ironwork.

courtesy HMRS ABN427

J. ROBINSON & Co. Ltd

John Robinson & Co. were seed crushers based at Bathurst Wharf. The business appears to have its origins in Gloucester, being started there circa 1850 by John Robinson who, when he moved to Bristol, left his cousin Thomas in charge. When this expansion to Bristol took place is uncertain but Robinsons Mill is said to date from 1874. A private siding agreement was taken with the GWR in August 1877 for a siding alongside the mill at Bathurst Basin.

The business grew to have several locations in the city with mills at Albert Road, St Philips and Bathurst Wharf and offices at 6-7 Redcliff Parade. Circa 1904 a new mill was opened at Avonmouth. The company's range of business was chemical manure manufacture, seed crushing, oil refining and compound cake makers. The main seeds crushed would probably have been linseed brought in to the Port of Bristol. The compound cake, made from oil and animal products, would have been sold as animal feed whilst various refined oils would have gone to paint manufacturers and linoleum producers.

In 1916 Robinsons became part of the British Oil & Cake Mills Ltd which had been incorporated in 1899. BOCM bought up a number of mills and oil refineries around the country and in 1925 Lord Leverhulme, of Lever Brothers, bought the controlling interest in BOCM and thus it came under the Unilever umbrella when that corporate giant was formed in 1930.

The history of Robinson's tank fleet seems rather confused. The company either frequently replaced its wagons or renumbered them, cascading earlier wagons down the number order. The first that can be traced is No. 1, built by Hurst, Nelson of Motherwell in the early 1900s. No details of the size of the order or who the registering company were have survived.

The next known wagons were 10-ton tanks numbers 5 to 6 provided by the Birmingham RC&WCo. in 1903 and registered by the Midland Railway. Of these number 5 was reported as being broken up in 1948 in which case it was either renumbered by Robinson & Co. or had changed hands, sadly such detail was not recorded in the ledger. No. 6 was recorded as rebuilt by the Manchester Wagon Co. in 1922 for J. & H. Roscoe. This suggests that number 5 may also have been disposed of ahead of new wagons arriving. There is also a record of a 20-ton wagon numbered 3 being built by Charles Roberts and registered by the Great Western in 1906.

The new wagons were 14-ton tanks, numbered 1 to 4, built by the Birmingham RC&WCo. in January 1924. They were followed by numbers 5 to 8 a year later.

As already mentioned Robinson & Co. became part of BOCM in 1916 but from the evidence of the 1924-built wagons they retained their own identity on the wagons although, no doubt, they eventually succumbed to the livery of the new ownership especially when part of the Unilever group.

F. SAGE

Little can be said about Sage apart from him being found in an 1889 trade directory trading from the Upper Railway Wharf, Midland Road. Thus far there is no evidence of wagon ownership.

The opposite side of tank No. 1 was also photographed, the image revealing little other detail. *courtesy HMRS ABP205*

This is an exceptional image of a 14-ton tank wagon and is from an official Birmingham RC&WCo. builder's photograph. It shows that wagons were still being painted for John Robinson & Co. Ltd long after they had become part of BOCM. Taken in January 1924 – although the builder's plate actually states 1923. The tank sits in saddles but is still held down by wires. The bottom discharge pipe is located between the legs of the 'V' hanger with the valve control wheel horizontal on top of the framing. It also shows that the lettering is shaded, probably in black, with the tank being a shade of red oxide.

Author's collection

An 11½-ton rated tank lettered for BOCM Bristol with the running number B.7. The wagon was built by S. J. Claye of Long Eaton and registered by the Midland Railway. When photographed in 1953 it was painted a light red oxide with black underframe and ironwork. The white lettering was shaded black. The wagon also carries a white painted star and a cast start plate on the right-hand end of the solebar denoting that the wagon was passed for running in fast goods trains averaging 35mph. The painted star was 2ft high as set down by RCH regulations.
courtesy HMRS Peter Matthews collection/ John Arkell

The one wagon in this volume for which the image is all that is known of the company! The five-plank side door only wagon was secondhand having originally been registered by the Great Western in 1924. It was purchased by the Sandwell Coal Co. in June 1935 on deferred purchase terms and carries a Gloucester owner's plate. Repairs were with Wagon Repairs Ltd. The livery would appear to be a black body with plain white lettering. *GRC&WCo.*

SANDWELL COAL Co.

No trace can be found of this company, despite having a wagon photographed at Gloucester in 1935. It is unfortunate that the order falls into the gap in the Gloucester order details. The business was based in the goods yard at Ashley Hill but there are no entries for it in the 1935 edition of *Kelly's* or in the 1938 *Colliery Year Book*. The problem might be that the wagons were ordered for an individual coal merchant who traded as the Sandwell Coal Co. Sidings at Ashley Hill were only provided in 1925.

CHARLES E. SHIRLEY

It would seem that Charles Edward Shirley, born in Stockport in 1873, began trading in coal in mid to late 1901 as on the census he is given as a cashier. The 1902 Kelly's *Bristol Directory* lists him as a coal merchant at 14 Sydenham Road, Stokes Croft whilst in 1914 he is at Montpelier Station; Station Road, Montpelier and at the Redcliff Railway Wharf.

One 10-ton wagon, numbered 3, built by the Lancashire & Yorkshire Wagon Co. was registered by the Midland Railway in 1901.

An impressive line up of Thomas Silvey's horse-drawn road delivery fleet, which includes four- and two-wheeled examples, in the Midland Railway Yard at St. Philips. They are posed alongside a rake of nine wagons which are probably freshly delivered from the Gloucester RC&WCo. in early 1920. Wagon numbers which can be identified are 84 and 97 and freshly painted 'G' plates can be seen on one wagon. Both of the wagon numbers fit in the batch registered in February 1920. The Silvey wagons have been propelled into the siding by the Midland Railway 0-6-0 tank whose crew are also posing in the cab with the shunter standing on the front footplate. There are a couple of interesting wagons in the background; two lettered H.G.L. belong to Henry Gethin Lewis, then comes the top of one believed to be a Huntley of Bristol and just discernible above the nearest Silvey wagon is one for A. G. Weeks who traded at several points on the Cheddar Valley line in Somerset.

courtesy Michael Silvey

Photographed in December 1905 at Gloucester was 8-ton, five-plank wagon No. 76. Lettered in white on a black body. The wagon was from the first batch that Thomas Silvey purchased from Gloucester having previously patronised the Bristol Wagon Works Co.
GRC&WCo.

THOMAS SILVEY & Co.

BASED in Midland Road the business of Thomas Silvey grew to be one of the largest connected with coal in the city. Thomas Silvey, born in Eastington, south of Gloucester, in 1839 first took a job with the Gloucester Wagon Co. and became an inspector, travelling around checking wagons in sidings for any repairs necessary. In doing so he saw opportunities in the coal trade. It would appear that he first went into business with Enoch and Edwin Hendy at St. Philips as has already been seen. Thomas Silvey left that partnership in June 1880 and was shown on the 1881 census as being a commercial traveller in coal, suggesting that he was still to set up on his own. An 1889 trade directory records Silvey & Co. at the Upper Railway Wharf, Midland Road, St. Philips.

Thomas was soon making an impression on the coal trade in Bristol and began supplying many large industrial users. These were to be the mainstay of the company over the years and included the gas works in Bristol and Bath and some further into the West Country and Gloucestershire. They also conducted a domestic delivery service.

As with Alfred Smith, Silvey also owned some ships as many customers were based alongside the water in Bristol. These ranged from Severn sailing trows, some converted to motor barges, through to the motor vessels *Denby* and *Wycliffe*. These traded across to South Wales whilst the smaller vessels ventured up to Lydney for loading with Forest of Dean coal. Indeed, it fell to Silvey's converted trow the *Yarrah* to load the last coal out of Lydney in 1960.

Thomas died in 1900 aged 61 and the reins were taken up by his widow, Elizabeth and their second son, Gilbert Ernest. This caused a little bit of a family rift as the eldest son, Frank, thought that he should have joined the business. He had been placed in the office of a flour mill at Avonmouth but now set himself up in the coal trade as well. It was to be almost seventy years before the two parts came back together.

Kelly's for 1914 has quite a feature for Thomas Silvey: 'coal merchants, factors and shippers for high-class house coal and all classes of steam and manufacturers' coals, Upper Railway Wharf, Midland Road, St Philip's. T N 1149'.

Despite Thomas Silvey's early links with the Gloucester RC&WCo. his first railway wagons did not come from that company. The first for which written evidence can be found came from the Bristol Wagon & Carriage Works Co. in November 1892 when 10-ton wagons, 49 to 53, were acquired and registered by the Midland Railway. It is from the Midland Railway private owner wagon registers, now in the National Archives, that details of more of the Silvey fleet can be found and these, together with Gloucester RC&WCo. records, have been tabulated below:

Wagon no.	Tonnage	Date	Builder
49-53	10	11.1892	Bristol Wagon Co.
54-55	8	03.1896	Bristol Wagon Co.
60-63	8	09.1901	Bristol Wagon Co.
209-214	10	10.1902	Bristol Wagon Co.
201-206	8	1905	Bristol Wagon Co.
71-80	8	01.1906	Gloucester RC&WCo. £59 each
215-224	10	08.1907	Gloucester RC&WCo.
231-236	10	11.1911	Midland RC&WCo.
234-239	12	01.1915	Gloucester RC&WCo. £79 10s each
251-260	12	09.1915	Gloucester RC&WCo.
Six wagons	10	06.1917	Gloucester RC&WCo. second/h £105 each
81-100	12	02.1920	Gloucester RC&WCo. £257 each
300-319	12	06.1923	Gloucester RC&WCo. £143 each

Another batch of 8-ton wagons, numbers 215 to 224 were purchased from Gloucester in August 1907 with the first of the batch being photographed in September. The oval plate on the solebar is an owner's plate for Thomas Silvey. The wagons were again painted black with plain white lettering. With the majority of the early wagon fleet being of 8-ton capacity or less it is suggested that the majority of the customers were still for housecoal. It should be noted also that these wagons were recorded by the Midland Railway in their register as being of 10-ton capacity whereas the order was for 8-ton wagons and clearly this is what was supplied. *GRC&WCo.*

401-420	12	12.1923	Midland RC&WCo.
501-530	12	07.1924	Gloucester RC&WCo. £163 each
531-590	12	10.1924	Gloucester RC&WCo.
601-620	12	1924?	Butterley
Thirty wagons	12	01.1936	Gloucester RC&WCo. £3,450 total
501-510	12	03.1939	Gloucester RC&WCo. £1,400 total
621-630	12	04.1939	Gloucester RC&WCo. £1,400 total

It can be seen from the above that the first twenty-three new wagons came from the Bristol Wagon & Carriage Works Co. What the wagon registers do not reveal are any wagons purchased secondhand. Does the fact that there are six numbers missing from the sequence suggest that some wagons were acquired from elsewhere? There is also the possibility that they were bought from other builders whose records have not survived and were registered with a railway company such as the Great Western whose records have not been found.

The first reference to Thomas Silvey in the Gloucester RC&WCo. records adds to the likelihood that there were further wagons that have not been recorded as in June 1895 a repair contract for 7 years was taken on fourteen 7-ton wagons. It is unlikely that these were the Bristol-built wagons. They were still in the fleet in 1902 when the repair contract was renewed for a further seven years albeit an extra wagon had been added. That there are no renewals of the repair contract after 1909 suggests that these wagons were withdrawn at around that time.

In December 1896 three secondhand 8-ton wagons were taken from Gloucester on simple hire for eleven months. Whether these would have been lettered up for Silvey is unknown, they may have been lettered in small italics as seen in other examples.

The first purchase of wagons from Gloucester came in November 1905 when ten 8-ton wagons, numbers 71 to 80, were bought new for cash at £59 each. A seven year repair contract was taken at the same time and this was renewed for a similar period in February 1913. In August 1907 a further ten 8-ton wagons were bought, numbered 215 to 224. As before a repair contract was taken for seven years and extended in October 1914.

The Midland Railway wagon registers now show a single order with the Midland RC&WCo. for six 10-ton wagons in 1911, the wagons numbered 231 to 236 being registered in November.

January 1915 saw a return to Gloucester with six 12-ton wagons being ordered. The fact that these had side and end doors suggests that Silvey now had more regular industrial customers who were using discharge facilities that would take advantage of the end door. The wagons were numbered 234 to 239 which sees a clash of numbers with those from the Midland RC&WCo. This is often a feature of the wagon registers and in

234 was a 12-ton wagon with side and end doors from an order for ten such wagons placed in January 1915 at £79 10s each, paid for in cash. It carries an oval owner's plate as well as the Gloucester builder's and repairer's plates. Angled commode handles are fitted on the end door. As well as for being used to raise a yardman up to look in the wagon these could have been useful for closing the end door after discharge, what is certain is that no hand or implement would be near them when the wagon was tipped as a heavy end door whose moment of opening could not be predicted would be a quick way to serious injury.   *GRC&WCo.*

No. 100 came from an order in February 1920 for twenty 12-ton wagons, numbered 81 to 100, purchased for cash at the high price of £257 each. The market price of wagons at this period was high after the shortages of the war but were soon to drop. However, despite the books saying that cash was paid the wagon carries a Gloucester owner's plate so perhaps the terms were altered to deferred purchase whilst the order was going through the works. The initial letters of Thomas and Silvey stand a little higher above the rest of the words than on No. 234 above, the result being that the rest are a little thinner in comparison. There is also no sign of a repairer's plate.
  GRC&WCo.

this case it is known that one of the Gloucester-built wagons was number 234 as it was photographed.

A few more secondhand wagons were obviously acquired in 1916 as a repair agreement on four unidentified 10-ton wagons was taken with Gloucester in March. Over the years Thomas Silvey did acquire other coal merchants' businesses around Bristol and south Gloucestershire and these may have been the result of one such buy-out. In June 1917 six 10-ton wagons were bought secondhand from Gloucester at £105 each with a repair contract for seven years also being paid for on each one.

In February 1920, twenty new 12-ton wagons, numbered 81 to 100, were bought for cash at £257 each. Compared to the price of a similar wagon of £79 10s only five years earlier it can be seen what effect the First World War had on costs. Coming into the early 1920s when a period of industrial unrest was brewing it was quite an investment for a trader to make, especially as they did not go for a deferred purchase option. Within three years the price of a wagon was to almost halve and with the failure of a large number of collieries, coal factors and coal merchants the secondhand wagon market was awash.

Silvey also had sixteen wagons on hire from the Bristol Carriage & Wagon Works Co. as in October 1920 there is a reference to Silveys offering to buy the wagons at £60 each with the wagon company asking for £65. The outcome of the deal was not recorded.

Silvey's next bought wagons in 1923 beginning negotiations for finance with Gloucester in April but finally taking twenty wagons for cash in June at £143 each. They were numbered 300 to 319. The debate over financing is interesting in that the previous batch of wagons put down in the minute books as having been paid for in cash carry Gloucester owner's plates suggesting that they were actually paid for on deferred purchase terms.

Towards the end of 1923 the company once more turned to the Midland RC&WCo. for a batch of twenty 12-ton wagons, numbered 401 to 420 and registered by the LMS in December.

In April 1924 the Gloucester RC&WCo. agenda books record an order for thirty 12-ton wagons at £163 each. These were to be numbered 501 to 530 and were registered by the LMS in July. In September a further fifty 12-ton wagons were ordered, numbered 531 to 590 they were registered in October.

The next new wagons, unfortunately at an unrecorded date, came from the Butterley Company at Codnor Park, Derbyshire. Twenty wagons, 601 to 620, were supplied.

It was back to Gloucester in January 1936 when the order of thirty 12-ton wagons was recorded, paid in cash at a total of £3,450. Running numbers are not known but they included number 723 photographed in February. Towards the end of the year Gloucester record the purchase of seven wagons from T. Silvey. These must have been old wagons taken in part exchange and probably added into Gloucester's South Wales Pool of elderly wagons used for spot hires.

The final recorded wagon purchases for Thomas Silvey & Co. come in March and April 1939 with two batches of ten

Wagon No. 300 was photographed in August 1923. It differs little to the previous two wagons seen and was to the 1907 RCH specifications. Again painted black with white lettering it was fitted with angled commode handles on the end door and was registered by the LMS.
GRC&WCo.

Examples from the wagon batches supplied by Gloucester in 1924. Both of them are to the RCH 1923 specification of seven-plank construction. No. 522 is the first to be branded for a specific traffic being lettered as emptying to Cannop Colliery in the Forest of Dean. This lettering has been placed where 'Empty to' and a label clip appear on previous wagons. On No. 559 there is no label clip and the fleet number has been moved. The main lettering is also taller with the top of the 'T' much closer to the top of the plank. Neither wagon appears to be fitted with commode handles. 522 was photographed in August and 559 in October. *both GRC&WCo.*

On the left wagon number 576 from the second batch of 1924 built wagons was caught in 1934 at Gloucester having been in for one of its regular refurbishments, probably at Wagon Repairs Ltd.
L. E. Copeland

Two later wagons for the company from the January 1936 and March 1939 orders. Both are built to the RCH 1923 specification with side and end doors. They also carry the RCH scheme symbols, the Cc and the star, which would have been added to the rest of the fleet after 1926 and 1933 respectively.
both GRC&WCo.

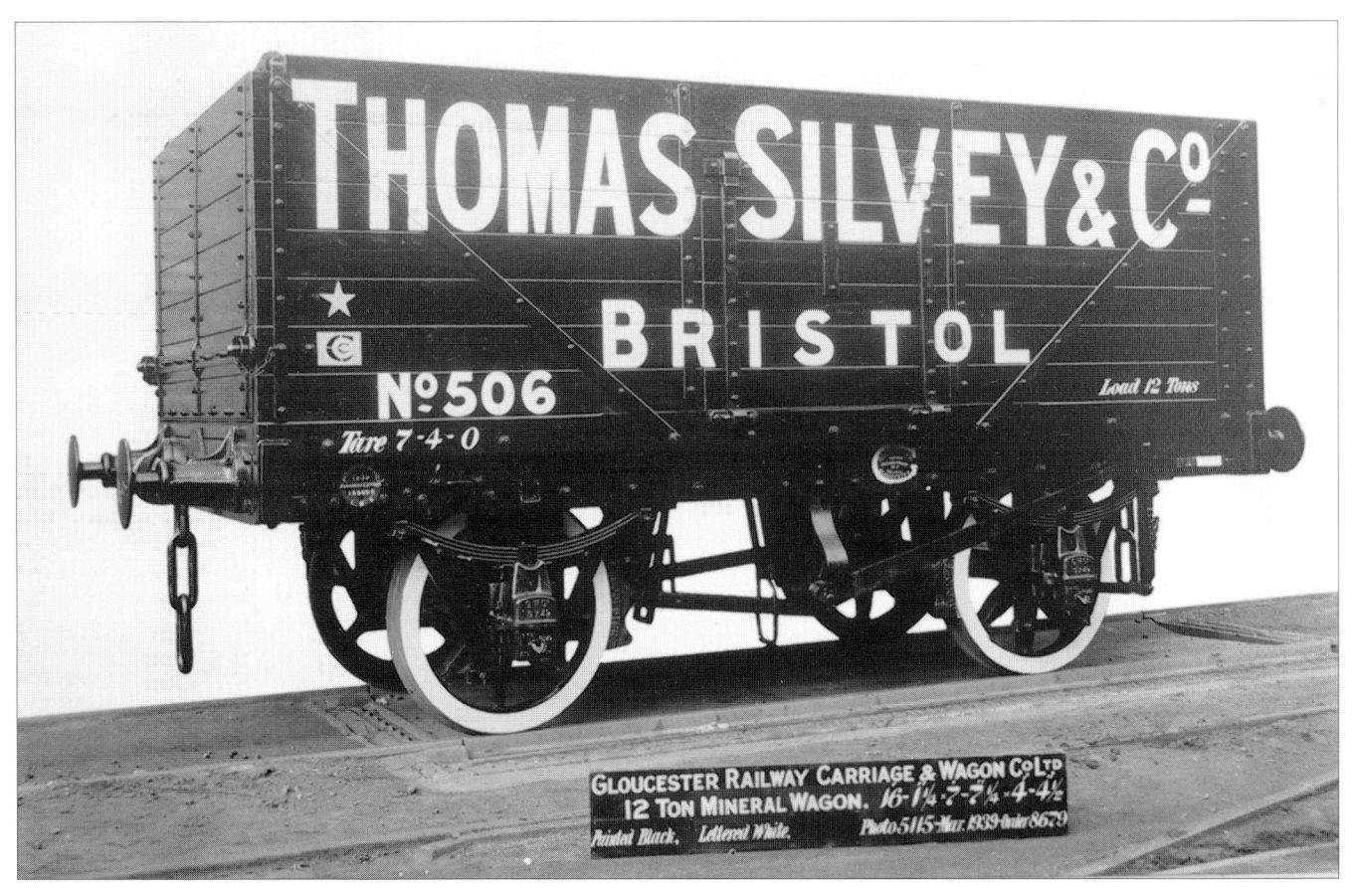

12-ton wagons at £1,400 each. The numbers were 501 to 510 and 621 to 630.

There is evidence also of one of the wagons obtained secondhand albeit undated. A 10-ton wagon originally supplied to Cwmteg Colliery at Pontardawe and numbered 223 in their fleet was rebuilt by Wagon Repairs Ltd, Gloucester and then sold on to Thomas Silvey & Co. becoming their No. 265.

The wagon fleet of several hundred passed into the pool in 1939 and on nationalization of the railways Silveys received £13,747 for them in compensation. From then on they were dependent on the wagons of British Railways to deliver the coal to their depots and coal sidings at various stations where they had a presence. Having had the supply of coal entirely in their own hands pre war – dealing with the collieries for which they held agencies and salesmen and agents they knew well – they now also had to rely on the National Coal Board and vagaries of its supply system with no guarantee as to where the coal had originated from. This was noticed by many customers who knew exactly the burning characteristics of their preferred coal. This loss of quality control was not just felt by Silveys but throughout the coal supply business.

In 1954 a change was made, moving away from supplying coal to supplying oil and this was soon to grow into the core business. A move was also made into sand and one of the old coal carrying vessels, *Nigel*, was converted in 1964 into a dredger. Being built originally as a landing craft for the Gallipoli campaign in World War One, its shallow draft allowed it to work longer on the Severn's sandbanks than competing dredgers.

One of the wagons built by the Butterley Co. was caught on the edge of a snapshot of the sidings at Cannop in the mid 1930s. These appear to be the only wagons not to be painted black and lettered white. Number 602 could well be grey with white lettering shaded black. Of seven-plank construction it has side and end doors.
Author's collection

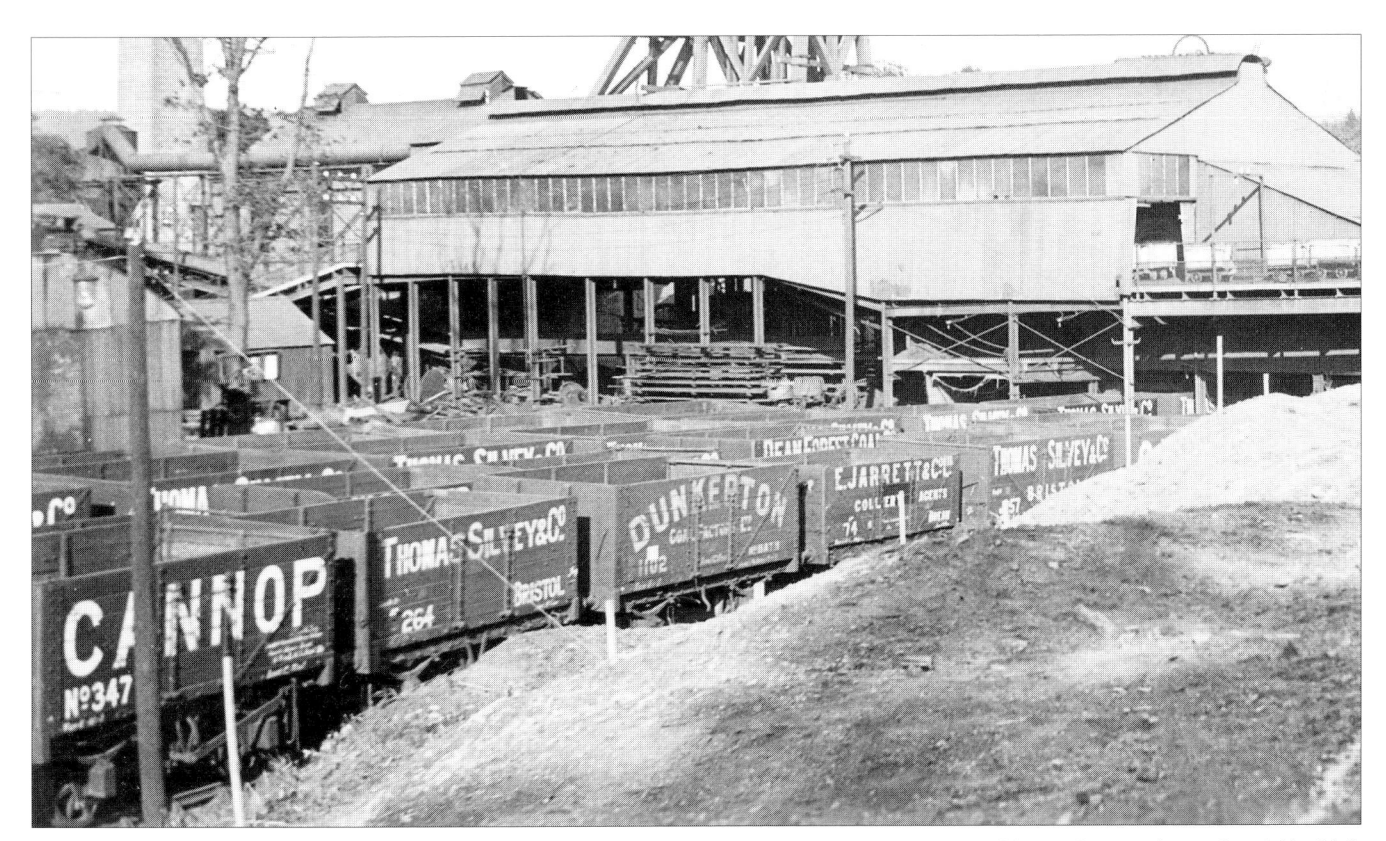

At least ten wagons belonging to Thomas Silvey can be seen awaiting loading at Cannop Colliery. Of most interest is number 264 which again displays a completely different livery with 'Bristol' set to the right. This could be a secondhand wagon as it does not appear in any of the known registered wagons.
Author's collection

Whilst taken in the 1950s this view of one of Silvey's delivery lorries, a Thorneycroft 'Nippy', contrasts with the horse drawn vehicles seen earlier. The internal combustion engine would have made life easier on the hills around the city but did it do away with the extra charge on delivery to hilly areas? Whilst the design for the 'Nippy' had been around since 1937 this example dates from post 1943 as it has a 'utility' grill and may have been acquired just post war. In the background Jubilee Street goes off to the right and it is thought that the delivery is taking place in Louisa Street which itself was off Midland Road where Thomas Silvey & Co. were based.

courtesy Michael Silvey

The business remained in the Silvey family passing from Gilbert to his son Thomas and then to his son Thomas Michael with other family members on the board. At the time of writing the company is still trading successfully although in early 2009 passing into German ownership.

Left: An unidentified Silvey sailing vessel in the River Ely at Penarth. *courtesy Michael Silvey*

Below: The *Nigel* at Lydney Harbour with its hold full and seemingly under full power astern – certainly it has attracted the attention of the crew of the ketch alongside. It may be manoeuvring to avoid the incoming steam ship before turning and heading out into the Rivern Severn with coal for Bristol. Later the *Nigel* was converted into a dredger for a Silvey subsidiary and as late as the 1960s was fitted with diesel engines. *Author's collection*

No. 205 for F. H. Silvey was photographed in September 1911 and was a fine example of Gloucester craftsmanship. Whilst similar in appearance to the two earlier wagons seen opposite this five-plank wagon with full height side doors has raised ends and buffer housings with four ribs rather than the smooth casing on the other two. Four wagons were taken at this time at a cost of £59 each. Like his brother Gilbert, Frank always seems to have preferred to pay cash for his wagons. *GRC&WCo.*

Five-plank wagon No. 191 was photographed at Gloucester in August 1905. Of 8-ton capacity it was painted chocolate, with white letters, shaded black and with black ironwork. Fitted with an oval owner's plate and registered by the GWR. *GRC&WCo.*

F. H. SILVEY & Co.

As mentioned under Thomas Silvey, Frank Herbert was the eldest son, born in 1870, but was not given control of the family business. He had initially gone to work in an Avonmouth flour mill but found that the dust disagreed with him and so returned to the family business. He now found that his younger brother Gilbert had been running the business with his mother and was set to take over. He thus went off on his own and set up in Fishponds but avoided clashing too much with the old firm as he traded mainly in housecoal.

Kelly's 1914 directory shows him trading at New Station Road, Fishponds with a branch depot at Montpelier Railway Station. At some point between 1933 and 1935 the business was converted to a limited company and in 1935 was advertising 'Best coal at lowest prices'.

The first known wagons recorded for F. H. Silvey were ordered from the Gloucester RC&WCo. in August 1905 and were six 8-tonners bought for cash at £56 10s each. They were registered by the Midland Railway in March 1906. All other purchases are listed below:

No. 204 was photographed in January 1909 and painted in a similar style. An angled commode handle is fitted on the right-hand end. *GRC&WCo.*

In January 1915 four 10-ton wagons were bought from Gloucester at £76 10s each. The wagons have raised ends and were fitted with lifting top planks above the side doors. Livery was now 'dark lead' grey with white letters shaded black and black ironwork excepting the diagonal braces. All of F. H. Silvey's wagons from Gloucester were fitted with the 'gap filler' at the base of the side door. *GRC&WCo.*

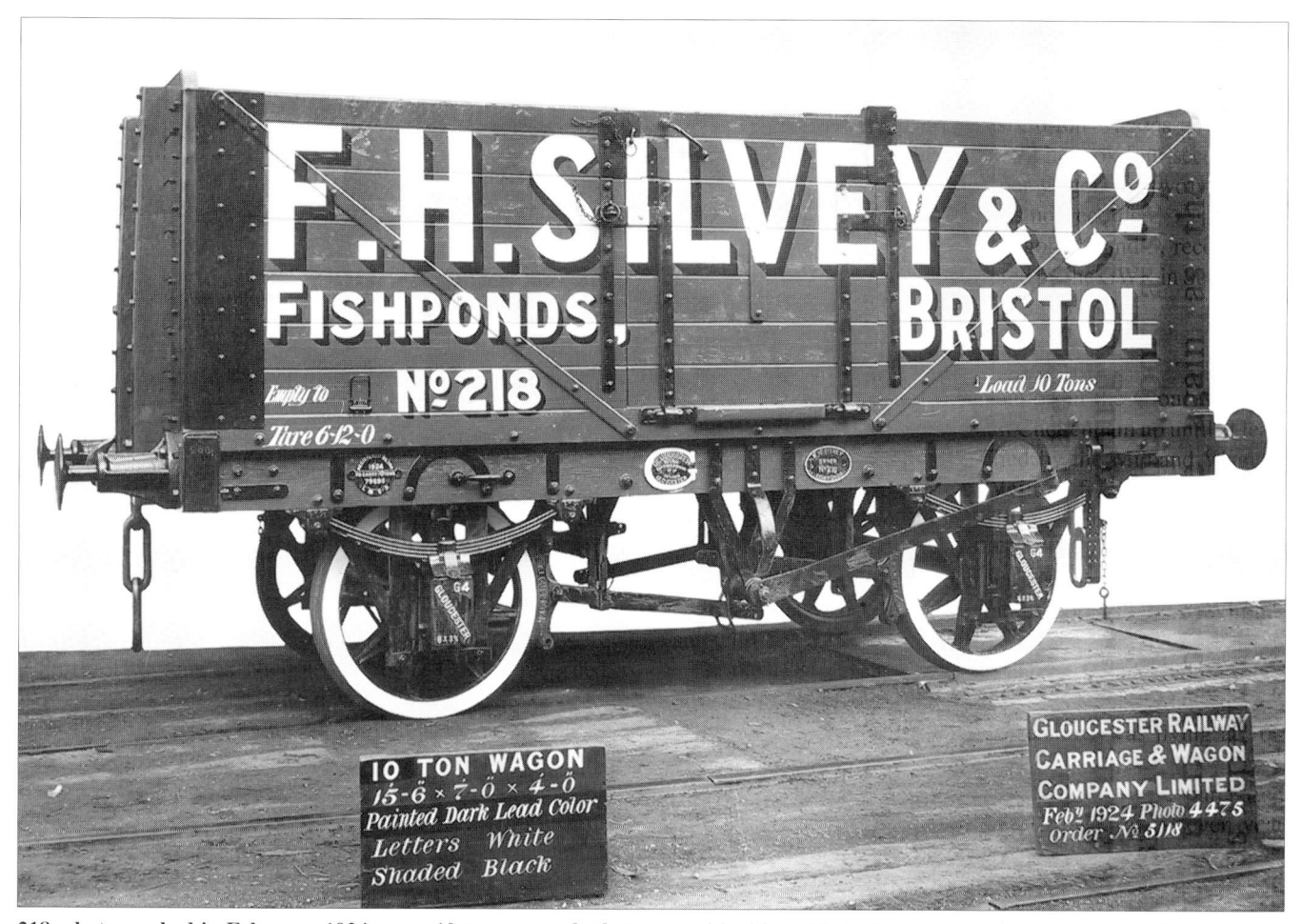

218, photographed in February 1924 was a 10-ton seven-plank wagon with either side brakes, hinged planks above the side door and raised end planks. Registered by the LMS, it was also painted 'dark lead colour' with white lettering and black shading. *GRC&WCo.*

Wagon no.	Tonnage	Date	Builder
191-196	8	03.1906	Gloucester RC&WCo. £56 10s each
197-199	10	09.1906	S. J. Claye
200-202	10	10.1906	S. J. Claye
203-204	10	01.1909	Gloucester RC&WCo. £60 each
205-208	8	09.1911	Gloucester RC&WCo. £59 each
209-210	8	12.1911	Midland RC&WCo.
211-214	10	01.1915	Gloucester RC&WCo.
215-218	10	01.1924	Gloucester RC&WCo. £148 each

It can be seen that most of the wagons were obtained from Gloucester although six came from S. J. Claye of Long Eaton, Derbyshire and two from the Midland RC&WCo. It is likely that this was the entire wagon fleet although there is a repair contract on six 8-ton wagons with Gloucester in January 1914 which cannot be fully explained but there are also no gaps in the number sequence. It is also known that F. H. Silvey & Co. had two wagons on hire from the Western Wagon Co. between December 1920 and December 1929 but the numbers allocated to these is unknown.

Ten 12-ton mineral wagons were built by Marcroft Wagon Works Ltd, of Coalville, in April 1937. They were numbered 1937-1946, had side and end doors only and were registered by the LMS.

SLADE & BAKER

Slade & Baker were brick, tile and coal merchants with an address of the Railway Wharf, Lawrence Hill. They were listed in the 1902 Kelly's *Directory of Bristol* but not in 1914. One of the partners appears to have been Henry Slade who can be found on the 1901 census aged 38 and a sanitary pipe and coal merchant. His son, Henry, 17, was also working in the business. There is, thus far, no evidence of them operating wagons.

Built in 1936 and painted red with white lettering shaded black, number 235 is quite a striking example with the main title on an arc. Of seven-plank construction with side and end doors it came from a batch of twenty wagons, 230 to 249.
GRC&WCo.

A much earlier wagon of unknown origin which originally had dead buffers. It carries the diamond-shaped at the left-hand end of the solebar and is fitted with self-contained buffers where the spring is housed within the buffer casing. Notice also the thick wooden internal diagonal brace and that both diagonals face in the direction of the end door. It was caught in a yard on the Southern Railway in 1930 leading to speculation as to where coal had been delivered. It is difficult to be precise about the livery, the body colour could be black or red whilst the lettering is plain white. *courtesy Lens of Sutton Association*

ALFRED J. SMITH Ltd

As has already been seen Alfred J. Smith commenced in the coal trade with Richard Charles Ring when he entered into an agreement in 1874, at which time he was an accountant. The 1881 census shows Alfred John Smith as being aged 37 and born in Bristol. He now described himself as a coal merchant and was living at Belleview House, Knowle Road, Bedminster, with his Jersey born wife Amelia, two daughters and a son, Sydney L. aged 7.

The partnership with Ring was dissolved in November 1884 after which Smith set himself up in business at 47 Queens Square as a shipper of steam, house and nursery coals and a contractor for freights. Smith seems to have traded under several styles at the same time throughout his business career and in 1889 can be found in *Kelly's* trading both under his own name at the Queens Square address and as the Cardiff & South Wales Coal Co. (Alfred Jn Smith, prop) at Avon Street, St Philips.

In 1893 Smith bought out the Newport Coal & Coke Co. Ltd as has already been seen and in 1910 obtained the sales outlet of the Princess Royal Colliery Co. Notes in the company files also record that he took over both Pearces and Summers & Co's coal businesses.

In November 1912 the business was converted into a limited company, Alfred J. Smith Ltd, with a capital of £30,000. The new company was to purchase the business carried on by Alfred J. Smith at 9 Queens Square and at Coleford, Gloucestershire; with branches at 2 Masonic Chambers, Ruperra Street, Newport; Bradford on Avon, Wiltshire; and Weston super

Number 260 came from a batch of ten wagons, the order for which was placed in September 1938. The lettering has subtle differences from number 235; the letters in 'Bristol' are all of the same height, the base of the title starts one plank lower hence it is more sharply curved which detracts slightly from overall balance. The Cc and star markings are on tinplate tacked to the wagon side, the Cc plate measured 6¾ in. x 4¾ in, black on old gold and the star was 6 in. square, yellow on black. *GRC&WCo.*

Mare, Somerset. Subscribers to the company included A. J. Smith, Brooklea, St. Annes Park, steam ship owner and coal factor; Alfred Sidney Livingstone Smith, managing director; H. Searle Smith, traveller and Pery Berril, manager.

Alfred J. Smith died in March 1920 aged 77 at 'High Grove', Wells Road after which the company was run by Alfred S. L. Smith and Harold Smith. Alfred S. L. Smith deceased in May 1943 and was replaced by Alfred Jocelyn Smith.

The company was listed as coal merchants in the 1938 *Colliery Year Book*, at the same address and also at Railway Wharf, Lower Queen's Road, Clevedon, Somerset.

Alfred J. Smith Ltd was wound up in January 1949 after being effectively taken over by its subsidiary, Coal Agencies Ltd which in turn was taken over by Renwick, Wilton & Dobson in June 1959.

There is no record of Smith's early wagon purchases suggesting that they were bought secondhand. They also bought comparatively few wagons after 1923. A total of fifty were acquired, all 12-tonners and all from 1936 onwards. Twenty came from Gloucester in August 1936; ten from Marcroft Wagons Ltd at Radstock in October 1937, numbered 250 to 259; ten from Gloucester in September 1938 numbered 260 to 269; and finally ten from Gloucester in May 1943 which the company were unlikely to have seen after delivery as they would have gone straight into the pool. All were registered with the LMS who consistently recorded the title as 'Alfred J. Smith (Coal Agencies)'. showing that they were just as confused as to which was the senior company in the Smith family empire.

The red livery with arced lettering was applied to the older wagons as seen here on five-plank number 204 photographed in the 1930s. *courtesy Paul Karau*

Above: A medley of different liveries for wagons belonging to Smith. Top left is an early dead buffered wagon photographed circa 1906 which has the main title along the top plank only whilst the bottom line probably reads 'Welsh Steam…'. Top right is what could be a wagon on short term simple hire and simply lettered in italics with 'A. J. Smith Queen Square Bristol'. More of the wagon is visible in the lower image although frustratingly the lower-left corner with the fleet number is obscured.

Alfred J. Smith, Ltd.
COAL FACTORS & FREIGHT CONTRACTORS

Distributors for West of England for Princess Royal Celebrated Highdelf Coals.

9 QUEEN SQUARE, BRISTOL

Telephone: 23011 Private Branch Exchange. Telegrams: "Carbon, Bristol."

BRANCH DEPOTS:
- PYLLE HILL, G.W.R.
- CANON'S MARSH
- WAPPING WHARF
- LAWRENCE HILL
- ST. PHILIP'S, L.M.S.
- ST. PHILIP'S BRIDGE WHARF

} BRISTOL

BRADFORD-ON-AVON, TROWBRIDGE, CLEVEDON, WESTON-S-MARE.

One of the ten war-time built 13-ton wagons which were finished with the utility style of lettering on a plain black body. It has a steel underframe and three-hole disc wheels. *GRC&WCo.*

Possibly the earliest view of a wagon for John Snow shows a four-plank dead buffered wagon with raised ends. Lettering is fairly basic with the company title along the top plank and with 'Bristol' in the centre of the side door. What a shame the chap in the boater hides the number!

JOHN SNOW & Co.

The founder of the company appears to be John Snow, born in Bristol in 1824 and by 1859 trading as J. Snow & Co. at Batch, St. Philips.

In 1881 Snow can be found on the census aged 37 and living at Tamworth House, Clifton. His occupation was given as coal and timber merchant employing seventy men and boys. That the business has become quite large is shown in Kelly's 1889 *Bristol Directory* which has Snow at '21 Kingsland Road, St Philips, Midland Road, Railway Stations Clifton Down and Lawrence Hill; and at Glastonbury, Wells, Castle Cary, West Pennard and most of the principal stations on the Somerset & Dorset Railway'. Snow appears to have been quite opportunistic in expanding the business with the growth of the railway network. As well as having wagons lettered for Bristol a large number were branded for Glastonbury which is where the company also operated a steam saw mills.

By 1901 Snow was trading at Clifton Down as the Clifton Coal Co. as already mentioned. Possibly he had bought out the business and kept the trading name on for a while. In *Kelly's* 1902 edition Snow is listed under his own name at Clifton Down Station only, with offices at 54 Whiteladies Road. In 1914, however, it gives a fuller listing with the head office at 54 Whiteladies Road and also 93 Alma Road, Clifton; 23 Kingsland Road, St. Philips & Wapping Wharf.

Snows signed up to the 1926 RCH scheme but not to the one in 1933. They appear in the 1928 *Colliery Year Book* as coal merchants at 98 Alma Road, Clifton and as Snow & Co. at the railway station, Wells. They do not appear in the 1935 Bristol section of *Kelly's* but are still listed at various locations in Somerset suggesting that they had moved headquarters to Glastonbury. Certainly the head of the business in 1929 had been Maurice Henry Stead of Glastonbury. They are not listed among coal merchants in the 1938 *Colliery Year Book* but were still trading as timber and builders merchants in Glastonbury in 1986.

The first reference to wagons comes in November 1866 when two 12-ton wagons were bought from the Cheltenham & Swansea Railway Carriage & Wagon Co. at a cost of £105. If this was the price per wagon then the likelihood is that they were broad gauge. In June 1876 an agreement was signed for the hire of four wagons for three years and for the repair of two wagons for three years.

A number of wagons were registered by the Great Western Railway in September 1872. All were ex-broad gauge wagons converted to standard gauge by J. Boucher at Bullo Pill. Whether they had originally been in the ownership of Snow is not known. The whole subject of privately owned wagons at the time of the gauge conversion is interesting but details are difficult to find. That Snow was operating them suggests he was getting coal from South Wales and this may be why converted wagons came from Boucher. The broad gauge wagons had to be worked to a place of conversion on the last day of broad gauge operation but narrow gauge wagons had to be ready for the recommencement of services. Conversion of the wagons could not be done that quickly so wagon operators would have had the expense of buying or hiring narrow gauge stock and of converting their old wagons due to a situation forced upon them. The Great Western paid no compensation. The wagons acquired from Boucher in

Above & below: Two images of John Snow & Co. wagons, both lettered for Glastonbury although identical main lettering layouts have been seen with 'Bristol' written on the side door. Both wagons are four-plank with raised ends of unknown origin. *courtesy Paul Karau*

September would still have been running as broad gauge on the South Wales main line in May. All were financed by the Bristol & South Wales Wagon Co. and the numbers were 223, 249, 254-256, 258, 260-263, 265, 268, 271-276, 278. At the same time 10-ton wagons numbered 402-416 were registered having been bought from the Midland Waggon Co.

There were further orders with the Midland Waggon Co. commencing in September 1873 when ten old broad gauge wagons were let for one year at £12 per wagon and were said to be 'late Tucker'. Tucker could well have been Joseph Tucker, coal merchant of Bath, who had bought ten 10-ton broad gauge wagons 'ex Carmarthen & Cardigan cattle trucks' from Midland in June 1870.

In January 1874 Snow cancelled an order for twenty-six wagons with Midland but in December 1878 hired 100 8-ton wagons for four months, presumably to perform a specific job and it is unlikely that they would have been lettered up.

Snow was also dealing with the Gloucester Wagon Co. at this time. In August 1874 he had a wagon rebuilt for cash and in October the same year five broad gauge wagons were converted and a repair contract taken on them.

Quite what was happening in December 1878 is unknown but having taken 100 wagons from Midland Snow also had fifty 10-tonners from Gloucester also on four months simple hire, either a harsh winter was expected over the Mendips or Snow had gained a contract which demanded regular supplies of coal.

returned to Midland in May 1887 with ten 6-ton wagons taken on hire for one year and this was renewed until at least 1891.

New wagons for Snow were registered by the Midland Railway in September/October 1909, with 10-ton wagons 483 to 489 being supplied by Hurst, Nelson of Motherwell.

It is believed that Snow wagons were painted grey, lettered white and shaded black.

EDWIN E. SOHIER

In 1880 Sohier was trading from the Midland Station at St. Philips but apart from trading out of the railway yard no evidence of wagon ownership has been found. The 1881 census shows him lodging at 5 Grove Place, Westbury on Trym, aged 27 and states that he was born in Victoria, Australia.

T. W. SQUIRE

There is a record in the Midland RC&WCo's books of three new 10-ton wagons being sold to a T. W. Squire on three years deferred purchase at £24 9s 6d pwpa in May 1889. It is unknown if this was the same T. W. Squire as was listed by the RCH in 1926 at 84 St. Mark's Road, Easton, Bristol. St. Mark's Road is close to Stapleton Road Station. Squire was not on the 1933 RCH scheme nor can he be found in trade directories or colliery year books.

STONE & TINSON

Stone & Tinson were chemical manufacturers with a works at Crew's Hole virtually alongside that of William Butler. They produced the salt muriate of ammonia by passing ammoniacal liquors collected from gas works over hydrochloric acid. The works was frequently in the local press due to the odours emitted. The company also operated a chemical works in Cardiff.

The business was originally two partnerships, one between Gerald E. Tinson and Chas. S. Webber who traded as The India Blue Company producing 'Blue' (ultramarine pigment) in Bristol and one between Thomas Stone and Chas S. Webber as manufacturers of sal ammoniac and other chemicals at Crew's Hole. Both partnerships were dissolved in June 1869 with Webber and one Nathaniel Smith taking over the Blue manufactory and Stone and Tinson the Crew's Hole operation. The partnership between Stone and Tinson was dissolved in February 1877 with Tinson retiring. Tinson appears to have had origins in the cloth industry being a worsted spinner at a number of mills in Worcestershire in the mid 1860s. Thomas Stone can be found on the 1881 census as a chemical manufacturer aged 58 and living at Cote House, Westbury on Trym.

Like Butlers most of the materials for use at the Crew's Hole works would have arrived by river with any transshipment to or from rail being done at one of the Bristol wharfs. They were operating wagons in the 1870s with the likelihood of them being rectangular tanks. All of those known were of 10-ton capacity built by the Bristol Wagon Works. Wagon number 11 was registered by the GWR in August 1874 followed by number 8 in March 1875 and 1 and 2 the following May. All of these were recorded as being for Bristol.

The works at Crew's Hole was closed in 1924 and the buildings transferred into the ownership of Butlers.

S. STONE & Co.

Samuel Stone & Co. were trading out of Lawrence Hill Wharf with an office address in 1902 of 1 Brighton Terrace, Easton Road and in 1914 of 201 Easton Road. The latter address was retained right through to 1935 and beyond. Stone & Co. signed up to both the 1926 and 1933 RCH but only one record of wagons can be found. In October 1924 12-ton wagons numbers 76 and 84 were registered by the LMS having been built by the Butterley Co. at Codnor Park. A partial wagon appears in an image of the sidings at Eastern United Colliery.

The business may go back through several generations of the family to the late 1870s or before as Samuel Stone can be found in 1881 living in Bridge House, Easton Road, aged 66 and trading as a coal merchant. His son, also Samuel, 27, was also there and working as a coal merchant.

The 1889 *Kelly's* directory lists S. & W. Stone, coal merchants at 8 Brighton Terrace, Upper Easton. This may well have been a partnership between Samuel and William Stone. They were both born in Mangotsfield and may have been brothers. William in 1881, when aged 63, was listed as a retired corn merchant living at Redfield House, St. George.

A wagon for S. Stone & Co. was captured on film in the empty wagon roads at Eastern United Colliery. The second line of text reads 'Lawrence Hill Station'. The image of the Pepler wagon on page 72 also reveals a little more of the lettering on Stone's wagon and shows it to be wagon number 76 built by Butterley. There does appear to be contrast between body side colour and the corner plates so red or grey might be the body colour.

ELAND SWEET

Nothing can be found on Sweet apart from a couple of entries in *Kelly's* albeit they were trading between 1902 and 1935. The business was based in Fishponds with *Kelly's* for 1902 giving two addresses, Ridgeway and Elmgrove Place. In 1935 Sweet Bros were trading at 530 and 532 Fishponds Road.

Two wagons were registered by the Midland Railway in September 1901. Both were of 10-ton capacity and were numbered 1 and 2. They were built by Wheeler & Gregory at Radstock.

ISAAC JAMES TANNER

It is only through an entry in the *London Gazette* that we know of Tanner. On his bankruptcy in July 1910 he was residing at Oxford House, 52 St John's Lane, Totterdown and carrying on business at Redcliff Railway Wharf as a coal merchant. The 1901 census has him aged 38, a coal merchant born in Bristol. There is no evidence yet of wagon ownership.

TILEY BROS

The business was started by Frank and Fred Tiley at some point between 1889 and 1902. The 1901 census shows Fred aged 53 and a coal merchant with Frank, aged 51, a clerk to an ironmongers. In the early 1900s a nephew, Frank Cockle, bought into the business and following the deaths of Frank in 1919 and Fred in 1920 he became the sole owner. In 1902 the business address was given as 114 Gloucester Road whilst in 1914 it was 146 Gloucester Road, Bishopston and Montpelier Railway Station.

The will of Fred Tiley is interesting in that he authorizes his trustees to let on hire eight railway wagons belonging to him. These were numbered 5, 6, 21, 37, 38, 40, 43 and 44 and were to be let to Frank Tiley and Frank Leonard Cockle for their joint lives. The lessees had to agree to keep the wagons in good condition by taking a repair contract with one of the wagon repairing firms. They had to pay out of the balance of the earnings of the wagons twenty-five shillings weekly to his wife and upon her death the wagons would become the property of Frank Tiley and Frank Cockle or the survivor if one or other of them predeceased Mrs Fred Tiley. Should these conditions not be met, or should the business have been disposed of then the trustees were empowered to hire out the wagons to another firm of coal merchants and any moneys received less repair expenses to be paid to Mrs Tiley and, failing that, the wagons were to be sold. As it turned out it would seem that the wagons went to Frank Cockle as Frank Tiley predeceased his brother Fred.

As the wagons listed above are the only ones for which details can be found it is assumed that Frank Tiley did not own any wagons in his own right, nor did Frank Cockle. As no trace of wagons registered to Tiley Bros can be found in the post-grouping period it would appear that the company only ever operated eight wagons unless others were obtained secondhand. All of the wagons bar number 8, an 8-tonner, were of 10-ton capacity and all were built by the Midland RC&WCo.

Tiley Bros were listed as coal merchants in the 1938 *Colliery Year Book*, at the same address. It is believed that following Frank Cockle's retirement in the 1940s the business was sold off to one of the larger merchants, possibly Huntleys, although by this date any wagons would already be in the pool.

LEWELLIN TWINING & Co.

The office address for Twining remained constant from 1889 through to the 1930s at 91 Alma Road whilst the depot was at Clifton Down Station. *Kelly's* for 1889 also gives an address of Portland Street, Kingsdown. In 1902 there was still a presence in Kingsdown but now in Henrietta Street. Twining was trading by the end of 1880 when his first wagons are recorded and in 1881 was given on the census as aged 29 and a coal merchant employing fifteen men and boys. Lewellin Twining had been born in Cheltenham and was the son of Edward Twining who traded as a coal merchant in Orange Grove, Bath. Edward was trading in Bath in the mid 1860s and was agent for the Parkfield Colliery. His eldest son, also Edward, and youngest son Henry, went into the Bath business whilst Lewellin moved to Bristol to trade.

The first wagons registered for the company appear in the Great Western Freighters Register. In January 1880 wagons

Photographed in November 1897 this 10-ton rated five-plank wagon with raised ends was one of sixteen bought at the same time. Internal measurements are 15ft 6in. x 6ft 11in. x 3ft 2in. and the wagon has full height side doors and brakes one side only. Livery was a lead grey body with white letters shaded black and black ironwork. Notice how the shading on the 'N's and the 'G' misses the letter in places – an error by the painter? *GRC&WCo.*

That a Twining wagon should be found at Culmstock on the Culm Valley line in Devon suggests that the company was supplying an industrial customer there. Straining to read the italic script it appears that the wagon emptied to a colliery in the Forest of Dean, possibly Crump Meadow. The wagon is of six-plank construction with a deep top plank and raised ends. All ironwork is painted black with 'Bristol' centred on the side door and the fleet number, 184, off to the right.
courtesy John Alsop

A selection of Twining wagons in the sidings of the Crump Meadow Colliery at Bilson Yard. All were caught on the same occasion on a panoramic three postcard view of the town of Cinderford. Whilst individual numbers cannot be discerned the views are useful for showing various wagon sizes in the fleet and variations in the lettering layout.
Author's collection

numbered 1 to 10 were supplied by the Bristol Waggon Works. The following January saw 11 to 16 bought from the Swansea Wagon Co. on seven years redemption hire at £10 15s pwpa including repairs.

Twining also dealt with the Midland RC&WCo. at this period taking a single 6-ton wagon on hire in December 1880 and then in August 1884 he took fifteen 6-ton wagons on a years simple hire. His first dealing with the Gloucester RC&WCo. was in July 1889 when a repair contract was taken on six 8-ton wagons for five years and this was renewed in 1894 and 1897. It is tempting to think that these were the six wagons built by Swansea Wagon in 1881.

It was not until November 1897 that Twining bought wagons from Gloucester but when he did it was for ten 10-ton wagons at £56 each and six at £57 each, all paid for in cash together with a fifteen year repair contract on them. This was to be his only purchase with the company. It does look as though he was pleased with Gloucester's standard of repairs as there followed a series of contracts as below for the repair of wagons:

13 January 1904	Repairs 4.5 years two 8-ton, renewed May 1908
13 June 1906	Repairs 10 years three 10-ton, renewed in June 1916
13 January 1913	Repairs 10 years twelve 10-ton (this looks to be for the 1897 built wagons but four are missing)

He also took secondhand wagons on hire terms from Gloucester in quite large numbers:

13 July 1914	Hire 5 years twenty 10-ton
14 September 1914	Hire 5 years twenty-five 10-ton
14 July 1919	Hire 5 years forty-five 10-ton (probably an amalgamation of the two 1914 hires)
17 March 1932	Let hire forty-five wagons for 5 years (possibly the same wagons as first hired in 1914, any intervening renewals not having been recorded)

The business continued trading until wound up voluntarily in October 1956 at which point the chairman was Brian Twining Harris.

Number 174 was photographed in the sidings at Cannop Colliery, Forest of Dean, in the early 1930s. Twining seemed to have a liking for wagons with raised ends. *Author's collection*

The 1897 order for new wagons from Gloucester was divided with six wagons being £1 dearer. It seems that this difference came through those wagons having an extra plank giving an additional six inches on the height. Registration of the wagons was with the Great Western. The body colour was now given as 'dark lead colour' showing how difficult it can be defining private owner wagon colours. Both this and number 150 from the same batch of wagons look to be the same shade so did Gloucester have two names for the same colour? *GRC&WCo.*

A sulphuric acid tank built by Charles Roberts at Wakefield for United Alkali when under the ownership of Imperial Chemicals specifically for traffic from Netham. The plate on the solebar reads 'U.A.Cº Netham Nº 2 Empty to Private Siding GWR Cᵒˢ Bristol East Depot, Up Side'. When constructed in 1929 such tanks were still built of separate sections bolted together at the flanges to allow the insertion of ebonite liners to protect the steel tank from the acid.
courtesy HMRS AAR528

UNITED ALKALI Ltd

The United Alkali works at Netham began as the Netham Chemical Works, and from a works at Crew's Hole, was extant by 1860. They imported copper ore for the production of sulphuric acid and this was one of the early cargoes carried by the vessels of William Osborn. The company were producing various acids. In the mid 1860s they began producing superphosphate of lime and bone manures as a riposte to companies making these chemical fertilizers using acid from United Alkali who had commenced making their own acid.

United Alkali was formed in 1890 when most of the

Above and opposite bottom: Three 12-ton wagon frames, numbered 1, 2 and 3, built in 1914 by the GRC&WCo., probably as 'internal users' within the complex at Netham albeit no evidence of major sidings around the works has been found. None of the wagons carry railway company registration plates although these could have been fitted after the photographs were taken. The purpose of these frames is also unknown. If destined for cylindrical tanks supplied by another builder then the saddles for the tank would have been fitted although the board alongside No. 2 does state that it is a tank frame. They may have been for a form of box tank used to move liquids around within the works. *GRC&WCo.*

British alkali producing companies came together. A similar rationalisation of the chemical industry came in 1926 when United Alkali were one of the four constituent companies in the formation of Imperial Chemical Industries.

Wagon details are scant, the best photographed examples being the wagon frames from the Gloucester RC&WCo. in 1914. United Alkali itself operated several other works around the country and it would seem that a few of their tank wagon fleet were branded for Bristol. In October 1916 five 10-ton cylindrical tanks for sulphuric acid, numbered 336 to 340, were built by the Midland RC&WCo.

In May 1929 three 10-ton ebonite lined steel tanks were built by Charles Roberts at Horbury Junction. These were numbered 1 to 3 and number 2 was photographed as seen opposite.

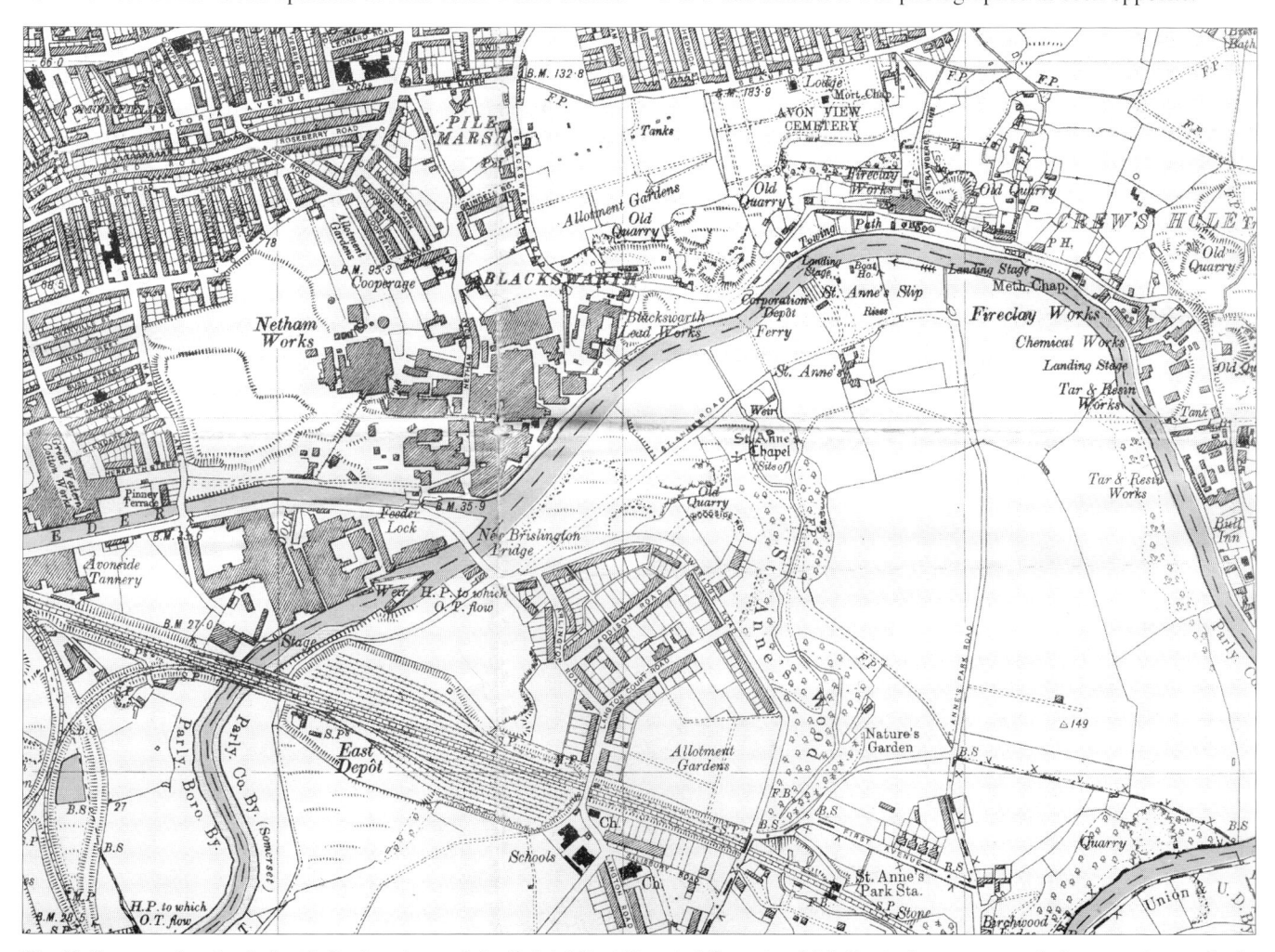

The Netham works stands just left of centre and the Bristol East Depot sidings, to which the tank wagon emptied, are to the south. At the date the map was surveyed the sidings both for Lysaght's works – in the V of the River Avon and the Feeder Canal – and for United Alkali which were provided in the open area to the north of Bristol East Depot sidings were not shown. As private siding agreements for both were taken out in 1923 it suggests that the map was surveyed well before its 1930 date. On the extreme right can be seen Crew's Hole, the location of William Butler's tar works. *Ordnance Survey 6-inch, 1930*

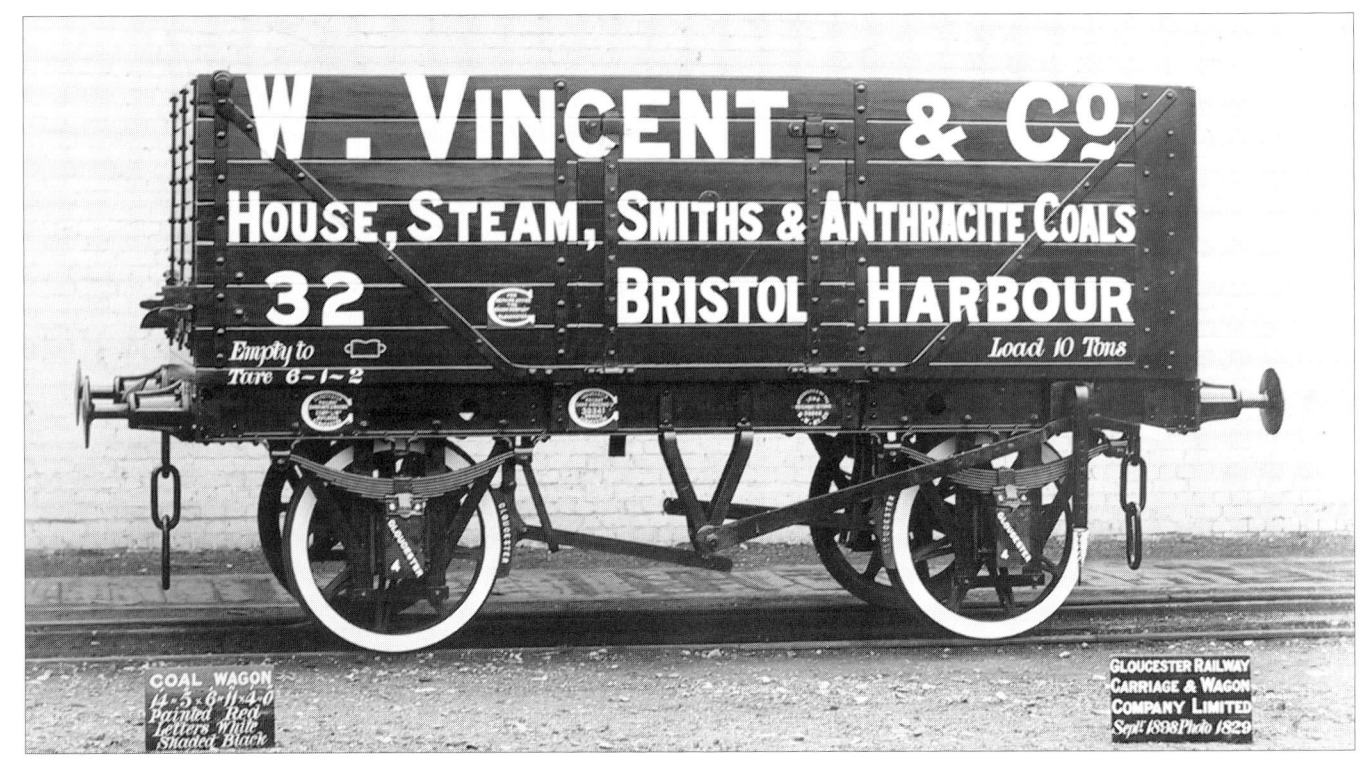

A wagon for William Vincent & Co. photographed in Gloucester in September 1898. Of seven-plank construction with side and end doors and steel underframe it looks very smart in its livery of red body with white letters shaded black. Ironwork was black apart from the diagonal braces and the likelihood is that the steel solebars were black.
GRC&WCo.

WILLIAM VINCENT & Co.

Trading in coal from at least 1865 through to post 1902 Vincent first had an address at Wapping Wharf and then, from around 1880, Commercial Road. He lived in Coronation Road, Bedminster and in 1881 when aged 45, he can be found at Chesterfield House, Bedminster.

The first records of wagons taken is not until May 1888 when two secondhand 10-tonners were taken on one years simple hire from the Gloucester RC&WCo. This hire may have been renewed in February 1890 when two 10-tonners were taken for one year and five months. Three months later three 8-ton wagons were taken on simple hire, again for one year and five months. These hires, for the two 10-tonners and three 8-tonners, were again renewed in May 1896 for one year.

In September 1898 five secondhand 10-ton wagons were bought on seven years deferred purchase terms plus repairs. October 1901 saw a further five 10-ton wagons taken on three years purchase terms and finally in November 1903 twenty-six 10-tonners were taken on seven years terms.

This rush of buying after 1898 may signify a change in ownership of the business as on the 1901 census William Vincent is described as 'retired coal merchant'. The 1902 *Kelly's* still lists the company in Commercial Road and a name change was about to take place. Into the business, probably prior to 1901, had come John Nutt who continued to trade as William Vincent & Co. In June 1904 a new limited company Vincent, Nutt & Co. Limited was formed with a capital of £10,000 in £1 shares. The subscribers included John Nutt,

Wapping Wharf Sidings are located in the centre of this extract of the 1930 6-inch map between the Floating Harbour and the New Cut. Coronation Road, the home of William Vincent is just the other side of the New Cut. Located on the Great Western's Bristol Harbour Branch which can be seen entering Redcliff Tunnel to the right. Just off the map were Redcliff Sidings. At the top edge can be seen the sidings at Canon's Marsh.

William Vincent and various members of the Hamblin family in Clifton. The directors of the new company were to be John Nutt and his son, Reginald J. C. Nutt, both living at 14 Great George Street off Park Street, Bristol. The shareholders list shows William Vincent with one share whilst his wife had 500 preference shares. John Nutt held 2,000 ordinary shares, his wife had 631 preference shares, Reginald held fifty ordinary shares.

The business continued to operate out of an office and yard at Wapping Wharf, the registered office address being the building there. The new company seems to have met with little success and was wound up voluntarily in March 1905.

There had been a desperate attempt to gain money for the business by refinancing the twenty-six wagons bought in 1903 by extending the payment period for a further five years. No doubt with the demise of the company other Bristol traders may have cast their eyes over the wagon fleet, the wagons bought in 1898 and 1901 might just have been paid for and therefore available for disposal. The other twenty-six wagons are likely to have returned to Gloucester's ownership and either entered that company's hire fleet or, being comparatively new, were probably sold off secondhand.

The voluntary winding up reported in the companies records did not prevent a petition being presented before the Gloucestershire County Court by Frank Beauchamp of the Radstock Coal Co. for the winding up of the business. Presumably this was a move on his part to try and ensure payment of monies owed for the supply of coal from his collieries at Radstock. The outcome is unknown.

WILLIAM WALLIS

In August 1878 two dead-buffered 8-ton wagons, numbered 1 and 2, were supplied to William Wallis by the Western Wagon Co. and financed by them. *Slater's* 1880 trade directory lists Wallis as trading at St. Philips Marsh and Kingsland Road Siding. The 1881 census has Wallis aged 53, born in Bedminster and living in 'House at coal wharf', Feeder Road. He had a son, also William aged 25, born in Risca, Monmouthshire, and working as a clerk. In 1889 the business had addresses of Feeder Road, St Philips and the Redcliff Railway Wharf, Pump Lane, Cathay.

Very little else can be found, the 1911 census has a Samuel Wallis aged 52 and involved with coal who seems to have taken over the business as in 1914 *Kelly's* lists him as a coal merchant at Feeder Road and Kingsland Road Siding. He did not sign up to the 1926 RCH scheme nor does the business appear in the 1928 *Colliery Year Book*.

WATKINS & LEONARD

Trading out of Lawrence Hill Coal Wharf this is another business which connects back to the Bristol coal mining industry. The partnership consisted of Thomas Watkins of St. George, Everett Leonard of Flax Bourton, Somerset and Herbert Frank Parsons Watkins of Fishponds. They were trading together as coal merchants at Lawrence Hill. The partnership was dissolved by mutual consent on the 30th November 1914 with the two members of the Watkins family to continue trading under the same title.

When the business was started is unknown but there is a reference to Watkins & Leonard in April 1898 to be 'late with Leonard, Boult & Co.'. In 1901 all three partners can be found listed on the census as coal merchants. Twenty years earlier Thomas and Herbert Watkins, father and son, are found living at Alderney Villa, St George. Thomas was 41 and a clerk at a coal works. Herbert was aged 5. Everett Leonard, 20, was a colliery clerk living with his parents at 9 Apsley Road, Clifton. His father, George Leonard, 54, was a colliery proprietor.

George Leonard was of the family connected with Easton Colliery, owned by Leonard, Betts & Boult. In 1879 the company became Leonard, Boult & Co. Ltd and were then operating Easton, Hanham and Whitehall collieries. It is tempting to think that Thomas Watkins was a clerk at one of these collieries. It is also likely that there would have been a connection with Edward William Boult Monks.

Watkins & Leonard were listed in *Kelly's* between 1902 and 1935 and also appear in the 1938 *Colliery Year Book*, at Lawrence Hill Coal Wharf.

The only record found thus far of wagons is of six 10-tonners bought from the Midland RC&WCo. and registered by the Midland Railway in August 1903.

RICHARD FRANK WEBB

Listed in the 1889 edition of *Kelly's* at the Lower Railway Wharf, Avon Street, St. Philips there is, at present, no evidence that he owned wagons.

WESTERN COUNTIES AGRICULTURAL ASSOCIATION Ltd

There were a number of agricultural associations and co-operatives that dealt in coal which they supplied to their members. Whilst delivering animal feed etc it was easy to pop a ton of coal on the lorry. The Western Counties Agricultural Association had their coal depot at Redcliff Wharf. Whilst there is no evidence of wagon ownership they signed up to both the 1926 and 1933 RCH schemes.

SAMUEL WALLIS,
Coal Merchant,
Kingsland Road Siding, G.W.R., ST. PHILIP'S.
Radstock, Somerset, Derby, Forest and Welsh Coals.
Sole Agent for the Late Countess Waldegrave's Celebrated Radstock Coals.   Prices on application.

A 1901 advertisement for Samuel Wallis trading out of Kingsland Road Siding.

The 10-ton five-plank wagon supplied by Gloucester in February 1907 to the Western Coal Co. Painted lead colour with white letters shaded black and with black ironwork the lettering layout makes for an attractive and striking wagon. It was a pity therefore that two years later it was all painted over as the wagon passed to a new owner. *GRC&WCo.*

WESTERN COAL Co.

This is the one business that has defied all attempts to track it down. There are several mentions of a Western Coal Co. in the Gloucester RC&WCo's books back in 1890 but that turned out to be a Swansea-based business which went into liquidation in 1892.

There then comes the Bristol-based wagon, purchased in February 1907 from the Gloucester RC&WCo. on seven years deferred purchase terms. The owner had a degree of optimism for his business as he took a fourteen year repair contract.

The only suggestion that can be made is that one John Western was behind the company as in Kelly's 1902 *Bristol Directory* he can be found as a coal merchant at Addison Road, New Brislington. The census of 1901 has a John Western aged 47 in Brislington as a grocer and shopkeeper, had he diversified into the coal trade? Was the Western Coal Co. title actually using his surname?

Whatever the case the company did not last long and appears to have been taken over by the Central Coal Co. (see page 34). In March 1909 they took over the purchase and the repair contracts on the wagon from Gloucester.

WESTERN PETROLEUM Co.

This is another mystery Bristol wagon operator and may have been a national owner with some wagons lettered for Bristol. Two tank wagons were built by the Midland RC&WCo. in 1903 and numbered 295 and 296 suggesting they were part of a larger fleet. The Western Petroleum Co. Ltd went into voluntary liquidation in March 1911 with a London office address.

WESTERN WAGON & PROPERTY Co. Ltd

The Western Wagon & Property Co. began life as the Western Wagon Company in 1860 to both build and hire out railway wagons. They were to primarily serve the demand for wagons in South Wales and a wagon works was built at East Moors, Cardiff.

The title was changed in 1881 to the Western Wagon & Property Co. Ltd to better reflect the operations of the finance house which had now moved into property. One figure who became a major influence on the business was George White who became Secretary in 1888. White had an incredible energy for the acquisition of shares in failing railway companies and selling them on. He also bought up many street tramway systems and improved them including systems in Reading, Dublin, Middlesbrough and London. Later he was one of the financiers behind the Bristol Aeroplane Company.

Wagons were still being built by the firm in 1916 (ten new 12-ton mineral wagons for Lydney & Crump Meadow Collieries Co.) but the large numbers of wagons hired out by Western Wagon were built mostly by others. The penultimate new acquisitions were 85 with side and end doors only, built by E. G. Ireland Ltd, of Newport. Western Wagon's last new wagons appear to be ten built by Hall Lewis, of Maindy, Cardiff, in April 1929.

The company effectively owned many hundreds of wagons at any one time with some being sold on to others whilst others were on simple hire. Many records of the business exist in the Bristol Records Office.

The Western Wagon & Property was wound up voluntarily in April 1935 with W. G. Verdon Smith (a nephew of George White) as chairman.

WETMORE & BIRD Ltd

Wetmore & Bird Ltd was incorporated in July 1912 with a capital of £2,000. It was set up to purchase as a going concern the business of a coal factor and merchant carried on by Robert Leonard Wetmore and that of a builders merchant carried on by Ernest Henry Bird at 10 Marsh Street.

The subscribers to the company included Wetmore and Bird, together with Leonard Scull, a coal merchant, A. Bedale, traveller (probably in coal on behalf of the company), Samuel George Burgess an accountant and Arthur Henry Richard Pope a civil engineer. The first directors were to be Wetmore, Bird and Scull. They were trading at Montpelier and in 1914 had a registered office in Station Road, Montpelier.

An order was placed with the Gloucester RC&WCo. in October 1912 for one secondhand 8-ton wagon on three years deferred purchase. In April 1915 a repair contract was taken for the remaining five and a half years on a 10-ton wagon ex C. C. Williams. As no corresponding take over of a purchase was recorded it is likely that the wagon was older than seven years and was now in its second or third repair contract cycle. One suggestion might be that the wagon was ex Clement Williams of Thornbury. In September 1915 a further repair contract for seven years was taken on two 8-ton and six 10-ton wagons. Again, these must have been from a previous owner.

In February 1916 Wetmore & Bird took two 10-ton wagons on seven years deferred purchase. They are likely to have been registered by the Great Western Railway hence no further trace of them can be found.

The business obviously floundered as it was wound up on the 31st May 1918. Wetmore, however, was to continue in the coal trade at Montpelier.

ROBERT WETMORE

Robert Leonard Wetmore appears to have been trading concurrently with Wetmore & Bird and in 1914 also had an office in Station Road, Montpelier. Wetmore had been born in Henbury in 1881 and the 1901 census showed him to be a clerk in a coal office.

He actually took a wagon from Gloucester prior to the formation of Wetmore & Bird Ltd, purchasing a secondhand 8-ton wagon in March 1910 paying for it over five years. There is then a gap until 1923 when two 10-ton wagons were purchased from Gloucester in November paid for over seven years. One of these wagons, number 27, was photographed prior to leaving the works in February 1924.

Wetmore also purchased a single 12-ton wagon from Thomas Hunter of Rugby in September 1927. It was numbered 17 and registered by the LMS.

Wetmore signed up to both of the RCH schemes and can be found at Montpelier Station in both Kelly's 1935 *Bristol Directory* and the 1938 *Colliery Year Book*.

The final evidence of Wetmore comes from the Gloucester RC&WCo's books when in June 1938 it is noted 'One wagon purchased from Robert Wetmore'. Whether this was Wetmore refinancing a wagon, disposing of an old wagon or ceasing trading is unknown.

Two 10-ton wagons were purchased by Robert Wetmore from Gloucester in 1924. Of these seven-plank wagon number 27 was photographed. That it has side and end doors suggests that Wetmore may have had industrial customers as well as supplying the housecoal trade of Montpelier. The wagons were painted red with white lettering shaded black. *GRC&WCo.*

Photographed at Newnham on Severn in the early years of the twentieth century was this 10-ton coke wagon of seven-plank construction with side and end doors and a three rail coke crate. It is clear how a load of coke occupies far greater space than a similar one of much denser coal. The wagon, numbered 223, looks to be painted black with plain white lettering. The device on the side door may be red and white. *Author's collection*

MARK WHITWILL & SON

The business was started in 1831 by Mark Whitwill and went through two further generations, all Marks. The business was in the main ship brokers and insurance and commission agents. They were also ship owners and ran services to North America from Bristol. Mark Whitwill II was a staunch advocate for building the docks at Avonmouth and Portishead.

At some point Mark Whitwill went into railway wagon ownership and began trading in coal and coke. This may have been diversification as the Port of Bristol began losing out to Liverpool for passenger and grain traffic. There appear to be no trade directory entries for Mark Whitwill to give any idea as to when he was trading in the coal business.

In 1912 he took the business into a new limited company, Whitwill, Cole & Co. Ltd.

Mark Whitwill's coke wagon number 237 is seen in the yard at Calne, Wiltshire. That the side door is down suggests the wagon is here for unloading, possibly bringing coke for a local foundry.
courtesy John Alsop

WHITWILL, COLE & Co. Ltd

Whitwill, Cole & Co. Ltd was a partnership between Mark Whitwill, William Henry Cole and Rose Gertrude Cole, incorporated as a limited company in 1912. The registered office was at 28 Baldwin Street, Bristol and the stated aims of the company was of colliery agents, coal merchants and shipping brokers.

One of the contracts held by the company was to supply the Bristol United Gas Light Company with up to 25,000 tons of coal a year. This came into Bristol by sea from Durham and Northumberland collieries.

Their trading as colliery agents was not apparently on a very large scale, a surviving trading ledger suggests that in the 1920s only about 40,000 tons of coal was sold. Wagons were also hired out for short periods, mainly to the Bristol United Gas Light Company and coal merchants Lowell Baldwin, Edgar Jarrett, C. R. Dowding, Peake, Oliver & Peake and others.

There appears to be no new wagon purchases made by the company between 1923 and 1938. In the latter year eighteen new 12-ton wagons were ordered with the contracts for their construction divided equally between the Gloucester RC&WCo. and Thomas Hunter of Rugby. For the nine wagons built by Gloucester Whitwills were charged £1,422. Gloucester-built wagons were numbered 700 to 708 and the Hunter-built wagons 709 to 717. All were registered with the GWR.

Whitwill, Cole & Co. Ltd were listed as coal merchants in the 1938 *Colliery Year Book*, at the same address. It appears that the company traded until 1971.

WILLIAMS & BIRD

This partnership traded out of the Midland Railway Wharf, St Philips. The partners were George Williams and John Bird who have already been encountered under the Midland Coal Co. They seem to have had an 'interesting' history of trading, using various titles, as they can be found taking wagons from the Midland Waggon Co. under the title Williams & Bird between November 1867 and May 1872.

However, at the same time they were also in partnership with one Henry Farley trading at the Union Coal Wharf, Avon Street, St. Philips as Farley & Co. This partnership was dissolved in January 1872 with Williams and Bird continuing and still using the title Farley & Co. The next entry in the *London Gazette* refers to the dissolution of the partnership between George Williams and John Bird by mutual consent on the 24th June 1878 with George Williams to continue the business. It was not to last long as in December 1878 Williams went into bankruptcy.

He was followed in July 1879 by Bird 'late of Midland Railway Wharf, West Street' where he was trading with Williams (as Williams & Bird), coal merchants, and then at the Midland Railway Wharf in Bath where he traded as the Midland Coal Co. At the time of his bankruptcy he was living in Seymour Villas, Stapleton Road with the occupation of 'agent' – presumably a coal agent. The residual Williams & Bird finally failed in December 1879. They had, in 1875, also opened a depot at Clifton Down Station.

Their wagon acquisitions were five 8-ton wagons bought secondhand on a five year purchase lease at £13 15s pwpa from the Midland Waggon Co. in November 1867. In June 1871

Taken in the sidings close to the Bristol Gas Works was wagon number 557. The wagon is of unknown origin as the large oval plate on the solebar cannot be read. Italic lettering on the solebar above the right-hand axlebox appears to read L&Y 11/14, does this refer to the Lancashire & Yorkshire Waggon Co. at Heywood, Lancashire? The wagon empties to one of the Clay Cross Company's collieries near Chesterfield.
courtesy Gerry Nicols

Two Whitwill, Cole & Co. wagons seen in the loaded roads at the Clay Cross Co's Moreton Colliery, Derbyshire. *Author's collection*

One of the nine Gloucester-built wagons from 1938. Of seven-plank construction with side, end and bottom doors it was painted black with plain white letters. The door was painted red with a white St. Andrew's cross. The rectangular plate on the side above the 'Empty to' instructions is a Thomas Hunter of Rugby repair plate. The wagon was lettered to empty to Thurcroft Colliery. *GRC&WCo.*

A Whitwill, Cole & Co. coke wagon partially obscured by a passing train but the running number of 601 is clear. The lettering style appears to be as per the example above. *courtesy Paul Karau*

ten 6-ton wagons were bought new at £18 13s 4d pwpa over three years. In January 1872 ten 7-ton wagons were taken on one years simple hire followed in May by another eight 6-ton bought on a three year purchase lease at £24 4s pwpa. The demise of Williams & Bird left the Midland Waggon Co. to write off a bad debt of £132 3s 7d.

WILLIAMS & Co.

It is believed that this is the same Williams & Co. as that operating at Cheltenham. Indeed, one batch of wagons recorded under Williams at Cheltenham, should have been marked up as branded for Bristol.

They appear to have been trading out of the Upper Railway Wharf, West Street, as early as 1859. In 1880 the address was given as St. Philips Railway Station and by 1902 had become St. Philip's, Clifton Down & Montpelier railway stations; the Upper Railway Wharf, Midland Road; Railway Wharf, Lawrence Hill & 113A, Whiteladies Road, Clifton. The same addresses appear in 1914 but no further references can be found.

It would appear that some of Williams' wagons were lettered up for Bristol and are recorded as such in the Midland Railway wagon registers. These included 10-ton wagon number 178 built by the Midland RC&WCo. in 1894, and numbers 56 to 85 built by Metropolitan RC&WCo. were registered in July 1902. The Midland RC&WCo. also supplied 10-ton wagons numbered 180 to 185 and 190 to 199 in 1907.

AND DISTRICT: OUT TO AVONMOUTH

BRISTOL SUBLIMED LEAD COMPANY Ltd

The Sublimed Lead company was incorporated in March 1885 and was to take over the plant and machinery of the White Lead Works near Broadmead carried on by George Thompson Lewis, William John Menzies and John Wesley Hall. The capital was £40,000 in £100 shares. They were also to buy the rights to a patent for the manufacture of pig lead, white lead and oxide of lead held by Lewis who originated from Philadelphia, USA. The registered office was at 51 Broadmead whilst the works were stated to be at Shirehampton. It was at the registered office on the 13th October 1893 that at an Extraordinary General Meeting it was decided that the company could not continue in business due to its liabilities and that it would be wound up accordingly.

On 29/1/1883 the Western Wagon Co. agreed to sell the lead company two 8-ton wagons on five years terms. The wagons were priced at £45 each and the plate numbers were 684-5. These might be the two wagons, numbered 1 and 2 which were recorded by the Great Western in January 1886 as being hired from the Western Wagon Co. and built by the Forest of Dean Wagon Co. at Bullo Pill.

THOMAS SHARPE

Thomas Sharpe was a long established coal merchant at Shirehampton who may well have traded by sea as well as by rail. There is some evidence of Cannock Chase coal for Sharpe being transshipped at Gloucester Docks from barges to larger sailing vessels for the trip down the Severn and up the Avon.

His trading address was the Shirehampton Coal Wharf and he appears in Kelly's 1889 *Gloucestershire Directory* at Sea Mills, Stoke Bishop. The 1881 census had shown Sharpe to have been born at Holme Pierpoint, Nottinghamshire in 1853. His occupation was coal merchant. By 1901 he had added 'farmer' to his commercial activities.

He appears several times in the minute books of the Great Western & Midland Railway Joint Committee who operated the line through Shirehampton. In January 1902 he was renting an office and land to which he added coal storage space in July. In January 1903 he rented a weighing machine and office. Trade was obviously good as in 1906 he increased his coal stacking ground from 80 to 100 yards and the following year took over a further 80 yards from William Hellings.

Thomas Sharpe appears to have died circa 1914 as *Kelly's* for that year records Mrs Sharpe as being the coal merchant at Shirehampton and in 1915 she took over the rent of the coal stacking ground. Sharpe signed up to the 1926 RCH scheme but not to that of 1933. It is known that he had two 8-ton wagons from the Midland RC&WCo. in 1893 with numbers 30 and 31 being registered by the Midland Railway in November. Of these number 31 was rebuilt in 1925 by Wagon Repairs Ltd, Gloucester, for Stevens & Co. of Oxford becoming their number 736. It is suggested that most of Sharpe's coal may have arrived by sea with the wagons being used for further distribution.

E. BAILY & SON, Ltd

Whilst being maltsters based in Frome, Somerset Baily also had mills at Portishead and at Avonmouth. That at Portishead was alongside the entrance lock to the dock and served by a siding. It was still extant in 1948 but was soon to be swept away by the building of the 'B' Power Station. Details of the Avonmouth facility are unknown but was probably one of the many granaries located about the docks area.

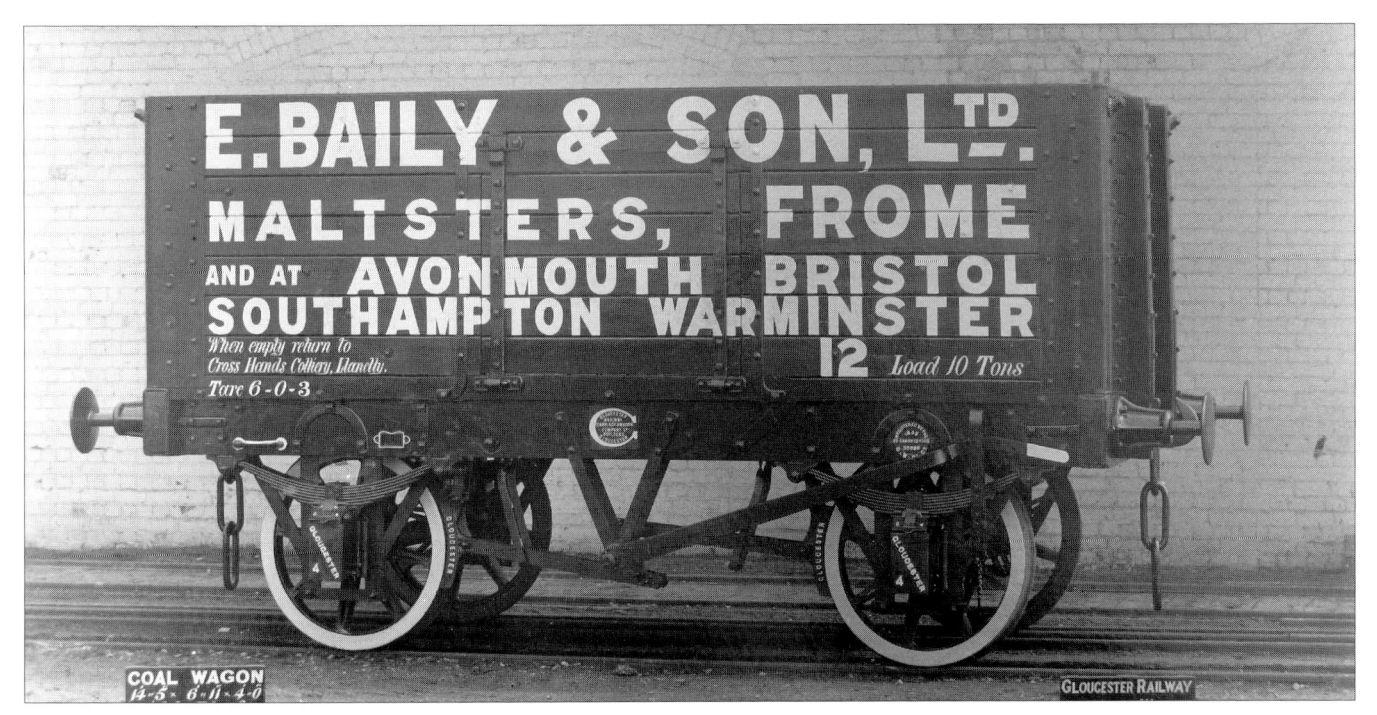

Photographed in October 1899 wagon number 12 for E. Baily & Son was painted black with plain white lettering. The locations stated on the wagon side include Avonmouth but do not mention Portishead. The wagon empties to Cross Hands Colliery, Llanelly, to load anthracite. *GRC&WCo.*

A later wagon for Baily & Son, photographed in January 1903 has lost Avonmouth from the listing and gained Portishead suggesting that a move may have been made around the turn of the century. The history of the business really belongs to a volume on Somerset and so only gets passing reference here. *GRC&WCo.*

Another wagon to which only passing reference will be made, mainly because it has proved impossible to discover who O.B. were. Obviously they are sugar refiners with a presence in Avonmouth as this 12-ton tank wagon built c1912 by Hurst, Nelson of Motherwell shows. Whether the molasses originated in Avonmouth or were brought in through the docks is unknown. *courtesy HMRS ABP214*

NATIONAL SMELTING Co.

The area north of Avonmouth alongside the Severn was to turn into a major chemical and metals production area after the First World War. One of the first companies into the area was the National Smelting Co. which was set up in 1917 to supply zinc. Prior to the war most zinc used in this country was imported from Germany but hostilities brought that trade to an end and supplies were sought from America and Australia. The National Smelting Co. was made up of British and Australian interests with a capital of £500,000 but despite an additional Government loan of £500,000 progress was slow. Possibly the end of the war delayed matters and it was not until the 1920s that work got underway at Avonmouth. When an additional share issue was made in 1924 the smelting works were still incomplete but alongside was a sulphuric acid plant built during the war by the Government. This was in operation but would not be producing strong sulphuric acid until the roasting of zinc concentrates was underway at the site. This rearrangement saw the company's capital increased to £1,700,000.

In 1929 the Imperial Smelting Corporation Ltd was set up as a result of a further reorganisation of National Smelting and they continued operations at Avonmouth until closure in 2003.

The only written references to wagons are three tanks built by Charles Roberts in December 1935 and numbered 294 to 296. They were registered by the LMS. Of these 295 appears in the register as belonging to National Smelting Co. whilst the other two are down to Imperial Smelting Corporation. Looking at number 294 and the varying information displayed on the tank side and the owner's plate it is easy to see how the clerk got it wrong! No details of the other wagons for Imperial Smelting have been found apart from that given in the captions.

National Smelting obviously took an unknown number of Great Western Railway 20-ton all steel 'Felix Pole' wagons on hire to supply the works with coal. What looks to be 110369 is seen waiting to go under the screens at Eastern United Colliery at some time during or just after the Second World War. *Author's collection*

A 20-ton tank wagon built by Charles Roberts of Wakefield in December 1935 although as delivery was probably not until January the work's plate actually gives 1936. Of the plates on the solebar that to the right of the load details reads 'For repairs advise owners 19 Parade Neath'. Next is a return empty plate 'Return empty to Hallen Marsh Sidings Avonmouth G.W.R.'. Then comes a standard Chas Roberts builder's plate and the rectangular owner's plate which still reads 'The National Smelting Co Ltd'. *courtesy HMRS AAS523*

Despite being built at the same time as the wagon seen previously 12-ton tank number 209 has a look of much greater antiquity. It was in fact photographed on the 26th January 1936. Details on the various plates are as before. Being a much smaller diameter tank the bottom discharge valve can be seen above the framing. The framing itself is a lighter colour, either grey or red. *courtesy HMRS AAS534*

This 20-ton Sulphite Liquor tank was photographed on the 23rd August 1940. Whilst the side boards proclaim it to belong to the Imperial Smelting Corporation the rectangular owner's plate gives Improved Metallurgy Ltd, Avonmouth. It empties to the Hallen Marsh Sidings. *courtesy HMRS AAT335*

A slightly more modern 20-ton tank for the carriage of ammoniacal liquor photographed by the builders, Chas Roberts, in March 1953. The owner's plate still gives The National Smelting Co. Ltd.
courtesy HMRS AAT936

National Fertilizers Ltd may well have been a subsidiary of National Smelting although the term National Growmore Fertiliser was in use by Fisons. It would be natural with the various phosphates, acids etc being produced in the Avonmouth area that chemical fertilisers would be a by product. This 14-ton ammoniacal liquor tank was from an order for three wagons placed with Chas Roberts in August 1939. The wagon empties to Hallen Marsh Sidings where Fisons did have a plant.
courtesy HMRS AAT308

A seven-plank wagon with side and end doors was lettered up for Crane & Company when obtained from Gloucester in October 1904. Why a firework manufacturer would require coal was a bit of a mystery, especially using a wagon with an end door. The likely explanation is given in the text and the wagon probably never carried coal for the works. It was finished with a 'bright red' body and lettered in white with black shading. Ironwork would also have been black. Whether the wagon continued to carry this livery after its first repaint is unknown. The Railway Clearing House were quite keen on wagon sides not being used for blatant advertising and for not carrying the true identity of the operator. *GRC&WCo.*

MIDLAND LINES: MANGOTSFIELD TO BITTON

CRANE & COMPANY

IT might seem odd that a fireworks manufacturer should have a coal wagon, especially with a number of 107 on its side. At first it was thought that it could have supplied coal to a boiler at the works, possibly for heating but further research into the company revealed the truth. No order for the wagon to Crane & Company can be found in the Gloucester RC&WCo's books. The fleet number does fit neatly into the sequence used by Alexander Crane, a Gloucester coal merchant whose wagons were seen in *Private Owner Wagons of Gloucestershire* and then a family link was discovered.

The fireworks factory at Warmley was started by Isaac Crane, brother of Alexander, in 1887. Previous to this he had been a grocer & tea dealer in Trevethin, Monmouthshire. It is possible that the wagon was never operated at all on behalf of the fireworks company, unless Alexander had the contract to supply coal to the works but it did fulfil a useful role as advertising for the business. This was a role that was forbidden by the Railway Clearing House although there were several well known breaches of the code such as wagons advertising Kodak and also Crystalline Billiard Balls. This wagon for Crane was slightly less blatant but was bought by Alexander and undoubtedly carried his coals.

The one job that Crane's fireworks were known for was the display put on for the visit of the Prince of Wales to Cheltenham in 1897. The firm did many other displays and operated until a major fire at the works in 1937. This was the second accident in two years, that in 1935 being an explosion which caused one fatality.

SIDNEY FUSSELL

BASED at Bitton and Warmley stations, Sidney has connections back to both the local coal extraction industry in the area and bootmaking. His father, Abraham Fussell, was owner of California Colliery at Oldland which he had acquired in 1876. The 1881 census describes Abraham, then aged 56, as a colliery proprietor and boot manufacturer. There were two sons, Philip, 24, and Sidney, 22, the latter a boot manufacturer. Abraham was trading as the Oldland Colliery Co. and prior to 1893 it became a limited company with Philip Fussell as managing director. Disaster struck in 1904 with an inrush of water and the whole workings were flooded. This proved too much for the company which was forced into liquidation. Sidney Fussell was now chairman and he must have negotiated the sale of some of the property to the West Gloucestershire Water Works in 1908 who began to extract water from the workings. Philip Fussell found himself a place on the board of the water company. With 'keeping it in the family' in mind it is interesting that the solicitors overseeing the final liquidation matters in 1912 were Fussell & Co!

When Sidney started trading in coal is unknown but may have been soon after the colliery closed, possibly filling a gap in the coal supply market left by the closure of the colliery, although there is no trace of wagon ownership until around the start of the First World War. Wagons were being acquired in April 1915 both from Hurst, Nelson in Motherwell and the Gloucester RC&WCo. Wagons numbered 18 and 19 were taken from Hurst, Nelson and financed by the Scottish Wagon Co. In the same month a single secondhand 10-ton wagon was taken from the Gloucester RC&WCo. and paid for in cash. Further secondhand wagons were acquired in September 1915 from Kimmins, Drew & Co., flour millers at Dudbridge (see *Private Owner Wagons of Gloucestershire*) which had originally been supplied by Gloucester to Edward Langford in 1901. Fussell took over the remaining 2½ years of the repair contract and extended it for a further seven years in November 1917.

Fussell signed up to both the 1926 and the 1933 RCH schemes and was listed until 1938 in the *Colliery Year Books* as a coal merchant at Warmley Station.

Sidney Fussell died on the 9th February 1939 at Durdham Down so would not have seen his wagons taken into the national pool. Whether the business ceased at this time as well is unknown.

CRANE'S FIREWORK DISPLAYS

Are proved by Testimonials to be **THE BEST ON EARTH**. Noted for their **Marvellous Designs, Beautiful Colours**, and the most **Comical Devices** yet invented.

FIRE PICTURES AND PORTRAITS
For Coming-of-Age Festivities, Wedding and other Fêtes.

FIREWORK DISPLAYS fired by Experienced Pyrotechnists from this, the only Firework Manufactory in the West of England holding a Licence from H.M. Secretary of State.

COMMITTEE MEETINGS ATTENDED and interviews arranged with the Managing Director, **Mr. I. CRANE**, who will, on receipt of letter or telegram, stating the amount and nature of display required, submit Special Programme.

Selected Cases of Fireworks for private use from **£2 2s.** upwards, with 50 per cent. discount added in Fireworks, making **THREE GUINEAS WORTH for TWO GUINEAS**, or same ratio of discount on larger purchases. All Carriage Free. Detailed particulars gratis.

ILLUMINATION GLASS LAMPS and CHINESE LANTERNS in great variety. BALLOONS sent by parcel post.

Illustrated Price Lists on application to—

CRANE & CO. LTD., Firework Manufacturers, Illuminators & Decorators,
ST. JAMES'S BARTON, BRISTOL.

Telegraphic Address: "CRANE, FIREWORKS, BRISTOL."   Telephone No. 06277.

An advertisement for Crane & Co. from 1902.

A harsh enlargement off a photograph which shows a wagon for the Golden Valley Paper Mills at Bitton. Of five-plank construction with side doors only the origin of the wagon is unknown. Livery would appear to be either red or grey with shaded white lettering. Underneath the wording 'Bitton. LMS' is 'C. K. Smith.'.

courtesy Gerry Nichols

GOLDEN VALLEY PAPER MILLS

The paper mill at Bitton was originally a brass mill but was converted to paper making in the 1830s. Following a fire in 1849 the mill was sold to one William Sommerville. The Sommerville family were very much a paper-making family with William's father, also William, having an interest in the Dalmore Mill, Midlothian. The younger William set his sons up with Charles taking over Golden Valley and two others having a mill at Creech St. Michael in Somerset built for them.

Like many paper mills fire was always a hazard and the Golden Valley Mill burnt down on several occasions, each time the opportunity being taken to rebuild and improve. In the mid 1890s it was recorded that some 200 to 300 tons of coal per week was being consumed (although this figure seems very high) by the work's boilers. Paper was made both from rags, which after processing had to be boiled by steam for about twelve hours, and from wood pulp. Perhaps it was the steaming of the rags that required such efforts from the boilers that a large tonnage of coal was necessary. The mill operated 24 hours a day, six days a week and employed about 450 men and women.

In July 1895 a partnership between William and Ernest Summerville, trading as W. & J. Summerville was dissolved by mutual consent. It was not to be long before the Summerville family sold out their interests in the mill to the King-Smith family.

The mills continued to produce paper until the 1960s and at a meeting of the Golden Valley Paper Mills Limited in October 1967 it was announced that all of the property and plant had been disposed off and that the company was to be wound up.

With the large consumption of coal it is not surprising that the company should operate its own wagons although undoubtedly the bulk of coal came in through one of the larger Bristol factors. No written evidence can be found of the number of wagons operated or of their origins suggesting that they may have been acquired secondhand. It is thought that they would have been registered by the Midland or LMS if bought new.

KINGSWOOD COAL & IRON Co. Ltd

The various collieries in the Kingswood area, to the east of Bristol and situated alongside the Midland Railway's main line from Gloucester into Bristol, have a long and reasonably complex history. There were originally a large number of individual workings but the potential was seen by Handel Cossham. Originally connected with Yate Colliery, Cossham formed a partnership with William Wethered and his sons Joseph, Henry and Edwin and traded as Wethered, Cossham & Wethered. They developed new workings at Pucklechurch which became the Parkfield Colliery. In 1863 the Speedwell and Deep pits at St. Georges were acquired and to run these the Kingswood Coal & Iron Co. Ltd was formed.

The Wethered interests were bought out with the formation of the Kingswood & Parkfield Colliery Co. Ltd in 1878 behind which was Handel Cossham and Charles S. Wills. Wills was of the tobacco family and his brother, Edward, was chairman of Bristol Collieries Ltd, owners of Malago Vale.

Cossham died in 1890 with his interests left to his wife for her lifetime. As a result the collieries did not come up for sale until 1900. The sale particulars make interesting reading giving some of the collieries' customers. However, if, as mentioned below, the wagons owned by the collieries had been sold off by this date then the coal would have been taken in Midland Railway wagons.

At the sale the collieries passed to the Bedminster, Easton, Kingswood & Parkfield Collieries Ltd. Behind the new company were the Bennett family who had had interests in the Bedminster collieries since the mid 1700s.

Several of the collieries were soon to close down and things do not seem to have gone well for the Bedminster, Easton, Kingswood & Parkfield Co. By 1914 the company was in receivership and was taken over by the East Bristol Collieries Ltd.

Behind the new company was Frank Beauchamp who owned a large number of collieries in Somerset. He was also the grandson of Zebedee Beachim of Beachim & Balmont. East Bristol Collieries kept Kingswood and Parkfield going until 1936 when both closed.

Very little is known of the wagons supplied but it is no surprise that some of the first recorded came from the Cheltenham & Swansea Railway Carriage & Wagon Co. as both Cossham and Wethered were directors. (Cossham also had interests in the Bristol & South Wales Wagon Co.) In November 1867 an order for 150 8-ton narrow gauge wagons with wooden floors at £62 10s each was placed. The only other order for Cossham & Wethered was in June 1874, by which date the Cheltenham & Swansea had become the Swansea Wagon Co., when fifty-eight old broad gauge wagons were disposed of to them at £33 each. Why they should be requiring broad gauge wagons is unknown.

The Kingswood Coal & Iron Co. placed an order with the Midland Waggon Co. in October 1873 for twenty 8-ton wagons, paid for in cash at £83 each. No other orders for the company can be found.

The Kingswood & Parkfield Colliery Co. sourced wagons from a more local builder in 1879 when fifty 10-ton wagons, numbered 500 to 549, where taken from the Bristol Wagon Works Co. on deferred purchase terms. They were registered by the Great Western in November.

It is possible that the colliery company sold off all of their wagons to the Midland Railway who had several attempts at ridding their system of the dreaded private owner wagon. Certainly all known images of the collieries have Midland Railway five-plank wagons in the sidings with no sign even of other traders' wagons collecting coal from the collieries.

MRS E. LACEY

Eliza Lacey can be found on the 1881 census aged 55, living at Warmley with the occupation of coal merchant. Whilst not marked as a widow there is no sign of her husband George. They had a large number of children amongst whom appear to be George and Frederick who on the 1911 census can both be found trading as coal merchants. It may be they who traded as Lacey Bros who could be found signing up to both the 1926 and 1933 RCH schemes. At no point do any of the Laceys seem to have bothered with advertising in trade directories or colliery year books.

It is only for Eliza that wagons can be traced with numbers 1 and 2, both 8-tonners built by the Bristol Wagon Co. being registered in April 1896 by the Midland Railway. In February 1897 numbers 3 and 4, again of 8-ton capacity built by Bristol, were registered whilst numbers 5 and 6 came later in the year being registered in December. In January 1905 10-ton wagons numbered 9 and 10 were supplied by the Midland RC&WCo. to Lacey & Co. of Warmley and registered with the Midland Railway. Had Laceys purchased two wagons secondhand to fill the gap of numbers 7 and 8?

FREDERICK MAYO

Mayo is listed in Kelly's *Gloucestershire Directory* for 1906 as a coal merchant trading at High Street, Oldland and the Railway Station at Bitton. No evidence has been found so far for wagon operation. He was still at the same address in 1931.

ARTHUR NICHOLS

Nichols can be found in the records of the Gloucester RC&WCo. as trading from the Old Station Yard, Mangotsfield. In May 1939 took two 10-ton wagons on eighteen months simple hire, followed, it would appear, by two more in July for the same period. No further details can be found.

WALTER SHEPPARD

Although listed in Kelly's 1919 *Gloucestershire Directory* through to the 1928 *Colliery Year Book* at the Railway Station, Warmley there is, so far, no evidence of wagon ownership.

SHORTWOOD BRICK & TILE Co.

The brick works at Shortwood grew up alongside Parkfield Colliery. They were operated by the Shortwood Brick & Tile Co. until in about 1903 they were taken over by the Cattybrook Brick Co. (see page 33). The works closed in 1969.

Wagons for the brick works are recorded in September 1872 when the Great Western Railway registered numbers 1 to 13 and 15. They had been built by the Bristol Waggon Works Co. In January 1873 numbers 17 to 20 followed from the same builder.

The brick works at Shortwood with a large number of Midland Railway wagons present. Did this company, like adjoining collieries, sell their wagon fleet off to the Midland and thereafter use railway company wagons? It is assumed that Cattybrook wagons may have been seen here after 1903 although the accompanying wagon label clearly relates to a railway company wagon.

courtesy Peter Smith & Steve Grudgings

ADDENDA & ERRATA

FOREST OF DEAN

OSMAN BARRETT
Barrett is now known to have taken forty 8-ton wagons from the Oldbury RC&WCo. in January 1872. Which of his several interests in the Forest of Dean they may have been used in conjunction with is unknown.

DEAN FOREST COAL Co.
The newly available records of the Midland Railway Carriage & Wagon Co. show that in August 1884 twenty secondhand 8-ton wagons were taken on six months simple hire.

The London & North Western Railway wagon registers show wagon number 547 as probably being acquired secondhand in 1926 when rebuilt as a 10-tonner ex Coppice Colliery (first registered in 1894).

DEAN FOREST CONSOLIDATED IRON Co.
A new wagon operator to add to the listing, although the company needs researching further to find where it was operating. Three 6-ton wagons were taken on one years simple hire in December 1878 from the Midland Waggon Co.

FOREST OF DEAN COAL Co.
It was noted that the Forest Coal Co. were, at present, an unknown company. There is still the possibility that the register actually referred to the Dean Forest Coal Company but another company with a similar name has now appeared in the records of the Midland RC&WCo. The Forest of Dean Coal Co. took five 6-ton wagons on three years deferred purchase terms in January 1890 and ten 10-ton wagons on five years terms in June. There is the possibility that the company title was a clerk's error for the Dean Forest Coal Co.

FOREST OF DEAN STONE FIRMS
This company had obviously had wagon dealing with the Midland RC&WCo. although details cannot be found. However, in October 1907 the wagon company noted that the stone firm had failed owing £182 19s 3d. By November 1911 this was down to £48 0s 9d which suggests that wagons were still on hire but it was decided to take proceedings for the recovery of the debt from the receiver, Mr Matcham.

ALFRED GOOLD
Two new 6-ton wagons were purchased by Goold from the Midland Waggon Co. in December 1863 on three years deferred purchase at £19 12s 6d pwpa. In April 1867 it was reported that Goold was in arrears to the sum of £110 12s 6d.

THOMAS GWILLIAM
In 1897 Gwilliam was working the Farmers Folly Colliery at Shortstanding, Coleford as well as being landlord of The Globe public house. In January 1898 the hire of one secondhand 8-ton wagon from the Gloucester RC&WCo. for one year by Gwilliam was recorded. The following month another 8-tonner was taken on hire for eleven months followed by another in April for nine months. All of the hires were obviously aimed to end at the start of 1899. Gwilliam appears to have had the colliery on lease and in June 1900 the colliery was up for sale. Output for the year ending December 1899 was 5,750 tons. Coal was won by shafts close to the main road and was put on rail at Bicknor Siding, a distance of about two and a half

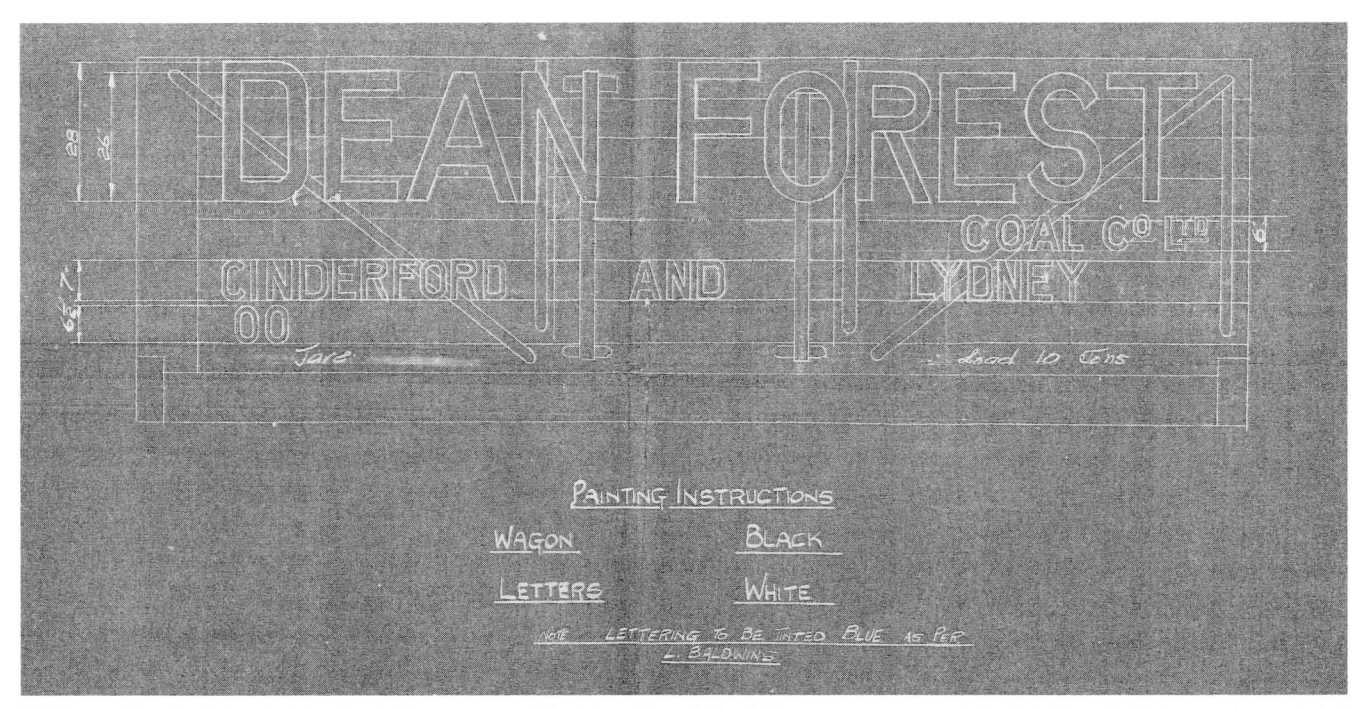

A Wagon Repairs Ltd painting sketch for wagons of the Dean Forest Coal Co. as seen on page 75 of the Forest of Dean volume. What should be noted is the painting instruction addition that 'lettering to be tinted blue as per L. Baldwins', thus the original photo caption which gave the lettering as white is incorrect.
courtesy Gordon Griffin

miles. The siding was on the Severn & Wye Joint Railway close to Lydbrook Junction Station. Farmers Folly was sold to Thomas Gwilliam for £500. The 1901 census has him, aged 49, and a colliery owner.

HAYWOOD COLLIERY Co.
The Haywood Colliery, located just off the High Street in Cinderford, was connected to the Great Western Railway's Forest of Dean Branch via a narrow gauge line. It was operated by the Littledean Woodside Coal Co. which, after a period of great financial difficulties was liquidated in 1882. It would appear that they may have had wagons lettered for Haywood Colliery from the Midland RC&WCo. as in February 1881 it was noted in their records that the company had failed but no previous mention can be found.

HIGH MEADOW COAL Co.
In *Private Owner Wagons of Gloucestershire* it was stated that the only references found came from an 1881 wagon register for Kemble with wagon No's 1, 4 and 6 being recorded. The records of the Midland Waggon Co. show that in October 1877 six secondhand 8-ton wagons were taken on hire for one year at £8 pwpa. In August 1878 five 8-ton wagons were taken on monthly hire. The six wagons taken on hire in October 1877 may have been kept on until 1884.

In February 1881 ten 8-ton wagons were taken on hire at £7 10s and, again, this hire may have been renewed through to 1884. At this date all were probably returned to Midland as the High Meadow Coal Co. was wound up in October 1884. The company's offices were at 3 Northgate, Darlington. One John Benton Ord of Gloucester was appointed liquidator.

HOLMES BROS
Working Kidnalls & Nags Head Colliery the company took a total of fifteen 10-ton wagons from the Midland RC&WCo. during 1886 in three batches of five ordered in March, November and December. Prices ranged from £9 10s to £10 10s per wagon per annum and all were on five years deferred purchase.

Prior to becoming Holmes Bros the business had traded as S. Holmes & Co. and it was under that name that the Midland RC&WCo. recorded a bad debt of £106 12s 7d in May 1896. In August 1903 it was noted that Holmes Bros had failed and that they too had a bad debt of £94 12s.

LYDBROOK COLLIERY Co.
The Lydbrook Colliery Co. Ltd was incorporated in July 1883, the company having a capital of £15,000. In January 1884 they took over a siding agreement on a siding just outside Upper Lydbrook Station and erected a bridge over the Severn & Wye Railway in order to carry colliery tubs from the Lydbrook Deep Level to the loading point on the siding.

In November 1885 four secondhand 8-ton were taken on hire from the Midland RC&WCo. at £6 10s pwpa for 1 year. In May 1886 one secondhand 10-ton was taken on a years hire at £7 pa and in September 1886 two further 10-tonners were taken on the same hire terms.

The Lydbrook Colliery Co. was wound up voluntarily in November 1892.

LYDNEY COAL COMPANY
It is believed that this was the company formed in Lydney albeit an earlier one of the same title had existed with an address of Weston super Mare, Somerset. In February 1887 the Midland RC&WCo. recorded that one secondhand 10-ton wagon had been hired to the company for one year, this was followed by a second wagon in March.

EDWARD MARMONT & Co.
In trade directories Edward Marmont appears as a coal dealer at New Town, Sharpness, Gloucestershire. On the 1901 census he can be found aged 63, born Stroud, and a coal merchant. Twenty years earlier he had been a fishmonger in nearby Stonehouse. He was, however, trading in coal by 1897 and in August 1905 purchased a secondhand 10-ton wagon from the Gloucester RC&WCo. This was followed by a second similar wagon in October 1906. The repair contracts were kept up until at least 1919 but when Marmont ceased trading is unknown. The last trade directory reference appears to be for 1914.

TITANIC IRON Co.
This may well be the Oldbury RC&WCo's shorthand for the Titanic Steel & Iron Co. Ltd of Milkwall which was formed in 1862 being promoted by Robert Forester Mushet. It was on the 10th August that Oldbury recorded an order for twenty wagons, ten to be delivered in September 1869 and ten in March 1870. Whether they were on hire or being purchased was not noted. The Titanic Works were closed down in 1871 and the company was wound up in 1874.

WILDERNESS PORTLAND CEMENT Co.
This is another totally new wagon operator based in Mitcheldean. The Wilderness Portland Cement Co. operated a cement works on the edge of the town and would have loaded cement onto the Great Western Railway's Gloucester-Hereford line at Mitcheldean Road Station. In December 1890 the Midland RC&WCo's books show that three secondhand 7-ton wagons were taken on hire for one year.

GLOUCESTERSHIRE

GLOUCESTER
ALEXANDER CRANE
Alexander's brother has already been encountered in this volume and it is now possible to update details of Alexander's fleet. As originally recorded it was thought that he was trading as early as 1879 but no details of wagons could be found until an order with Gloucester in 1902. With the availability of the Midland RC&WCo's records it is possible to see that he took wagons from that company as early as July 1883. In that month one 6-ton was taken on hire for one year at £5 per annum. He seems to have taken another in November 1884 as in March 1889 the hire of two 6-ton wagons ex-Crane to Henry Merchant (also of Gloucester) was recorded.

Crane, however, must have had other, unrecorded, wagons on hire as a renewal of four is given in September 1889, another one in December and one in August 1890. These hires may have continued for some time but again are unrecorded.

T. GEORGE & SONS
Thomas George proclaimed that he started in business in 1860 with the first record of wagons being 1892. It is now possible to take his wagon operation back to 1867. In September of that year he took one secondhand 7-ton wagon on simple hire for one year from the Midland Waggon Co. In April 1870 two 6-ton wagons were purchased over seven years for £9 pwpa. In October 1872 a secondhand 6-ton wagon was purchased. In August 1883 he took a 6-ton wagon on 1 years simple hire and in November 1889 and August 1890 there were records of one wagon's hire being renewed.

The number of 6-ton wagons taken may explain the repair contract taken with Gloucester in August 1892 on five unidentified 6-ton wagons.

GLOUCESTER CO-OP IND. SOCIETY Ltd
The record that the Society purchased its first wagon in 1865 may have to be amended as the Midland Waggon Co's records only show a single 6-ton wagon being taken for one year in July 1865 at a cost of £12 per annum. It is most likely that it was taken on hire. In September 1867 one 7-ton wagon was taken at £12 pa for one year, again probably on hire.

Two 8-ton wagons were purchased for cash in August 1875 at £63 each. Only four years later, in October 1879, two 10-ton wagons were bought for just £49 each. In February 1881 two 8-ton wagons were bought on seven years deferred purchase at £8 15s pwpa.

SAMUEL HIPWOOD
That Samuel Hipwood had wagons from other builders can now be confirmed as in August 1883 he hired one 6-ton wagon for one year from the Midland RC&WCo.

J. LANGSTON & SON
Langston who were known to have had two wagons can now have their fleet increased considerably through the records of the Midland Waggon Co. and its successor, the Midland RC&WCo. In March 1872 two 6-ton wagons were bought on seven years deferred purchase at £11 4s pwpa. In November 1875 two 8-ton wagons were bought at £60 each, cash.

February 1879 saw two 6-ton wagons taken on hire for one year. The hire of two 6-ton wagons was also noted in November 1880 (put down to W. J. Langston); in August 1883 and December 1889. There is the possibility that it was the same two wagons with the hires being renewed.

In September 1878 the partnership between James Langston and William James Langston trading as Langston & Son, coal merchants, Gloucester, was dissolved by mutual consent. William James Langston will continue. This was undoubtedly the retirement of James with son William taking over.

JOHN KNIGHT
In February 1865 the Oldbury RC&WCo. noted an order from Knight, Gloucester for 'wagons like Scudamore' to be delivered to West Bromwich.

HENRY MERCHANT
As already mentioned under the addenda for Alexander Crane in March 1889 the Midland RC&WCo. recorded the hire of two wagons to Henry Merchant ex Crane. He also had other wagons from Midland as in February 1890 the renewal of a hire on a single wagon was recorded. The two ex Crane wagons appear to have had their hire renewed in June 1890. There was also the renewal of a hire in February 1890 on four wagons put down to A. Merchant which could be a transcription error for H. Merchant.

GEORGE MERRYLEES
Merrylees lived at Dalkeith, Longlevens and, at his death in 1908, was described as a 'general factor'. The 1901 census shows him to have been born in Scotland and to be aged 65. He traded as George Merrylees & Co. as leather belting manufacturers, leather factors, engineers' store factors and contractors, oil & colour merchants, and importers of oil, grease etc at St. Nicholas Works, 113 Westgate Street.

In November 1892 George Merrylees & Co. took three secondhand 8-ton wagons on hire from the Gloucester RC&WCo. for two years and eleven months. In January 1896 two 10-ton wagons were taken on hire for an unspecified term but it may have been these wagons which, having proved their worth, were purchased by the company in August 1899 when two 10-tonners were bought on seven years deferred purchase terms.

At the beginning of the 1900s the company name became Merrylees, Pugh & Co. Ltd.

NICHOLSON BROS & Co.
This is another 'new' operator of wagons tracked down via clues found in the records of the Midland Waggon Co. and its successors and the *London Gazette*.

Slater's *Gloucestershire Directory* for 1859 has T. & J. B. Nicholson trading as coal & coke and stone merchants at New Street, Cheltenham and as stone & marble masons in George Street, Gloucester with, in brackets, 'and at Reading'. The *Post Office Directory* for the same year has Thomas Nicholson, coal merchant, GWR Wharf, Cheltenham.

It was in September 1858 that the Midland Waggon Co. noted the hire to T. S. & B. Nicholson of Gloucester of twenty wagons at £11 pwpa yearly then three monthly. In September 1859 D. Radford offered to take over wagons at £12 pwpa on a yearly basis and in February 1860 the transfer from T. B. Nicholson to D. Radford of ten wagons for the remainder of contract was concluded. The suggestion that the Nicholsons might have been in difficulties was confirmed in July 1860 when the Waggon Co. wrote off a bad debt of £126 14s 5d although paid 16s 8d in £. In July 1863 a final bad debt of £25 6s was written off.

Knowing that the business had failed the *London Gazette* was checked where in May 1860 it was reported that a petition for bankruptcy was filed on the 19th March, 1860 against Thomas Nicholson the younger, and Isaiah Birt Nicholson, of the city of Gloucester, coal and slate merchants. In November 1862 it was noted that the partnership between Thomas Nicholson the younger, Isaiah Birt Nicholson, and John Miles, trading as coal and general merchants, in Gloucester and elsewhere as

Nicholson, Brothers, and Miles was dissolved due to the death of John Miles on the 17th day of April.

Finally the *London Gazette* noted in July 1863 that the partnership Thomas Nicholson and Isaiah Birt Nicholson, coal, coke, and slate merchants, and factors in Gloucester, trading as Nicholson Brothers & Company was dissolved by mutual consent but would be continued by Isaiah Birt Nicholson.

This was obviously not the end of the company's woes as in March 1867 the Cheltenham & Swansea Wagon Co. issued a writ against Nicholson Bros & Co. for an overdue account amounting to £700. In the same month it was noted that the Bristol Wagon Co. were stating that Nicholson Bros & Co. had asked for arbitration on their claim for detention. This suggests that Nicholsons also had wagons from the Bristol Company and that they had been detained somewhere for non payment of dues. The Cheltenham & Swansea received a letter in February 1868 from Nicholson's solicitor, Mr Goold, urging the settlement of the claim by accepting a dividend of £600 but this was declined.

The Gloucester Waggon Co. were also caught up and in 1867 a flurry of wagons ex Nicholson Bros & Co. are recorded as being sold off or hired out to new operators albeit the original sales details were not recorded. In August 1867 twelve 10-ton wagons were sold to R. C. Cole of Cirencester. In October Cole & Leigh took eight wagons on hire for six months. In December Edward Medlicott hired one 9-ton wagon for three years and finally in January 1868 one 10-ton wagon was hired for three years to George Stephens and two 9-ton wagons were sold to Davies & Roberts. Thus Nicholsons had at least twenty-four wagons from Gloucester.

JOSEPH SCUDAMORE

That Joseph Scudamore traded from Gloucester can be confirmed from the written records of the Oldbury RC&WCo. In August 1864 Scudamore asked Oldbury for prices on 6, 8, 10 and 12-ton wagons for both broad and standard gauges. In October a quotation for a 10-ton broad gauge wagon at £100 was given and an order for ten such wagons on seven years deferred purchase terms at £20 pwpa was given.

LEMUEL SEYERS

Seyers is known to have taken one secondhand 6-ton wagon from the Midland Waggon Co. in November 1879 on simple hire at £5 pa for one year.

W. H. WORTH

There are several entries in the books of the Midland RC&WCo. for W. H. Worth. In August 1885 two secondhand 6-ton wagons were hired at £5 pwpa for one year. In November 1885 a single 6-ton wagon was hired on the same terms. These wagons still appear to have been on hire in 1889 and 1890 when the contracts were renewed for a further year.

There is also the possibility that Worth hired three 8-ton wagons from Gloucester in October 1894 for two years as this entry was mis-transcribed for W. H. North – one of the perils of attempting to read the difficult hand of the company secretary writing up the minutes of meetings!

CHELTENHAM

JOHN BARRELL

The records of the Midland Waggon Co. reveal that in December 1871 Barrell bought six 6-ton wagons at £10 10s pwpa over seven years. In May 1872 he took four secondhand 6-ton wagons at the same price per wagon for two years but whether this was purchase or hire is not recorded.

It is also unknown if the two wagons, 2 and 3, recorded as being built by Midland and registered by the GWR in September 1872 were any of these.

CLIFT & WHITING

Ezra Whiting did get a quick mention in the Gloucestershire volume as being a coal merchant in Cheltenham up until at least 1894. A check on wagons supplied by the Midland Waggon Co. in August 1873 to 'Clift & Whiting' found the dissolution of a partnership between John Clift and Ezra Whiting trading as coal merchants at 14 St. George's Parade and Tewkesbury Road, Cheltenham. The dissolution came on the 30th September 1876 and stated that they were trading both as Clift & Whiting and Clift & Co.

On the 1881 census John Clift can be found aged 44, born in Hampshire, living at the St. George's Parade address. Ezra Whiting, 64, born Bisley, Gloucestershire, was living at 109 Moors Parade, Tewkesbury Road.

Three 6-ton wagons for Clift & Whiting were purchased from Midland in August 1873 at £13 pwpa on a seven year purchase lease.

EZRA CROOK

Ezra Crook also got a mention in the Gloucestershire volume as being an old established Cheltenham merchant. Again he can be found taking wagons from the Midland Waggon Co. with two secondhand 8-ton wagons bought on five years deferred purchase at £13 9s pwpa in May 1870. In September the same year two new 7-ton wagons were bought over five years at £13 5s pwpa. In November 1876 two new 8-ton wagons were bought over three years at £21 10s pwpa. The likelihood is that these wagons joined the fleet of Crook & Greenway.

HANKS & GWINNELL

The partnership took two 7-ton wagons at £51 each for cash from the Midland Waggon Co. in May 1870. In August 1881 two 6-ton wagons were bought from the renamed Midland Railway Carriage & Wagon Co. on five years deferred terms at £12 4s 6d pwpa.

HENRY JORDAN & Co. Ltd

Jordans are now known to have taken four 8-ton wagons at £70 10s each for cash from the Midland Waggon Co. in April 1872. These were followed by the hire of six 6-ton wagons at £9 10s pwpa for one year in December 1875.

J. LLOYD

Possibly this was the J. Lloyd who took one new 8-ton wagon on three years deferred purchase at £23 15s per annum from the Midland Waggon Co. in January 1869. In November 1871 one 6-ton was taken on hire for one year at £10 per annum.

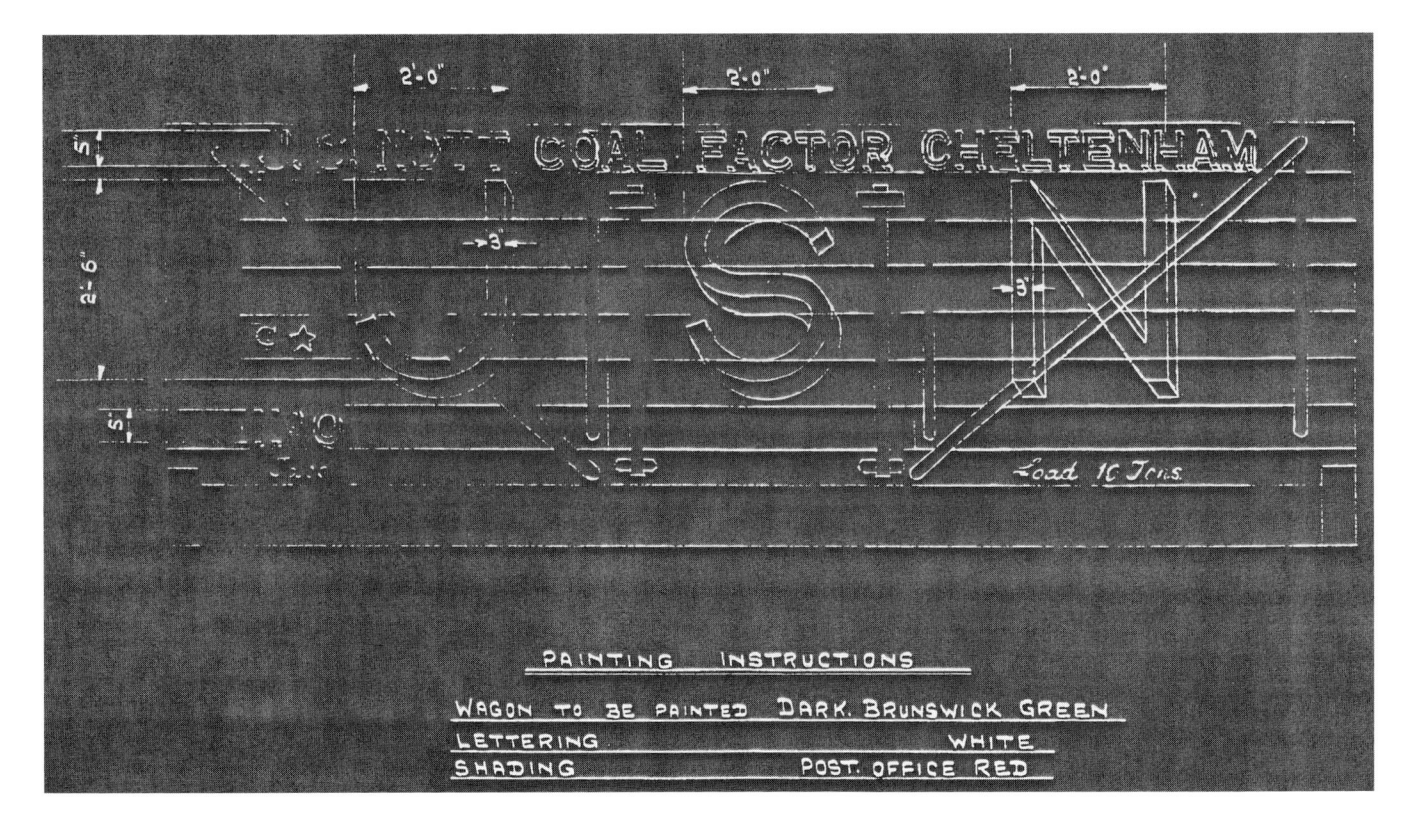

J. S. NOTT

It is always good when evidence turns up to prove a previous doubt. For example the photograph of the J. S. Nott wagon was accompanied by a reminiscence that it was painted green with white lettering shaded black. The Wagon Repairs drawing above shows that the wagons were painted dark Brunswick green with white lettering albeit the shading was to be Post Office red. However, that does not preclude the possibility that the instructions were altered and the shading was done in black.

A. G. STOCKWELL

It is now known that the two new 8-ton wagons registered as 5 and 6 in October 1890 were ordered in August and paid for in cash at £62 each.

JOHN WILLIAMS & Co. (CHELTENHAM) Ltd

As noted Williams was a very early user of private owner wagons and quickly grew to operate out of a large number of depots including Bristol as recorded earlier in this volume.

He had dealings with the Midland Waggon Co. virtually from the formation of that company when they were only hiring out wagons. In April 1854 he enquired about hiring thirty wagons at £14 5s pa although this was not listed as approved. In March 1857 the hire of thirty 6-ton coal wagons for seven years is recorded at £11 10s pwpa. In June 1857 William Adams who built the majority of the wagons for Midland in their early days advised that thirty wagons let to J. Williams had been declined by the Midland Waggon Co. for finance.

In November 1857 Williams enquired about two further wagons and in December it was noted that Adams had offered to build twenty wagons for Williams. Whether any of these were taken up is unknown.

HENRY WORKMAN

Workman too was early in his dealings with the Midland Waggon Co. who received an application in May 1853 for eight wagons. It is unknown if these were supplied.

NORTH OF CHELTENHAM
W. J. OLDACRE & Co.

Oldacres also dealt with the Midland RC&WCo. taking wagons on hire in 1871. Two secondhand 7-tonners in January and one 6-ton wagon in December. All were hired for one year at least.

TEWKESBURY
E. W. F. EDGWICK

Edgwick was another trader who took wagons from the Midland RC&WCo. commencing in March 1881 with one secondhand 6-ton wagon taken on a years simple hire at £5 pa. This hire may have been renewed right through to 1891 as once hire renewal details appear in the records a single wagon is recorded in November 1889. In July 1890 a single 7-ton wagon was taken on hire for a year at £7 pa.

SAMUEL HEALING & SONS

In September 1884 four 8-ton wagons at £7 pwpa were hired for one year from the Midland RC&WCo. In April 1887 five 8-ton wagons were taken on hire for one year at £6 pwpa. This hire continued as in November 1889 the renewal of a hire on five wagons for a further year was noted.

OXFORD, WORCESTER & WOLVERHAMPTON
RICHARD CLIFFORD

There are a number of mentions of R. Clifford in the records of the Midland Waggon Co. and it is believed that they apply to Richard Clifford of Moreton-in-the-Marsh.

In July 1854 the fact that a lease was due to expire on two wagons was noted suggesting that Clifford had had wagons from at least 1853. October 1854 saw a report that one of Clifford's wagons was damaged in an accident at Moreton on the Oxford, Worcester & Wolverhampton Railway. Also damaged were two wagons hired by Wilson Carter and one by Benjamin Pearson of Stratford-on-Avon. In December 1863 Clifford took one 6-ton wagon on hire for one year.

The Midland books note that in June 1871 a bad debt accrued by Richard Clifford to the sum of £18 6s 8d had been written off. The *London Gazette* for the 25th June 1869 gave Richard Clifford the younger, of Moreton-in-the-Marsh, farmer, coal merchant, and horse dealer, being adjudged bankrupt on the 22nd.

CIRENCESTER
RICHARD COLE
As recorded in the Gloucestershire volume ten wagons were registered by the GWR in June 1872 to Richard Cole having been built by the Midland Waggon Co. The wagon builder's books reveal that they sold ten 8-ton wagons to R. Cole in April at a cost of £60 each. In July 1872 four 7-ton wagons were also bought from them secondhand.

DAVIES & ATTWATER
Known to have been in business in 1889 they took a total of three secondhand wagons from the Midland RC&WCo. in February 1889. They were two 6-ton and one 7-ton wagon taken on simple hire at £6 10s pwpa for 1 year certain. Again, it is possible that the hire was renewed but not recorded.

STROUD
STROUD GAS LIGHT & COKE CO.
The North British Railway Register shows that the Stroud Gas Light & Coke Company obtained four secondhand 10-ton wagons, numbered 17, 19, 20 and 21 ex James Richmond of Kirkaldy. All had been built by the Chorley Wagon Co. in 1896. All survived to be broken up in 1949.

WOOD & ROWE
A Wagon Repairs Ltd drawing for wagon number 22 has been discovered courtesy of Gordon Griffin. This shows the wagon to have been painted black with lettering in lemon yellow. Whether this applied to all wagons in the fleet is unknown. The rather indistinct drawing is reproduced above.

NAILSWORTH BRANCH
SAMUEL JEFFERIES & SON
In November 1862 the sale of two coal wagons at £50 each to Jefferies was recorded by the Oldbury Railway Carriage & Wagon Co. In February 1864 a quotation was given by the company for 'two more wagons like the last'. The price now was £62 but the result of the quotation is not given.

R. WILLIAMS
One 6-ton wagon was bought secondhand from the Midland Waggon Co. in October 1871 on seven years deferred purchase at £9 8s per annum.

BERKELEY ROAD TO YATE
WICKWAR QUARRIES Ltd
It was speculated that the company may have had wagons prior to the purchase of wagons from the Gloucester RC&WCo. of which number 51 was the first. The Midland Railway registers now reveal that 12-ton wagons numbered 21 to 50 were purchased from Clayton Wagons Ltd of Lincoln and registered in September 1924.

YATE
BRISTOL MINERAL Co.
The *London Gazette* records the dissolution of a partnership between Thomas Sherwood Smith, Edmund Lloyd Owen and E. L. Owen jnr trading as the Bristol Mineral Co. on the 25th May 1872. This may follow on from Owen's connection with the Frampton Haematite Mining Co. and, even earlier, the Chillington Iron Co. Whether they were working the iron mines at Frampton Cotterell is unknown but is a distinct possibility.

It would also appear that Thomas Sherwood Smith kept the business running for a while.

The Gloucester RC&WCo's agenda books contain several references to wagon hire contracts. In July 1871 four 10-ton wagons were taken followed in August by two more. All were secondhand ex the Bute Hematite Co. In December 1871 another eight 10-ton wagons were hired then in February 1872 the hire of six 7-ton and ten 10-ton was recorded. No periods were put on any of these hires.

At least six of the 10-tonners had been returned to Gloucester by March 1873, for they are recorded as having been re-hired to Bullivant & Allen that month. However, the GWR registered four new 10-tonners to the Bristol Mineral Co. in April 1873, all financed and built by Gloucester, with paint numbers 1, 2, 25 and 26. However, there were no orders for wagons from Gloucester at this time.

Other wagons ex Bristol Mineral Co. were passed on via Gloucester in 1874/5 with fifteen 10-ton going to Consolidated Collieries Co. Ltd and six 8-ton to Edwin R. Payne.

YATE COAL & LIME CO.
This company remains a bit of a mystery as the only record comes in the books of the Midland RC&WCo. in September 1882 when they note 'Bills dishonoured'. No previous mention can be found.

THORNBURY BRANCH
TYTHERINGTON STONE Co.
Under Tytherington the lack of an image of wagons in their livery was mentioned. Now, thanks to Gerry Nichols we have a view of two of their wagons.

In February 1913 the Tytherington Stone Co. took twenty wagons from the Midland RC&WCo. on deferred purchase through the Bristol & South Wales Wagon Co. No details of the wagons were given.

It is also now known that they had at least one rectangular tar tank built by the Bristol W&CWCo. in October 1914 and numbered 2.

SOUTH WALES & BRISTOL DIRECT
FREDERICK BISS
Biss has been included again thanks to the observation and keen eyesight of Chris Baston. He was able to point out that on the door is actually painted the letter 'B'. By playing with the contrast on the image the 'B' can be seen, probably painted black on a red triangle.

GEORGE E. DOWDING
Dowding took an unknown number of 6-ton wagons from the Midland RC&WCo. in October 1882 on one years simple hire at £5 5s pwpa. In September 1884 two secondhand 7-ton wagons were again taken on one years hire at £7 pwpa which may have been renewed through as far as 1890. In July 1888 five new 10-ton wagons were bought on a five year deferred purchase lease at £11 18s pwpa.

Further new wagons were taken from Midland in July 1890 but no details are recorded. Two new 6-ton wagons were bought in February 1891 at £61 each, cash.

RESEARCH
It is very unlikely that all has yet been discovered on the wagons of Gloucestershire as new material is still coming to light. The recent availability of the records of the constituent companies of Metropolitan Cammell has revealed a great deal of new material. We still have the problem, as with the Gloucester RC&WCo. records, that orders are just written down to a name, such as George Merrylees with no place given. Reliance then has to be put on trawling the census and trade directories. In the case of a company or partnership the *London Gazette* is of great help whilst occasionally limited company records will be found in the National Archives. For photographic images we are now down to staring intently at postcard views of collieries and railway stations in the hope of finding an elusive wagon.